THE LEAVEN OF THE SAINTS

DAWN MARIE BEUTNER

The Leaven of the Saints

Bringing Christ into a Fallen World

Dear Roger,

May God bless you and all your loved ones through the saints!

Dawn

IGNATIUS PRESS   SAN FRANCISCO

Nihil Obstat: Very Reverend William P. Saunders
Censor Deputatus

Imprimatur: + Michael F. Burbidge
Bishop of Arlington
November 1, 2022

The *nihil obstat* and *imprimatur* are official declaration that a book or pamphlet is free of doctrinal or moral error. There is no implication that those who have granted the *nihil obstat* and the *imprimatur* agree with the content, opinions, or statements expressed therein.

Cover art:
Coronation of the Virgin
Fra Angelico
Uffizi/Florence/Italy
© Alinari Archives/Art Resource, New York

Cover design by Riz Boncan Marsella

© 2023 by Ignatius Press, San Francisco
All rights reserved
ISBN 978-1-62164-561-0 (PB)
ISBN 978-1-64229-207-7 (eBook)
Library of Congress Control Number 2022934001
Printed in the United States of America ∞

CONTENTS

The Leaven of the Saints

Moses told the Israelites that the Lord wanted them to eat only unleavened bread at the first Passover meal.[1] Jesus told His disciples to beware the leaven of those who opposed His teachings,[2] and He told a parable about a woman who added leaven to other ingredients when making bread.[3] In our modern world of store-bought bread, low-carb diets, and gluten intolerance, many people might find these passages archaic, mystifying, and perhaps irrelevant.

But God knew exactly what He was doing when He commanded the Israelites to prepare unleavened bread for a meal. Unleavened bread, as bakers know, merely requires flour, water, and a heat source. Flavorings like salt will make it more palatable, and fire is a better heat source than that used by the poor who have no wood to burn,[4] but unleavened bread can be prepared quickly when, say, you are running for your life from the Egyptian army. Today we have the luxuries of modern products like baking powder, baking soda, and packaged yeast, rather than needing to cultivate a yeast starter slowly and wait for it to cause a loaf to rise enough to be both edible and desirable, as ancient cooks were forced to do. But the Israelites understood the not-so-hidden message conveyed by the unleavened bread of the Passover meal: be ready to let go of many of the comforts of life, when needed, if you want to be saved.

What was the "leaven" that Jesus warned His disciples to avoid? The Pharisees and Sadducees didn't listen to Jesus to learn from Him; they listened in order to pick fights with Him. It wasn't that they didn't worship the true God. It's just that they thought they understood God better than the Son of God Himself. Unfortunately, this situation can be easily proved; we have all met people

---

[1] Ex 12:15.
[2] Mt 16:6–12; Mk 8:15; Lk 12:1.
[3] Mt 13:33; Lk 13:21.
[4] See Ezek 4:12–15 for an example of an unusual heat source.

who were utterly convinced that whatever they wanted was the best thing to do, no matter how obvious it was that their decision would be a disaster. More unfortunately, all of us have *been* that sort of person too. Only by avoiding the "leaven" of the Pharisees, the insidious lie that we know more than God Himself, can we know the truth.

Jesus' parable about the woman making bread is perhaps the most cryptic reference to leaven. Jesus merely says that "the kingdom of heaven is like leaven which a woman took and hid in three measures of meal, till it was all leavened."[5] But in both the Gospels of Matthew and Luke, Jesus precedes this sentence with the parable of the mustard seed, which, though small, grows into a tree. One message from this passage is that the leaven and the seed, though small, gradually and silently produce a mysterious abundance, an abundance so profound that Jesus calls it "the kingdom of heaven".

What does this teach us about leaven? And what does this have to do with the saints?

When Jesus Christ ascended into Heaven, He did not leave behind an autobiography, a completed code of canon law, a diagram for the hierarchy of the Church, or an outline for a decree for the canonization of saints. When He rose into Heaven, it is fairly certain that none of the apostles who witnessed it realized that the Church would develop the concept of the "communion of the saints", an idea enshrined in the Apostles' Creed. But it didn't take many years for the members of the Body of Christ to recognize that our Lord might not return this very day and that Christians who had already died while in the embrace of the Church were embraced "on the other side" of their journeys as well. Saint Stephen, a deacon and the first martyr of the Church, surely started people thinking along these lines when he said he could see Jesus in Heaven,[6] even as people were stoning him to death. Other New Testament passages refer to deceased Christians as those who have merely "fallen asleep",[7] showing the Christian understanding of what happens after our earthly lives have ended.

[5] Mt 13:33.
[6] Acts 7:56.
[7] Acts 7:60; 15:6, 18, 20; 1 Thess 4:13–15.

But even here on earth, some Christians throughout the millennia have demonstrated that they are more *alive* than the rest of us. These holy men and women have ended wars, healed the sick, levitated in the air, fed the hungry, preached to huge crowds, and changed the course of history. Sometimes—as with levitation—only a supernatural explanation is possible once the natural explanations have been exhausted. At other times, the actions of the saints seem miraculous to us because of the sheer number, brilliance, and effectiveness of them. It's difficult to even list the achievements of some of our greatest saints—Augustine, Thomas Aquinas, John Paul II—without appearing to exaggerate. But these men and women are not stars; they are leaven.

That is, like the unleavened bread of the Israelites, the saints show us the importance of letting go of anything that will separate us from God. The joys of family life, the pleasures of food, and emotional and physical comforts are all good things, but no earthly thing or person is worth keeping if that thing might cost us salvation. The saints, therefore, show us how to live our lives in readiness to meet Christ.

The saints also show us that the leaven of the Pharisees, pride, is always ready to keep us from hearing the voice of God. They teach us this precisely because they do the opposite, welcoming Christ into their hearts at any cost and listening to His voice.

But the most profound way that the saints are truly leaven in our world is shown by their quiet, steady witness to Jesus Christ. While there are certainly saints who have confronted emperors, led troops into battle, and become a household name, most saints have spent almost all their lives being a leaven within their families, villages, and religious houses, not at the center of the world stage.

In this latter meaning of leaven, any individual with the ability to consume solid food can appreciate the difference between unleavened and leavened bread. An unleavened loaf of bread is essentially a cracker. Compare the taste of a cracker to the taste of the best loaf of leavened bread you have ever eaten—flavorful and *light* because the action of the leavening agent makes it more appealing and healthful.

Saints are one of God's crowning achievements. It is no wonder that reading about the saints can make them seem not quite human and make us feel insignificant in comparison. But we make a mistake when we don't see the saints the way God sees them.

Seeing the humanity of the saints

One of the mistakes we make when we speak and write about the saints is sometimes called, pejoratively, hagiography. That is, we tell the story of a saint's life, but we do so with such a credulous, reverential attitude that the person hardly seems human. For example, if you list only the miraculous events in a holy person's life, he will sound superhuman. A similar phenomenon occurs at funerals, where eulogists are always careful to mention the deceased person's finest personal attributes and omit everything else.

The opposite extreme is common in circles both inside and outside Catholicism. It's possible to examine the behavior and actions selectively of any person, apply the desired "spin", and make anyone seem stupid, cruel, or crazy. The Pharisees and Sadducees were experts at this behavior when they dealt with our Lord and Savior Jesus Christ Himself.

In a more recent example, in 1917 the local government of Fátima, Portugal, tried very hard to make three young children appear to be a danger to public safety. Why were these children so dangerous that they needed to be kidnapped, arrested, and threatened with death? Because they said they had seen a beautiful woman (whom everyone gradually realized was the Blessed Virgin Mary) who told them to pray.

Sometimes secular attempts to make holy people look ridiculous backfire, as they did with Saints Francisco and Jacinta, along with their cousin Lucia Santos, when thousands of witnesses—not all of them Christian believers—saw a miraculous, inexplicable vision, just as the three children had predicted, on October 13, 1917. At other times, the innuendo of disbelievers and unbelievers poisons the cultural atmosphere against holy people for decades, as, for example, false accusations that Blessed Anne Catherine Emmerich had broken her vow of chastity have delayed her cause for sainthood for more than a century.

Another problem we face when we try to learn from the saints is a result of a lack of understanding of history. This occurs painfully and frequently in today's news, as happened recently when some individuals objected to the canonization of Saint Junipero Serra and even destroyed statues of the Franciscan saint. Their complaints seemed to focus on the modern-day fallacy that all Europeans, particularly Spaniards, who came to the Americas in the eighteenth century had only one goal: to kill, enslave, and profit from the native peoples of the continent.

But, one might ask the couch potatoes of our culture, why did Franciscan priests like Junipero Serra bother to come to the New World in the first place? Why did they undertake a potentially life-threatening sea journey, knowing that they would probably never see their families and homeland again? Why did they choose to live in real poverty alongside the people they served? Why did Junipero Serra walk barefoot, though he suffered from a lifelong limp (which he earned as the result of a mosquito bite in the New World), across the American continent? Why did he gather so many communities of native peoples together and establish cities in locations so wisely situated that his cities still exist today?

As Catholics, we understand that he wanted to bring the greatest of treasures, faith in Christ, to people who had never heard of Him before. But even our enemies should be able to respect the acts of charity that he performed, which literally saved the lives of the people he served. When he established communities, he gave the native peoples protection, allowing them to live in peace away from the deadly warfare that commonly occurred between native tribes and protecting them from European officials who didn't always recognize the dignity of the native peoples. Father Serra taught them about agriculture so they could feed themselves and become self-sufficient. He helped the native peoples out of poverty—both spiritually and materially—so that they could live alongside the Europeans who had come to their country.

Another distortion in our understanding of the saints occurs when we apply the argument of "nature versus nurture". Are these holy people now known as saints because they were born with better dispositions than ours? Does God have favorites—that is, people to whom He grants great personal abilities or perfect families or ideal communities—while the rest of us are, and will always be, second-class citizens in the kingdom of God?

That lie is easy to disprove. Saint Francis de Sales (1567–1622) admitted that he had a problem controlling his temper when he was a young man. In the early twentieth century in Italy, Blessed Maria Gabriella Sagheddu's family thought she was a typical teenager—rebellious, critical, and a pain to be around. Saint Eugene de Mazenod's parents had a bitter, stormy marriage that ended in divorce, which was highly uncommon in nineteenth-century France. The families, culture, and dispositions of the saints were often just as flawed and imperfect as ours are today.

There are antidotes to these misunderstandings. We can learn about the culture and historical circumstances in which the saints lived, in part so that we can understand their lives, but also so that we can learn from their successes and failures. We can place ourselves in their shoes and imagine how we would have dealt with their trials, which can help us do the same in our own lives. And we can pray.

After all, asking God for help is the key. God's grace, not white-knuckled human will, is what helped Francis become the epitome of gentleness and a brilliant bishop; it's what helped Maria Gabriella joyfully embrace life as a contemplative nun among the Trappists; and it's what helped Eugene weather a troubled childhood and become a priest, missionary, and founder of a religious order. It's what allows each of us to see through our personal weaknesses and see holiness the way God sees it. Humility, prayer, virtue, and living a sacramental life helped them become the leaven of their culture, and, by God's grace, we can become saints the same way today.

This book contains descriptions of dozens of saints, many religious orders, and other topics related to saints, but it is not exhaustive. Your favorite saint, favorite story about a saint, best-loved religious order, or other specific details about a historical event or group may not have been included. This book was written for ordinary Catholics, and experts in a particular area may find that some details have been oversimplified. If so, the author apologizes in advance.

The Greatest Witnesses: Martyrs

The secular world knows what a martyr is and also that it is generally a good idea to avoid creating one. For example, many people hated Martin Luther King, Jr., for his forceful but peaceful attempts to point out that American segregation laws were offensive to human dignity, and his death by assassination only helped more people understand his point. Even totalitarian dictators tend to avoid killing their critics—or at least their well-known ones—out of fear of backlash.

But Christians mean something different when we call someone a martyr. The English word "martyr" comes from a Greek word implying a witness who would be willing to testify in court. The glossary definition of "martyr" from the *Catechism of the Catholic Church* is "a witness to the truth of the faith, in which the martyr endures even death to be faithful to Christ". *That* kind of martyr can teach us lessons that transcend politics and culture, pointing us to Someone far greater.

Blood and gore

The details of the deaths of some early saints are positively gruesome. For example, Saint Apollonia was a consecrated virgin living in Alexandria, Egypt, around the year 249 when an anti-Christian mob attacked and killed her. They broke out her teeth with pincers before she was burned alive. Catholics have made her the patron saint against toothaches. Saint Agatha was living in Sicily around the year 250 when she was arrested for being a Christian. She was tortured by having her breasts cut off before being executed, which is why she is the patron saint for healing from breast cancer.

Why do Christians record and remember their deaths in such agonizing detail? Doesn't that make us guilty of the same mistake

commonly found in modern secular entertainment—that is, glamor-
izing violence?

Not at all, because the reason we discuss the violence perpetrated
against the martyrs has nothing to do with making a profit, stirring up
our lower human desires to experience violence and sin vicariously,
or attracting attention. We discuss Christian martyrs because they
show us Jesus Christ, albeit by reminding us of His Passion rather
than more pleasurable events in His life.

Jesus was explicit when He told His disciples that following Him
would come at a price. He said that, as followers of Christ, we will
be hated,[1] we will be beaten,[2] we will be betrayed by our own family members,[3] and we will be persecuted.[4] But He not only *spoke*
about the cost of discipleship; He also *showed* us the cost of being
faithful to God when He poured Himself out, to the last drop of
blood, on the Cross.

Jesus' words and living witness to the demand to remain faithful to
God at any cost, through God's grace, inspired the Twelve Apostles
to preach the Good News to everyone, even at the price of their own
lives. Many Christians over the centuries have done just that. Only
those who explicitly reject the Christian faith would fail to notice
that Martin Luther King, Jr.'s motivation for speaking out against
racial injustice and thereby placing his life in danger was precisely
because he was a follower of Christ.

There are innumerable stories of Catholic men and women who
were willing to face death for their love of Christ and who were sub-
jected to horrific pain and suffering as a result. Here are just a few of
the more vivid ones, as well as the lessons they teach us.

Saint Maria Goretti (1890–1902) was only twelve years old when
a teenage boy, fueled by pornography, tried to rape her. When she
resisted and pointed out that it was a sin, he brutally stabbed her to
death. Years later, he was unrepentant and in prison when he had a
dream. In that dream, he saw Maria offer him flowers and forgiveness.

Saint Dorothy was a consecrated virgin living in the early fourth
century in modern Turkey when she was arrested and condemned

[1] Mt 24:9.
[2] Mk 13:9.
[3] Lk 21:16.
[4] Jn 15:20.

to death. On the way to the site of her execution, a lawyer made fun of her for being a Christian, and she told him she would send him flowers from Heaven. When he miraculously received roses after her death, the lawyer—just like Maria's murderer—repented and became a faithful Christian. Do we need any further evidence of the power of martyrdom to lead some of Christianity's worst enemies to become Christians themselves?

Saint Andrew Bobola was a Jesuit priest from Poland living in seventeenth-century Lithuania. Because of anti-Catholic persecution, he was forced to live in secret to bring the sacraments to the faithful. When he was found and arrested by Cossack soldiers, they tortured his body through scourging, whipping, burning, and other methods too many and too horrific to describe. What annoyed his persecutors most of all was that Andrew continued to pray throughout these tortures. Finally, in anger and disgust, they killed him. Decades later, his casket was opened, and his body was found to be incorrupt. That is, more than three hundred years after his death, one might think that Andrew Bobola is merely asleep, awaiting the Second Coming of Christ. Do we need any further evidence that the physical sufferings that martyrs experience are unnoticed by God? And that God gives at least some of His martyrs special graces to bear incredible sufferings in that moment, if only they will ask?

Blessed Franz Jägerstätter was a husband and father of three little girls when the Nazis ordered him to serve in the Austrian army. He offered to serve as a noncombatant but refused to fight for Hitler or the Nazi anti-Catholic program to enslave the world. He was executed by the guillotine in 1943. Do we need any further evidence that, whether execution is torturous or swift, martyrdom shows what is in the heart of each martyr?

Accounts of the brutality inflicted on Catholic martyrs may turn our stomachs, but we miss the point completely when we numb our feelings to the very real sufferings that they endured. None of the martyrs stoically faced suffering and death like third-rate actors in a fourth-rate movie. They show us that our own physical sufferings, when offered up to Christ, can truly bring His presence into our world. This can give us courage when we face real persecution from those who dislike or despise Christ and Christianity in our own communities, right here and right now.

When to run, and when to stand and fight

Precisely because persecution of Christians lasted for so long and was prevalent among so many different peoples of the ancient Roman Empire, it is easy to draw some conclusions about martyrdom from the years of the early Church, specifically the years 64–313.

Some early Christians were surprised to find themselves arrested, imprisoned, and threatened with torture and death because of their faith in Christ. When the Roman emperor Nero blamed Christians for starting a great fire in Rome and made them into living torches to light his banquets (do you think his guests got the hint about what would happen to anyone who opposed the emperor?), it came as a shock to the established Christian community already living peacefully in Rome—the men, women, and children we now know as the First Martyrs of Rome. It was certainly a surprise to many Christians in later decades each time a succeeding emperor or local governor renewed the persecution and sent soldiers into the streets to hunt down and find Catholics. But it wasn't *always* such a surprise.

For example, Saints Nereus and Achilleus thought they could escape the persecution of Christians in early fourth-century Rome by running away to a nearby island. They were wrong. They were found and executed with their fellow Christian, fourteen-year-old Saint Pancras. The same thing happened to Saints Rufina and Secunda in the third century when they tried to hide from the authorities; they were found and executed.

Some people clearly hoped that their wealth, friendships, and position in society would protect them from martyrdom. Flavia Domitilla was a second-century Roman noblewoman who was related to emperors. She embraced the faith and brought others into the Church; for a time, her connections protected her. But ultimately, she was sentenced to exile—which was not the romantic fate it might appear since most people condemned to exile died slowly from poor treatment or starvation—and died a martyr and saint.

Not every local governor punished every Christian with execution. The Roman emperor Maximinus Daia reigned over the eastern half of the empire during the years 311–313, and his persecution of Christians was particularly brutal. However, some Christians, perhaps those who seemed able-bodied, were blinded in one eye, hamstrung in one leg, and sent to the mines to serve as slave labor for their punishment, instead of being executed. One of those who was sentenced to this punishment was the Egyptian bishop Saint Paphnutius, who had previously lived as a desert monk under the direction of Saint Anthony the Great. We know that Paphnutius did not die a martyr because years later, when Catholics were no longer persecuted and were able to hold public meetings to settle doctrinal and moral issues, Paphnutius noticed another survivor of the same punishment at a Church council, Bishop Maximus of Jerusalem. Paphnutius also saw that Maximus was sitting among those who followed the Arian heresy. He led Maximus outside the meeting hall and told him that he could not bear to think that someone who had suffered so much for the sake of the Gospel would ally himself with those who distorted the Gospel. Maximus was convinced; both men died as saints of the Church.

On the other hand, there are reports that some Christians were brazen in offering themselves for martyrdom, showing up on the governor's doorstep and proclaiming their faith publicly, which generally led to swift and painful death. Saints Justus and Pastor (ages thirteen and nine, respectively) did exactly that when the persecution of Christians was renewed in their native city of Alcalá, Spain, in the year 304. The two boys, who wanted to prove that they were as strong in their faith as adults, bravely encouraged each other while they were being flogged. This shamed the emperor's representative, so he ordered them to be executed quickly.

But not every Christian, whether arrested by surprise or self-identified as a follower of Christ, was faithful during torture or the threat of torture. Some gave in, which was particularly easy when all you had to do was put a little incense on a brazier in front of a pagan god, whom, after all, you did not believe in to begin with. For those who think they could easily endure torture for Christ, read the horrific modern-day autobiographies of the men and women who were tortured under Communist regimes.[5] Like the ancient Romans, Communist torturers had no pity for those who went against the almighty state; some Christians, very humanly, broke down under the pain.

In the ancient world, the situation of "lapsed Catholics" led to a fierce internal debate within the early Church, both before and after the Roman emperor Constantine allowed the practice of Christianity

[5] For example, see Walter J. Ciszek, S.J., *With God in Russia* (San Francisco: Ignatius Press, 2009).

in the empire. Each time the persecutions lessened, some of those Christians who had apostatized under threats of death and torture would ask to return to the Church. Though great saints took their positions on both sides of this argument, eventually the Church recognized that martyrdom, while a great grace, is not *required* for every Christian. The Church began to develop her beautiful, complicated teaching about free will and grace—about whether a person can be considered guilty of an act if the act was done under duress, and about mercifully allowing *all* repentant sinners to return to the Church, provided they do penance to atone for their sins.

These real-life stories lead us to a personal question: What would you do? If you knew that being a Christian was illegal and that soldiers might arrest, torture, and kill you, most likely with gladiators and wild animals ready to make your death look exciting to the crowds, would you even become a Catholic? Would you try to avoid detection and move to a new city if it looked like you had been identified as a Christian? Is escape prudence or cowardice? Is staying in danger bravery or foolhardiness?

Perhaps the lesson that we can learn from the early Church martyrs is that God does not have a one-size-fits-all pattern for martyrdom, any more than He does for other vocations. Christ also promised that He will give us what we need when we need it, and that includes the wisdom to make tough decisions when the time comes.

Who are the real enemies?

When the secular world celebrates the bravery of victims of violence, it is often done as the reputation of the perpetrators of that violence is simultaneously smeared. For example, we talk about the victims of a serial killer precisely so we can hate and demonize the murderer, pointing out his worst faults and most dreadful deeds, typically so that we can shake our heads in puzzlement that anyone could be so evil.

But Jesus said to love our enemies.[6] Jesus also said, while hanging from the Cross in agony, "Father, forgive them; for they know not

[6] Mt 5:44; Lk 6:27.

what they do."[7] He wasn't just talking about forgiving the soldiers who nailed him there or Pontius Pilate or the Jewish leaders. He was asking for forgiveness for all fallen men and women, which includes all of us, everywhere and at every time. If the men and women who have participated in the execution of Catholic martyrs are not our enemies, then who (or what) are we fighting against?

As Saint Paul explained it, "We are not contending against flesh and blood, but against the principalities, against the powers, against the world rulers of this present darkness, against the spiritual hosts of wickedness in the heavenly places."[8] There *is* a devil, and there *are* demons who follow him and who torment us. There are many ways that they encourage us to avoid what is good and seek out what our fallen human natures desire, those words and actions that seem to promise happiness but only make us miserable—lies, for example.

Jesus said, "I am the way, and the truth, and the life."[9] Since God *is* Truth itself, it is an offense against Him to speak lies, with our mouths or our bodies. The more egregious the lie, the more egregious the offense against God.

John the Baptist lost his head for publicly stating that it was wrong for King Herod to marry the woman who had already married Herod's own brother.[10] Failing to speak up about an act that violated the Ten Commandments would have been a lie. When the pagan king Nebuchadnezzar told three young Jewish men, Shadrach, Meshach, and Abednego, that he would throw them into a fire and burn them alive if they refused to worship an idol, they explained why they could not acquiesce to the king's demands to tell a lie with their bodies by bowing down to a false god:

> O Nebuchadnezzar, we have no need to answer you in this matter. If it be so, our God whom we serve is able to deliver us from the burning fiery furnace; and he will deliver us out of your hand, O king. But if not, be it known to you, O king, that we will not serve your gods or worship the golden image which you have set up.[11]

[7] Lk 23:34.
[8] Eph 6:12.
[9] Jn 14:6.
[10] Mt 14:3–4; Mk 6:17–18; Lk 3:19–20.
[11] Dan 3:16–18.

During the reign of King Henry VIII, every Catholic bishop of England sided with the king and supported the lie that the king was the head of the Catholic Church. Every bishop except for one: the martyr-saint John Fisher. For Saint John, the truth was worth dying for.

Blessed Antonia Mesina (1919–1935) was a pious Italian girl gathering wood for her family when a would-be rapist attacked her. She fought back but was killed. The secular world understands that her death was a tragedy but completely misunderstands why we consider her a martyr. After all, does this imply that we expect every woman to give her life to avoid rape?

No, the Church understands rape to be a crime, like many others. But the Church also understands sexual intercourse to be an intimate personal act in which a man and a woman give themselves to each other, both for procreation (to become co-creators with God) and for union, so that they will be physically, emotionally, intellectually, and in every other way united with each other. Antonia, whose personal devotion was known by her family and friends, understood that rape was a lie and tried to stop it.

Can you name even one of the apostate English bishops who betrayed the Church for the sake of appeasing an angry king? Of course not. Each of those men thought they could betray Christ and His Church and remain a friend of the world. But, as Christians, we can hope that each of those men—and all the men and women who have offended God through lying and other sins—later became soldiers for the truth, precisely because of the witness of the martyrs.

Deaths that inspire us to live

One of the ironic results of martyrdom is that, although all human persons naturally abhor death, the example of Christian martyrs inspires us to want to follow them.

We have so little information about many of the early Church saints that it is sometimes a challenge to figure out why Christians have remembered their names for so long. There were many brutal persecutions in the Roman Empire between the years of 64 and 313; many thousands of Christians were executed during the reigns of the Roman emperors Nero, Vespasian, Domitian, Trajan, Hadrian,

Marcus Aurelius, Alexander Severus, Maximinus Thrax, Decius, Valerian, Gallienus, Diocletian, Maximus Galerius, Maxentius, and Maximinus Daia,[12] among others, during that time. Why do we still celebrate Saints Marcellinus and Peter of Rome, Cosmas and Damian, and Apollinaris of Ravenna when we know so little about them?

The supernatural answer is surely that Christians have been begging for the help of these five men—along with many other martyrs—and been receiving their assistance from Heaven for centuries. But it is not too difficult to discern more practical reasons for the fact that all five of these saints are still remembered in the Church's liturgical calendar.

Saint Marcellinus was a priest, and Saint Peter was an exorcist; both were living and serving the Church in Rome when they died as martyrs in the year 304. Since that is all we know for certain (although there are later legends about them), why have their names been included in a Eucharistic Prayer of the Mass for seventeen hundred years? A reasonable guess is that something about Marcellinus' and Peter's public witness for Christ during their trial and execution was so striking that the Catholics of Rome continued to ask for their intercession from Heaven at every Mass and never wanted to stop.

Saint Apollinaris of Ravenna was the first bishop of Ravenna, Italy. Some traditions say died around the year 75 and knew Saint Peter and other apostles. Other traditions say he was sent into exile because of his faith, survived a shipwreck, and either died a martyr or just narrowly escaped martyrdom more than once. Perhaps the Christians of Ravenna continued to pray for the intercession of Saint Apollinaris not just because he was the first bishop of the city but because he was exactly what a bishop should be: a holy shepherd who not only served God and His flock but also protected His people by remaining faithful despite opposition.

Saints Cosmas and Damian, who were tortured before being beheaded around the year 303 in Cilicia (modern Turkey), were also

---

[12] Some modern scholars question the severity of the persecution of Christians under these emperors, and it must be admitted that anti-Catholic persecution was sporadic, sometimes localized, and did not always involve execution. However, the Roman law that made being a Christian an act of treason against the state was not revoked until the reign of the Roman emperor Constantine; blaming Christians for a problem—plague, an unsuccessful war—was always an option for an emperor or even a local governor when a scapegoat was needed. The most bitter persecutions of the Church occurred during the reigns of the emperors Nero, Decius, and Diocletian.

physicians. The high cost of medical care is not a modern invention, and people throughout history have spent themselves into debt trying to find healing for their loved ones. The fact that these two men used their medical skills to care for the poor for free would make them notable in any time and place.

Saint Wenceslaus (d. 929), the duke of Bohemia (modern Czech Republic), died as a martyr for two reasons: because he was a faithful Christian who ruled by balancing justice and mercy and because his jealous brother wanted to take his place. Few men have imitated Christ so perfectly as to be betrayed and killed by someone who had previously been so close.

Saint Fidelis of Sigmaringen (1578–1622) was a lawyer-turned-priest who traveled to Switzerland to explain the teachings of the Church to Protestants and bring them back to the fold. Saint Peter Chanel (1803–1841) was a French priest sent as a missionary to the South Pacific to bring the faith to the native peoples living there. Both men knew that their lives were in danger from those who hated the faith, but both men knew that bringing people the Good News about Jesus Christ and His Church was worth the risk. Both died violent deaths.

Saint Maximilian Kolbe (1894–1941), a Franciscan priest in the Auschwitz concentration camp, offered to take the place of a condemned man and die a slow, agonizing death by starvation as a Nazi punishment after a prisoner escape. Some might argue that he did not die because of his Catholic faith, overlooking the fact that he was in that camp precisely because he was a Polish Catholic priest. But when Father Kolbe literally laid down his life for another person, he proved that Jesus' words[13] were worth dying for.

Whether we have complete biographies of these martyrs or not, in each case they show us that laying down one's life for another person is an act of love that we can all imitate in perhaps ordinary daily actions.

Be prepared

Not every persecution of Catholics is a persecution to the death. Sometimes the fight is more subtle but just as real.

[13]Jn 15:3.

Most Catholics know that "jolly old Saint Nick" was inspired by the real-life example of the fourth-century bishop of Myra (now in Turkey). Saint Nicholas confessed his faith in Jesus Christ when the Roman emperor Diocletian renewed his persecution of Christians, and he was sent to prison. For unknown reasons, he was not executed. But he remained faithful throughout his imprisonment, was eventually released, and participated in the Council of Nicaea after Constantine ended the persecution of the Church. The Church calls him a Confessor, in that he confessed his faith and was ready to die as a martyr, even though he was not executed. Another early Church leader, Saint Eusebius (283–371), bishop of Vercelli, wrote vigorously and effectively against the heresy of Arianism. He survived exile and imprisonment, and most traditions say that he managed to escape martyrdom.

Saint Rose of Viterbo was only twelve years old when she became a thirteenth-century public figure. At the time, Emperor Frederick II ruled much of Italy and constantly challenged the reigning pope's control of the papal states that surrounded his territory. Some modern historians like to call Frederick "the first modern ruler" in European history; if they mean Frederick was the first European ruler to govern like a twentieth-century totalitarian despot, they are right. The people of Rose's hometown of Viterbo were justifiably divided over how to deal with such a powerful leader; should they try to appease the tyrant and take his side in the fight, or should they side with the pope and perhaps endanger their own safety when Frederick retaliated with his army? Rose had been devout since she had received a vision of the Blessed Mother at the age of eight, but her devotion alone couldn't have given her the ability to draw huge crowds of listeners as she encouraged her fellow citizens to remain faithful to the pope's side in the ongoing war. By God's grace, she defended a just cause in public for two years. At that point, those who supported the emperor rose up and demanded that she be executed, but the city's mayor commuted her punishment to banishment from the city. Rose predicted that the emperor would die soon; when he did, she returned to the city.

The system of government known as Communism always tries to destroy the practice of religion because those in authority want complete control of their people's lives. Perhaps millions of Catholic mothers and fathers in China, Russia, and Slavic nations have been given the ultimatum: give up your faith or go to prison. But evidence shows that innumerable faithful Catholics have clandestinely taught the faith to their children and received the sacraments in secret.

Sometimes the dangers we fear do not materialize. Sometimes we are called upon to speak the truth. Sometimes we remain faithful in silence.

But we deceive ourselves if we pretend that being a Christian can ever be a safe decision in this world. For proof, see the waves of persecution that have accompanied the expansion of Christianity as it has traveled over the globe, as described below.

Persecution over the centuries

The following table summarizes the persecution of the Catholic Church as it has occurred over the centuries and in many different regions of the world.

Century	Location	Cause of Persecution
1st	Holy Land	Early Jewish rejection of Christianity
1st–3rd	Roman Empire	Official persecution of the Church by Roman emperors
4th	Roman Empire	Intermittent persecution by Roman emperors
5th	Europe	Invasion of pagan tribes: Goths and Huns
8th–15th	Spain	Muslim conquest of Spain
8th–9th	East	Iconoclast heresy promulgated by Byzantine emperors
9th	Europe	Invasion by pagan Vikings
11th–13th	Holy Land	Muslim invasion of the Holy Land, leading to the crusades
16th–17th	Europe	Wars of Religion between Catholic and Protestant nations

Century	Location	Cause of Persecution
16th–17th	Japan	Anti-European, anti-Catholic persecution by the Japanese government
16th–18th	England and Ireland	Persecution of Catholics by the Church of England
17th–19th	Vietnam	Practice of Catholicism outlawed by Vietnamese government
18th	France	Large-scale persecution of Catholic Church during the French Revolution
18th–21st	China	Anti-Catholic persecution by Chinese government
19th	Korea	Anti-Catholic persecution by Korean government
19th	Uganda	Pagan leader rejection of the spread of the Gospel by Catholics and Protestants
20th	Mexico	Repression and persecution of Catholic Church by Mexican government
20th	Spain	Particular targeting of Catholics and Catholic institutions during the Spanish Civil War
20th	Russia and other Slavic countries	Explicit rejection of God and religion due to Communism
20th	Global	Promotion of pagan beliefs and persecution of Jews, Catholics, and other religious believers due to Nazism

Like a Father

As Catholics living in the twenty-first century, we have a tremendous library of resources, beginning with Scripture and ending with the latest official Church documents, to help us make decisions about our faith and how we practice it. The Christians who lived in the first several centuries after the life of Christ did not have that luxury. Instead, through prayer, hard work, robust debate, and, most importantly, an abundance of the Holy Spirit, the early Church began the process of developing Catholic doctrine.

Just as a father sometimes has to think carefully when he answers questions raised by his children, so the leaders of the early Church had to think carefully as they developed answers to the many questions raised by their brothers and sisters in Christ and the surrounding culture. Those questions included how Jesus Christ could be both God and man, how a Christian could remain faithful while living in an anti-Catholic culture, and how to distinguish true visions from false ones, as well as how to distinguish true visionaries from false ones. The early leaders who put forward the most convincing arguments for their positions, both through their writings and their living witness, came to be known as Fathers of the Church.

Unlike the martyrs, who clearly established their right to be honored as saints by dying for Jesus Christ, there has always been debate over which men should be granted the title of "Fathers".[1] This is in part because the Church has sometimes lacked complete information about the personal lives and writings of early Church leaders. Even today, there is still debate over whether to consider certain men as Fathers of the Church, but many names are widely accepted.

What does it mean to say that a man is a Father of the Church? The first criterion is obviously that he has been given that title by the

---

[1] Women of the early Church who are sometimes referred to as Mothers of the Church will be discussed at the end of this chapter.

Church; official approval must come from a general council of the Church or from the pope himself.

There are other criteria, such as being named in the *Roman Martyrology*, a list of saints of the Church that has been compiled since the sixteenth century. If that document lists a saint who lived in the first several centuries and who was known to be both holy and learned, he is considered a Father of the Church. Another criterion is whether there's evidence that a person's writings were read publicly in churches during those centuries, showing respect for the orthodoxy of those writings from the earliest times. Finally, if one of the more celebrated Fathers of the Church praised that person as a reliable authority about the faith, he could be considered a Father.

Leading by example

All the early popes of the Church risked martyrdom when they accepted election as leader of the Catholic Church, which was a powerful witness to their faith in Christ. But several of the early popes did much more than that.

Saint Peter was the first pope. He was followed by Linus, then Anacletus,[2] and then Clement. Pope Clement I reigned during the years 88–97 and, according to tradition, was martyred by being thrown from a boat into the sea, weighed down by an anchor. But Clement is known as a Father of the Church more for a letter that bears his name than for his brave martyrdom.

This letter, known as *I Clement* (*First Letter of Clement*) or his *Letter to the Corinthians*,[3] was written in response to a schism that was occurring among the Christians in the city of Corinth, Greece. In the same way that Saint Paul wrote to encourage the feuding Christians of Corinth in the biblical books we know as First Corinthians and Second Corinthians, so Clement later wrote a long letter encouraging Christians in that same city. He wrote about virtuous living,

---

[2] Some older records separated references to "Anacletus" and "Cletus" and identified them as two popes; modern scholars generally believe they are the same man.

[3] Another document, called *II Clement*, is sometimes attributed to Clement, but it is a homily rather than a letter, and since the time of Saint Jerome of Stridon, there have been doubts that Pope Clement wrote that document.

explained truths about God, and offered solutions to internal conflict in the Church. Because of details included in the letter, some say it is possible that Clement wrote it as early as the year 70, before he became pope, but it is also possible he wrote it during his pontificate. One of the most moving passages of that letter is at the end, in a prayer he offered to God.

> We beseech thee, Master, to be our helper and defender.
> Save those of us in affliction,
> Have mercy on the humble,
> Raise up the fallen,
> Show thyself to those in need,
> Heal the sick,
> Turn back those of thy people who have gone astray,
> Feed the hungry,
> Release our imprisoned ones,
> Revive the weak,
> Encourage the fainthearted.
> Let all the heathen know that thou art God alone, and
>   that Jesus Christ is thy Servant, and that we are thy
>   people and the sheep of thy pasture.[4]

Clement was a true shepherd to his flock, and so were several other early popes. Pope Dionysius I became pope soon after Roman emperor Valerian had been defeated in battle and imprisoned by a Persian king during the middle of the third century. Valerian had ruthlessly persecuted Christians while he was in power, and Dionysius comforted and reorganized the decimated Church as she recovered from that bitter persecution. In the year 382, Pope Damasus I presided over a council in the city of Rome; a major document of that council was the list of books that should be accepted as Sacred Scripture. That list, which dates from the year 382, is the same list that defines the contents of Catholic Bibles today. Pope Leo I was not only a great fifth-century negotiator who could deal with a brutal leader like Attila the Hun and convince him not to attack Rome,

---

[4] Clement I, *The Apostolic Fathers: Modern Translations of These Early Christian Writings*, ed. Jack N. Sparks (Nashville: Thomas Nelson Publishers, 1978), chap. 59, pp. 50–51.

but he was also a theologian who could explain Church teaching so effectively that he was able to resolve painful schisms over heretical teachings that were plaguing the Church during his reign. Pope Gregory I was a very influential pope of the sixth-century Church; his administrative actions involved development of sacred music and strength in leadership, but he was also a prolific writer of sermons, letters, and other works.

Ninety-one men reigned as pope from its beginning to the year 749, the year that the last Father of the Church, Saint John of Damascus, died. Most of those men are acclaimed as saints, but the five great popes described above are particularly honored as Fathers of the Church because of the Christlike way they served as Chief Shepherd of His Church.

Another way that the Fathers of the Church acted with fatherly concern for the Church was through their reliance on tradition, rather than innovation, in their teaching. From the beginning, Christians remembered Christ's warning that there were wolves and thieves who would come and try to snatch His sheep away from His flock.[5] They consciously expressed their arguments for or against certain positions by relying on Christ's words, as well as the words of those Christians who had faithfully followed Him all their lives. Saint Jerome of Stridon was probably the first Christian to establish his interpretation of a biblical text through a string of passages from other writers, and Christian thinkers from Saint Thomas Aquinas to the apologists of today do the same. As the *Catechism* says:

> The apostles entrusted the "Sacred deposit" of the faith (the *depositum fidei*), contained in Sacred Scripture and Tradition, to the whole of the Church. "By adhering to [this heritage] the entire holy people, united to its pastors, remains always faithful to the teaching of the apostles, to the brotherhood, to the breaking of the bread and the prayers. So, in maintaining, practicing, and professing the faith that has been handed on, there should be remarkable harmony between the bishops and the faithful."[6]

[5] Jn 10:12.
[6] *Catechism of the Catholic Church*, no. 84, quoting Vatican Council II, Dogmatic Constitution on Divine Revelation *Dei Verbum* (November 18, 1965), no. 10.

This common practice of relying on both the Bible and the Tradition of the Church seemed so obvious to the early Christians as to be uncontroversial—until someone failed to do it. For example, when the fifth-century abbot (later judged to be a heretic) named Eutyches was brought before a council to explain his belief that Jesus Christ did not have both a divine and human nature, he referred only to Scripture and refused to put forward arguments from the writings of the Fathers or previous councils. His judges were horrified. How could you claim to be speaking the truth if you refuse to accept the unbroken Tradition of the Church? In some senses, the Fathers of the Church *are* the Tradition of the Church.

Saint Augustine of Hippo would have been one of the greatest thinkers at any time, in any place, in history. He could have been named a Father of the Church for just one of his accomplishments, but he influenced the Christians of his time in several different ways.

As bishop of Hippo (a city in modern Algeria) in the fifth century, Augustine served as the chief shepherd of his diocese. His numerous sermons not only inspired his flock, but they still sparkle with his insights and personality, while remaining rooted in Christian thought. As the founder of a small monastic community prior to his election as bishop, he personally inspired his clergy to live lives of simplicity and deep prayer. His philosophical works have provoked philosophical discussions among Catholics and non-Catholics alike for centuries; only a brilliant man could write in such a way that men and women would still be writing doctoral dissertations explaining his thought fifteen centuries later. He responded to popular heresies of the day so astutely that one almost feels sorry for the Manichaeans, Donatists, and Pelagians who were no match for his intelligence. He may not have created the genre of autobiography with his *Confessions*, but that book has inspired Christian conversions ever since and is still studied by the secular world. Finally, in the realm one might expect to be of the greatest importance to a Father of the Church, he created a corpus of Christian writings explaining theological and moral topics such as original sin, grace, free will, the Trinity, the nature of the human soul, marriage, consecrated virginity, and virtue, as well as Scripture commentaries. In the *Catechism of the Catholic Church*, Augustine is quoted more often than any other writer, except for the Bible itself.

These Fathers, perhaps more than others, show the Catholic Church to be a *living* Church, in that the words of these great men still lead and guide the Church away from error and toward the truth today.

Fathers to the death

Several of the early Church Fathers sacrificed their lives for their faith in Christ. But it was how they lived and how they died that causes them to be described as "Fathers" more often than "martyrs".

Unlike most of the other Fathers described here, we do not know a great deal about the actual martyrdom of Saint Cyprian of Carthage (d. 258). All we do know is that during the anti-Catholic persecution initiated under the Roman emperor Valerian, soldiers showed up at Cyprian's house, probably because he was the city's bishop. When he both admitted he was a Christian and refused to renounce his faith, they beheaded him.

However, that was not the first time that a Roman emperor had tried to kill Cyprian. Several years before, a previous Roman emperor named Decius had also persecuted Christians; that time, Cyprian had fled the city and escaped arrest. Cyprian later defended his decision to run away in writing, pointing out that, as head of the Church in Carthage, his death would leave the Christians there without a leader. As anti-Catholic governments for the eighteen centuries since have demonstrated, it is much easier to destroy the Christian community if it does not have a visible head. When the persecution ended in Carthage, Cyprian returned. While many Christians had died during the persecution, some had survived, and Cyprian had to rebuild the Christian community. At this point, he faced a serious problem that most Christian bishops faced during the first few centuries of the Church: What do you do about the apostates?

That is, when threatened by death, torture, and threats against family members, some Christians renounced their faith. Later, when the persecution had passed, some wanted to return to the faith. Should they be allowed to do so? In time, the Church recognized that, while accepting martyrdom rather than renouncing one's faith was a heroic and holy act, not everyone was called to such an act.

Moreover, because these threats were coercive, the person who gave in to such pressure was not making a decision of his own free will. In time, the Church allowed Christians who had apostatized under pressure to return to the Church, after completing a suitable penance. Cyprian was one of the bishops who developed a moderate practice—between the extreme of never allowing such people to return or letting them all return without doing penance—to respect both the shining example of the martyrs and the mercy of God toward those who had not accepted a brutal martyrdom. On the other hand, Cyprian put himself on the wrong side of the Church in a different matter: Could Baptism performed by heretics be valid? Eventually, the Church said yes, while Cyprian had said no. But by then, he had already witnessed to his faith in Christ by dying for Him.

Saints Justin Martyr (c. 100–165) and Severinus Boethius (c. 480–524) lived almost four hundred years apart. However, they were both Christian philosophers and lived in a Rome that was ruled by an emperor who opposed Catholic teaching. The brilliant explanations each man publicly gave for his faith in Christ were uncomfortably effective in bringing people to faith in Christ. Both were therefore arrested for the crime of being Christian, both gave brave and intelligent answers to questions about their beliefs, and, sadly, both were later executed. Justin explains in his writings that the truth and moral beauty of Christianity led him to become a believer, though it appears another factor in his conversion was watching real-life Christians face death with an inexplicable serenity. Severinus Boethius' most famous work is his *Consolation of Philosophy*, a writing he composed while in prison and awaiting death, in which he points out the great truth that happiness can be found in God alone. As philosophers who recognized the compatibility of faith and reason, both men are still excellent examples to Catholic apologists today.

While Justin and Severinus were philosophers living centuries apart, two other great Fathers of the Church—Saints Polycarp and Ignatius—lived at the same time and knew each other.

Ignatius (c. 50–107) was bishop of Antioch (Syria); Polycarp (69–155) was bishop of Smyrna (Turkey). While Polycarp's pastoral letter to the Christians of Philippi still exists, both men are best known for the writings surrounding their deaths by martyrdom.

The Roman emperor Trajan decided that the natives of recently conquered lands should worship the pagan gods of the Roman Empire, and his order, which was designed to ensure his control over all those in the empire, caught Christians in the same trap. Trajan, unlike some other emperors, did not seek out Christians for persecution, but he saw nothing wrong with executing them if individuals were publicly identified as Christian. While Trajan was visiting the city of Antioch, Bishop Ignatius' opposition to the emperor's order to worship pagan gods got him arrested and brought before the emperor himself. He bravely defended his faith—and was sentenced to death by Trajan.

And not just any death. Since Ignatius was a well-known figure, the emperor decided to send him to Rome so that he could be publicly and brutally executed as entertainment for the bloodthirsty Roman populace. As Ignatius traveled, chained to the soldiers he characterized as "leopards", the boat he was on stopped in cities along the Mediterranean coast. Christians from these cities and the surrounding countryside came to see, pray with, cry over, and encourage the valiant bishop. During the journey, he wrote letters to those Christian communities. His six letters describe his journey and include his words of encouragement to his fellow Christians. In one of his most powerful letters, he not only showed his vivid awareness of the brutality awaiting him but also asked his fellow Christians in Rome *not* to use any influence they might have with local authorities to stop his death, which he knew would likely involve being attacked and killed by wild animals in the arena.

> I am writing to all the churches and I command all men: I am voluntarily dying for God if you do not hinder me. I exhort you not to be an "inopportune favor" to me. (Let me be food for the wild beasts, through which I can attain to God. I am the wheat of God and I am ground by the teeth of wild beasts so that I may be found the pure bread of Christ.)[7]

Not only did Ignatius know that his death for Christ would bring him to eternal life with Christ in Heaven, but he also knew that Jesus

---

[7] Ignatius, *Letter to the Romans* 4, in Sparks, *Apostolic Fathers*, p. 99.

was not merely symbolically represented in the Eucharist. Ignatius wanted to become like Christ, broken down in the arena as kernels of wheat were broken down to become bread, to become the food of animals as Jesus Christ becomes our food in Holy Communion. Catholic teaching on the Real Presence didn't start in the Middle Ages; it started in the Upper Room on Holy Thursday—Ignatius' awareness of Christ's Presence in the Blessed Sacrament less than a hundred years after His death demonstrates that.

Another letter that Ignatius wrote was to Bishop Saint Polycarp of Smyrna. He had met Polycarp on his journey, was impressed by the man, and encouraged him in his duties as a bishop and reminded him of the duties of the laypeople in his flock.

Almost five decades passed before Polycarp himself was threatened with death. When the persecution started this time, his flock, who greatly loved their elderly bishop, begged him to hide from the authorities. He complied with their request, but two Christian boys who were slaves were tortured into giving up Polycarp's hiding place. Polycarp was found and arrested. Ever mindful of Christian charity, the elderly bishop offered the soldiers food to eat when they arrived and left cheerfully with them. When he was brought before the Roman proconsul, he refused to give up his faith but spoke respectfully to him. To appease the crowd watching the trial, the proconsul ordered Polycarp to be burned at the stake. Being burned to death—while alive—is an extremely painful way to die, but Polycarp's death was full of signs of God's grace. Polycarp convinced the guard to only tie him to the stake, not nail him there, saying that God would give him the grace to stay in place. As the flames encircled Polycarp's body, witnesses smelled something like baking bread, not burning flesh. When a guard was ordered to end Polycarp's life quickly—since this was certainly not turning out to be the agonizing example of Christian weakness they'd hoped for—witnesses also recorded that they saw a dove fly out of Polycarp's side, and the blood from Polycarp's body extinguished the fire. Perhaps because the whole experience of Polycarp's peaceful death was so surreal, the proconsul ordered his body to be burned to ashes. He thought those crazy Christians might start worshipping Polycarp next.

But in all the examples of martyred Fathers of the Church—their persistence, brilliance, and serenity—no one has ever been confused about the source of those virtues. In each case, the man is honored precisely because he followed the example of his Lord.

Fighting heresies

Racial segregation in the United States was not a heresy against the Catholic faith, but it was certainly an ugly injustice. Though we may find it an incomprehensible practice today, those Americans who supported it offered arguments to explain its necessity, mostly based on flimsy explanations of science or religion designed to show that segregating people by race was somehow better for those races and for society. But the American people did not just wake up one morning and see through these lies; it took time, and, more importantly, it took good arguments.

Whether it involves motivating Americans to reject racial segregation, convincing Europeans that the earth is round and not flat, or even teaching modern people to wear their car seat belts, encouraging a large number of people to change their lives and beliefs cannot be done instantaneously. When Arius proposed his false interpretation[8] of the Christian faith in the fourth century, his convincing arguments initially won over many people, particularly powerful people. Winning the hearts and minds of Catholics back to a true understanding of the nature of Jesus Christ could not be done in a day or by one man. Instead, God inspired a team of great men to explain and witness to the truth about Christ. Each one of those Fathers of the Church contributed in his own way to the ultimate defeat of Arianism.

While the great archenemy of Arianism, Saint Athanasius (d. 373), bishop of Alexandria, wrote voluminously against this heresy and was bitterly persecuted for it, he was certainly not the only great thinker of the early Church who fought against it. Saint Alexander (d. 328) was bishop of Alexandria—Athanasius was his secretary before he succeeded him as bishop—when Arius began promoting his theology. Alexander corrected him publicly and wrote letters to other bishops explaining Arius' errors. Saint Hilary (d. 368) was bishop

[8] Arianism is described in the following chapter.

of Poitiers in France when he first started speaking out and writing against Arianism. He saw that Arius' error was rooted in a misunderstanding of the Blessed Trinity, so he wrote *On the Trinity* to explain the truth and expose errors. Saint Cyril (d. 444), a later bishop of Alexandria, combatted both Arianism and the heresy of Nestorius in a unique way: he was so prolific in his writings that his opponents couldn't keep up. Saint Fulgentius of Ruspe (d. 533) wrote against Arianism as well as the heresy of Pelagianism, and he, like a good son of the Church, used the writings of an earlier Father, Saint Augustine of Hippo, to explain the false teachings of Pelagius about God's grace and human free will.

Before Arius became a byword for controversy, strange ideas that sound a lot like today's New Age teachings became a problem for the early Church. Saint Irenaeus (d. c. 203) was the bishop of Lyons in France when Gnostic ideas began percolating throughout his diocese. In his greatest work, *Against Heresies*, he poked fun at the theology proposed by the Gnostics. What Gnostics taught sounded very complicated, intelligent, and mystical, but Irenaeus, by carefully laying out all their theology for everyone to see, showed their ideas to be absurd and ridiculous. Irenaeus parodied the made-up names Gnostics had created to describe their made-up theology by making up his own mock theology, with names like "gourd", "cucumber", and "melon". It made people laugh, and it made them recognize the foolishness of Gnosticism.

Saint Sophronius (d. 638) was patriarch of Jerusalem; Saint Maximus the Confessor (d. 662) was a monk who wrote about the Bible and mysticism when many aspects of Christology were being debated. Followers of Christ agreed that Jesus was both the Son of God and a man, but they were still trying to understand how one person could be both. (Not that we are not still trying to understand better this great mystery ...) The heresy that came to be called Monothelitism tried to explain this complex situation by saying while Jesus did have both a divine nature and a human nature, He had only a divine will, not a human will. Sophronius and Maximus confronted the errors that followed from this assumption through their writings and public witness, seeing any misunderstanding of the nature of our Savior to be a matter worth suffering and dying for. When Maximus refused to bow to political pressure and accept the false teaching, he was tortured, mutilated, and sent into exile, where he later died.

Building up the Church in other ways

When we think of the Fathers of the Church and how they defended and explained Catholic teaching in the first few centuries, we tend to think of Saint Augustine preaching homilies, Saint Athanasius hiding in the desert from assassins, and Saint Jerome translating the Bible. These larger-than-life figures have a right to be respected for their great intellects and greater sacrifices. But there were other ways to defend Christ and His Church; the following men became both saints and Fathers in their own unique vocations.

Saints Hippolytus (d. 236), Theodoret of Cyrrhus (d. c. 458), and Andrew of Crete (d. 740) are all considered saints for their brilliant arguments and for their final adherence to the authority of the Church. (Note the word "final".) Hippolytus was so emphatic about the proper understanding and practice of the faith that he criticized more than one pope for lack of rigor in papal statements and eventually gathered followers who claimed that he, Hippolytus, was the true pope, not the man sitting on the papal chair. When the Roman emperor arrested both Hippolytus and the true pope and sent them to work as slaves in the mines, Hippolytus reconciled with the Church and with the pope before both men died as martyrs. Theodoret was a brilliant man who sided with Nestorius, the patriarch of Constantinople whose heretical teachings, including a refusal to accept the title of "Mother of God" for the Blessed Mother, caused great controversy in the early fifth-century Church. Theodoret was condemned by a Church council, and his writings were ordered to be burned. Later, he was able to convince his fellow bishops that he accepted Church teaching in these matters; therefore, he was reconciled to the Church and thus is now considered a saint of the Church. Andrew was the bishop of Crete (Greece) and sided with those in favor of Monothelitism, a heresy that was condemned by the Church. Since Monothelitism was, in some ways, simply a teaching that was proposed to reconcile those following a different heresy (Monophysitism) back to the Church, it's easy to see why he and others would have briefly accepted a faulty teaching before the ramifications of that teaching were fully understood. All three of these men show us how difficult it is to remain on the side of truth when the Church has not fully examined proposed teachings—but how easy it is to return to the Church when one loves our Lord and follows His teaching and example of obedience.

Apologetic arguments are not the only way to build up people's faith. Saint Serapion (d. c. 370), bishop of Thmuis, Egypt, wrote a beautiful prayer book called the *Sacramentary*, which was used by early priests during the celebration of Mass, Baptism, Benediction, and funerals. Saint Venantius Fortunatus (d. c. 600) was the bishop of Poitiers, France; his Latin hymns and poems inspired Catholics during his own lifetime and for centuries afterward. Saint John Climacus (d. 649) was a monk on Mount Sinai in Egypt; he wrote *The Ladder of Divine Ascent* about his own experiences of prayer and to help his fellow monks pray.

During their homilies at Mass every Sunday, our priests today try to teach us how to draw close to God and live the Gospel. Some Fathers of the Church—Saints Gregory of Nazianzus (d. 389), John Chrysostom (d. 407), and Peter Chrysologus (d. 450)—were exceptionally good preachers. The surnames of the latter two saints mean, respectively, "golden mouthed" and "golden tongued" in Greek, nicknames indicating how much the people in the pews looked forward to hearing them preach. The sermons of these men were that rare and wonderful intersection of profound teaching and excellent delivery, with a message that one could walk out the church doors and *live*—a unique ability, which inspires the laity in every time and place.

But not every Father of the Church was a priest serving a parish of families. Saint John Cassian (d. c. 435) was a monk in Marseilles, France. He collected the teachings of the early Desert Fathers[9] in his *Conferences*, and he codified the lessons from the Desert Fathers about how to live a monastic life in his *Institutes*. Monastic communities still read and learn from Cassian's writings today. Saint Benedict of Nursia (d. c. 550) wrote a simple, practical, holy Rule of Life that has

---

[9] The Christian men who lived as monks and hermits in the Scetes desert of Egypt beginning in the third century are commonly called the Desert Fathers. The women who lived and prayed in the desert are known as the Desert Mothers.

been the inspiration of multiple religious orders, including his own Benedictine monks.

Saint Vincent of Lerins (d. 445) was a monk and priest who is sometimes criticized for his views about the role of grace and free will, which seem to side with the heresy of Semi-Pelagianism. In his defense, Vincent died before that heresy was rejected by the Church, so we have no way of knowing what he would have said if the Church had presented the dangers of that teaching to him. But Vincent provided the Church with an invaluable tool when he composed his *Commonitory*, a document he wrote to summarize all the teachings he had learned from his study of the previous Fathers of the Church. He had a bad memory, he said, and wanted to write down all that he had learned. We can thank God that he did, because he wrote, among other things, this powerful explanation:

> Moreover, in the Catholic Church itself, all possible care must be taken, that we hold that faith which has been believed everywhere, always, by all. For that is truly and in the strictest sense "Catholic," which, as the name itself and the reason of the thing declare, comprehends all universally. This rule we shall observe if we follow universality, antiquity, consent. We shall follow universality if we confess that one faith to be true, which the whole Church throughout the world confesses; antiquity, if we in no wise depart from those interpretations which it is manifest were notoriously held by our holy ancestors and fathers; consent, in like manner, if in antiquity itself we adhere to the consentient definitions and determinations of all, or at least of almost all priests and doctors.[10]

Those three characteristics of true Catholic teaching—that it be held universally, from ancient times, and with the consent of all, or at least most, of the leaders of the Church—are now recognized as essential. Want to propose a new doctrine of the Church on any subject? That doctrine must be measured against those three benchmarks

---

[10] Vincent of Lerins, *Commonitory* 2, 6, trans. C. A. Heurtley, in *Nicene and Post-Nicene Fathers*, 2nd series, vol. 11, ed. Philip Schaff and Henry Wace (Buffalo, NY: Christian Literature Publishing, 1894). Revised and edited for New Advent by Kevin Knight, NewAdvent .org, 2021, http://www.newadvent.org/fathers/3506.htm.

of universality, antiquity, and consent: it has been believed every-where, always, and by all.

Fathers but not saints

All of the following men said they loved Jesus Christ. All of them were intelligent and well read. All of them appear to have been bap-tized members of the Church. Yet, none of them are currently con-sidered to be saints by the Church. In today's culture, which seems to assume that everyone except Adolf Hitler goes to Heaven at the time of death, this might seem surprising.

It should first be said that some of the Fathers of the Church who do not have the title of "saint" may well be saints in Heaven. The Church here on earth, however, cannot canonize some of them for complicated reasons, sometimes because we simply lack enough information about them. For this reason, it has often become the practice to refer to them as "ecclesiastical writers" rather than Fathers of the Church today. But they were influential Christians in their own time, and many of them are still studied today.

Clement of Alexandria (d. 215) is a perfect example of an early Christian writer about whom we have very little information. He was a layman who served as the leader of a catechetical school in Alexan-dria, Egypt, and several of his writings still survive. Unsurprisingly, his writings deal with the sorts of things that you would expect from a Catholic educator: how to deal with the non-Christian philosophy of potential converts to the faith, why the faith is true, and how to lead a person to live a life of Christian virtue. But in the seventeenth century, the famous ecclesiastical historian and cardinal Cesare Baro-nius convinced the pope that there wasn't enough proof in surviving records about Clement to be certain that he'd lived a holy life, as well as no evidence that the early Christian faithful had considered him a saint in Heaven. Additionally, Clement had apparently espoused some of the early Christian writer Origen's problematic theories. So, for lack of positive evidence that Clement was a saint, he officially lost the title three hundred years ago.

In other cases, the reason the following men are not considered saints is easier to understand. Tatian (d. second century) was a Syrian who was born a pagan but became a Christian. His *Diatesseron* was one of the first attempts to harmonize the four Gospels into one complete account of Jesus' life. But he also left the Church to establish his own church, one which considered both marriage and alcohol illicit. Tertullian (d. c. 222) wrote beautifully about many topics of Christian life, so beautifully that he is quoted multiple times in the *Catechism of the Catholic Church*. But Tertullian was attracted by the teachings of a man named Montanus, who oddly combined a rigorous approach of dealing with sinners with a reliance on subjective charismatic experience (some say he thought that he was the incarnation of the Holy Spirit, in the same way that Jesus was the incarnation of the Son of the Father). Tertullian eventually left the Catholic Church for the heretical church of Montanus; Catholics generally consider his writings "safe" up to that point in his life.

Falling for false teachings is not an irrevocable mistake, as was proved by Eusebius (d. 340). He was the bishop of Caesarea in Palestine and the author of *Ecclesiastical History* and other works that are still greatly respected. But he strayed into the camp of Arianism for a time before formally accepting the Nicene Creed and rejecting that heresy.

It could be said that a few of the early Fathers should have listened to Saint Jerome, who encouraged Christians to become so familiar with the Bible that they should fall asleep with a copy in their hands. Though no one faults the polished, educated writing style used by Lactantius (d. 323) in his writings about the faith as a Christian teacher, those writings seem to lack a familiarity with Sacred Scripture. Similarly, Arnobius (d. 330) apparently wrote his apologetic work about the Christian faith too soon after his conversion, so it seems weak on Christian doctrine.

The reason that Didymus the Blind (d. 398), a layman-turned-theologian, and Rufinus of Aquileia (d. 410), a monk-theologian, are not known as saints today could be summarized by a single exhortation: choose your friends carefully. Both men were a bit too uncritical in their acceptance of the teachings of the great Scripture scholar Origen.

Origen (d. c. 254) was the leader of a catechetical school in Alexandria, Egypt. He can be fairly described as one of the greatest biblical exegetes in the history of the Church; like Tertullian, he is quoted in our modern *Catechism*. He was born into a family of Christian martyrs and died after being imprisoned and tortured for the faith, thereby proving his faithfulness to Christ. He was a prolific scholar, although many of his works have been lost to us over time. But he was also a very speculative thinker; that is, he proposed innovative theories to explain some aspects of the faith, which later scholars studied and expanded upon. Problematic areas included his use of allegorical explanations of Scripture, his explanation of the relationship between the Persons of the Trinity, and his answers to questions about the Second Coming. Some of his controversial teachings were later rejected by the Church.

There were also rumors that, taking Jesus' encouragement to "cut off your hand if it causes you to sin",[11] Origen had himself castrated. It is possible that this is merely a later rumor started by those who opposed his teachings, but we will never know for certain. Because of the controversies surrounding Origen's teaching—perhaps more than Origen himself—the Church will always greatly respect him as a Father of the Church but probably never give him the title of saint.

The last Father to be discussed here can also never be considered a saint because we do not know his real name. Acts 17:34 explains that a man named Dionysius converted to the faith as a result of the Apostle Paul's teaching in the Areopagus in Greece. Tradition says Dionysius became a bishop and died a martyr. In the sixth century, a Christian theologian wrote several works under the pen name of Dionysius the Areopagite. Now often called Pseudo-Dionysius the Areopagite, this man was greatly respected and his writings were studied by medieval thinkers. Saint Thomas Aquinas himself quotes liberally from his writings, apparently assuming them to be written contemporaneously with the Bible. Since that time, scholars have become convinced that they were written at the later date. Since we know nothing about the man's personal life or real identity, we can hardly propose him as a candidate for sainthood. But God, who inspired him to write so profoundly about the inner life of the Trinity, the choirs of angels, and the names of God, knows the whole story about both Dionysius and Pseudo-Dionysius.

Mothers of the Church

The lower level of the Basilica of the National Shrine of the Immaculate Conception in Washington, DC, contains a crypt church. Built

[11] See Mt 5:30.

in a cruciform shape, this church locates the tabernacle containing our Lord in the Blessed Sacrament at the head of that cross shape, with Saints Joseph, Elizabeth, John the Evangelist, and Anne in side chapels on each side. The left and right arms of the cruciform shape also contain several side chapels dedicated to saints. One might expect such important side chapels to be dedicated to saints who were famous, powerful, or well educated while they were alive. But most of these side chapels are dedicated to early virgin martyrs of the Church, such as Saints Agnes of Rome (d. third or fourth century), Agatha of Sicily (d. 251), Cecilia of Rome (d. 304), Anastasia of Sirmium (d. third or fourth century), Margaret of Antioch (d. 304), Catherine of Alexandria (d. unknown), Susanna of Rome (d. unknown), and Lucy of Rome (d. c. 300). Each small chapel features a beautiful golden mosaic image of the lovely young woman, including, as is typical in saint iconography, an image that shows how the woman was executed or tortured. Saint Agnes is shown with her traditional symbol, a lamb, since "agnes" means "lamb" in Latin, as well as the sword that was used to behead her.

To those who claim that the Church hates women, the virgin martyrs are the perfect answer.

The ancient world, much like today's culture and almost every culture in between, expected men and women to marry. While Christianity was not the first religion to espouse the practice of virginity as a religious virtue, its reason was based on a fact: Jesus Christ lived a celibate life. He renounced God's gift of marriage to serve God more completely as a celibate man, and Christian men and women have done the same ever since. Ancient culture and modern culture alike consider this practice to be impossible, embarrassing, and laughable.

But no one was laughing when grown men, faced with the prospect of torture, renounced their faith in Christ during the brutal persecution of Christians in the Roman Empire, while young women outshone them in courage by refusing to do the same, even during torture. These brave Christian women, like the nuns and sisters of today, had willingly chosen to give up the blessings of marriage and children to espouse themselves to Jesus Christ, their Heavenly Bridegroom. When discovered by the Roman authorities—and they were probably not hard to find because of their countercultural way of life—they refused to renounce their faith, even enduring brutal tortures and attempts at forced prostitution.

It is commonly believed that up to 50 percent of the population of the Roman Empire were slaves; neither slaves nor women were generally considered worthy of receiving an education. It is therefore not surprising that the greatest female Christians from this early time period did not write treatises on the mysteries of the Blessed Trinity. But that is exactly why the behavior of the virgin martyrs was so astonishing to their pagan contemporaries.

The ancient world used capital punishment routinely and brutally as a deterrent to crime. People were used to seeing public executions and crucifixions, as well as seeing living human beings slaughtered in the arena. They were used to watching thieves, robbers, murderers, and even respected people who had fallen from power cry, curse, scream, and beg during these gruesome and very public deaths. What an amazing sight it must have been to watch young women peacefully and prayerfully walk to their executions! We know that this is exactly what happened because the pagans remarked upon it and were mystified by it. Often enough, the terrible sight of a martyr "falling asleep",[12] in death, opened the minds of some of the onlookers to want to find out more about that mysterious religion that claimed its Founder rose from the dead.

In that way, the deaths of the virgin martyrs are the most perfect examples of the parable Jesus described in John 12:24; by dying to themselves, they brought new life to the world.

Though Saints Perpetua and Felicity died as martyrs too, they were not virgins; they were mothers. Although we can identify only a general time period for the dates of the deaths of some early martyrs, we know exactly when and where Perpetua and Felicity died: March 7, 203, in the city of Carthage (Tunisia).

Perpetua had a pagan father and a Christian mother. She married and gave birth to a child before deciding to become a Christian. She and four other people, including her slave, Felicity, were catechumens receiving instruction in the faith when the leaders of Carthage resumed the persecution of Christians. All five of the catechumens were arrested and interrogated, but they refused to give up their faith in Christ. While in prison, Perpetua was allowed to keep and nurse her baby, and Felicity gave birth to her own child. Perpetua's father tried repeatedly to convince her to change her mind and save her life,

---

[12] See Acts 7:60.

but she refused. All five—two women and three men—were baptized in prison, though one of the men died while they were awaiting their execution. The other four Christians were led into the amphitheater on a March day in the early third century, where they were killed and devoured by wild animals.

We know so many details about this group of martyrs because Perpetua left behind her diary describing the end of her life and a Christian eyewitness later added his account of their deaths. Even skeptical modern scholars generally accept that this document, *The Passion of the Holy Martyrs of Perpetua and Felicity*, is a contemporary account of an actual event, not fiction. After all, the description of Perpetua's father crying and pleading with her to change her mind, the dreams she received in prison, and her concern about the baby she would have to leave behind are deeply moving, powerful, and true to life. It is easy to understand why, a few centuries later, this account was so popular among Christians that Saint Augustine of Hippo would have to remind Christians that it was not part of the canon of Scripture. Every woman grieves the possibility that she might have to choose between her faith in Jesus and her child.

Saint Paula (347–404) was born into a wealthy, powerful family in the city of Rome; she married and had four daughters and a son. When her husband died, she was only thirty-two years old. Another wealthy woman of Rome, Saint Marcella (325–410), was also a noblewoman who had been left a widow, in her case after less than a year of marriage. But Marcella was a deeply devout woman who gathered other Christian widows to her home and inspired them to live holy lives.

Unlike Perpetua and Felicity, these two women lived during the time after Constantine's edict permitted the practice of the Christian faith. Although there were periodic persecutions of Catholics during their lifetimes, they were generally protected by their wealth and nobility. More importantly, they discovered around the year 382 that they had a kindred spirit in the pope's secretary, the man we know as Saint Jerome of Stridon.

Although Jerome was known for his sensitive nature and intolerance of bad ideas and weak men, he met his match in Marcella and Paula. Jerome taught the devout women who gathered at Marcella's home, encouraging them to embrace a virtuous, holy way of life as Christian wives, widows, and mothers. And he became a fast friend.

When Jerome left Rome to live in solitude in the Holy Land, Paula did the same a month later, bringing her daughter Eustochium with her. Paula wrote to others about her pilgrimage to sites throughout the Holy Land and then settled down in a monastery in Bethlehem. Jerome lived in a monastery for men in the same city. The money used to establish both monasteries was Paula's, who gave up everything to live a life of poverty with other holy women. She died among them in that monastery, and Saint Jerome wrote a long, consoling letter to her daughter afterward.

Saint Marcella remained in Rome, where she was known for her life of prayer and study, as well as visits to the tombs of the martyrs. (There were many tombs to the martyrs in the city of Rome.) When she was eighty-five years old, the Vandals invaded Rome and looted it. They captured and tortured her to try to force her to relinquish her goods—but she had already given away everything to the poor. When they realized she had no treasure, they released her, and she died soon afterward.

The lives of Saints Monica (333–387) and Helena (c. 250–330) are fairly well known. Helena was the wife of the Roman emperor Constantius Chlorus (250–306) and the mother of the Roman emperor Constantine the Great (272–337). She was only the daughter of an innkeeper when Constantius married her, and he was later convinced to divorce her in order to marry more profitably. When her son became emperor, she was no longer rebuffed as the "lower born first wife" and was allowed to return to polite society. She apparently became a Christian after her son's rather public acceptance of the faith. She was very generous with donations to the poor and to churches; on a pilgrimage to the Holy Land, she built churches to honor the Lord and is said to have brought back portions of the True Cross on which Christ died.

Monica was the Christian wife of a pagan official in Tagaste (North Africa); her husband was known to be bad-tempered, perhaps unfaithful, and certainly annoyed by her habit of praying. She had three children; we know little about two of them, but a great deal about the third: Saint Augustine of Hippo. It's due to Augustine's *Confessions* that we know about her faith in God, her many attempts to lead her son to become a Christian and live a moral life, her many tears over the fact that he refused to do either, and her eventual rejoicing when he accepted the faith.

The pain of unilateral divorce, abusive husbands, and wayward children is not unique to the ancient world, which is why these two saints have been commonly invoked by suffering wives and mothers up to today. Either woman could have chosen the paths of bitterness, anger, and separation, but instead they chose Christian patience, perseverance, and charity. The dangers of escalating violence in a marriage or apathy about a child caught up in a sinful lifestyle are, at present, more prevalent than the dangers of public execution, so these latter saints can more easily be seen as motherly intercessors as we deal with our own family dysfunctions.

All these holy women—from the virgin martyrs, to Perpetua and Felicity, to Paula and Marcella, to Monica and Helena—show themselves to be foundation stones in the edifice of the Church, just as surely as the Fathers of the Church, who defined dogmas, composed creeds, and battled heretics.

Saint Catherine of Alexandria, who defended her faith to the emperor though she was only eighteen years old, proved true Christ's prediction that Christians would have to stand before kings for His sake.[13] Saint Perpetua showed that she perfectly understood Christ's admonition that "He who loves son or daughter more than me is not worthy of me"[14] when she refused to renounce her faith. Saint Paula demonstrated that she was a better Christian than the rich young man who went away sad, more enamored of his possessions than following Christ,[15] when she died in poverty. Saint Monica lived out Christ's command to "forgive, and you will be forgiven"[16] by continuing to seek reconciliation with her husband and son. In these women's lives, we learn that being a Christian begins and ends with the love we show in our families and communities. It is this love that has changed the world before and will change it yet again.

Summary

The following is a summary of most of the men commonly accepted as Fathers of the Church or ecclesiastical writers, as well as the ways that

---

[13] Mk 13:9.
[14] Mt 10:37.
[15] Mt 19:16–22.
[16] Lk 6:37.

these men are sometimes categorized. For example, sometimes the Fathers of the Church are grouped by the time period in which they lived.

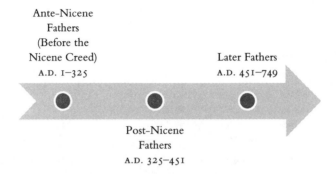

Ante-Nicene
Fathers
(Before the
Nicene Creed)
A.D. 1–325

Later Fathers
A.D. 451–749

Post-Nicene
Fathers
A.D. 325–451

Century	Best-Known Fathers
1st–2nd	Apostles and apostolic Fathers Greek apologists Western apologists Fathers who responded to the heresies of Gnosticism and Marcionism
3rd	Writers from Africa, Alexandria, Asia Minor, Palestine, and Rome
4th	Apologetic and historical works Writers from Africa, Cappadocia, France, Italy, Spain, and Syria Writers from Alexandria known as the "Allegorical school" Writers from Antioch known as the "Literal school"
5th	Responses to Nestorian and Eutychian controversies Great popes and historians

Sometimes Fathers are grouped by their location, the language they spoke, or the manner by which they explained the faith. Note that those who lived under the authority of the Roman emperor (whose seat of power was Rome) are considered part of the Western empire; those who lived under the authority of the Eastern or Byzantine emperor (whose seat of power was generally Constantinople) are considered part of the Eastern empire.

Which Church leaders should be included as Fathers of the Church?
That is open to debate, but the following table includes those who
are most commonly considered to be Fathers, along with their notable contributions to the faith.

Name	Year of Death	Description	Notable Contributions
Saint Clement I	97	Pope	His *Letter to the Corinthians* (*I Clement*) still survives. Internal evidence in the letter indicates it may have been written around the year 70, meaning it was written at the same time as some books of the New Testament.
Saint Ignatius of Antioch	107	Bishop of Antioch (Turkey); martyr	He wrote six letters to Christian churches and another letter to Saint Polycarp of Smyrna while on his way to execution in Rome for being a Christian. These letters are an excellent source of information about the early Church and her teachings, particularly through Ignatius' descriptions of the Eucharist.
Saint Polycarp of Smyrna	155	Bishop of Smyrna (Turkey); martyr	He wrote a letter to the Philippian church, but the account of his martyrdom, *The Martyrdom of Polycarp*, written after his death, is also an important work.

(continued)

Name	Year of Death	Description	Notable Contributions
Saint Justin Martyr	165	Philosopher of Rome (Italy); martyr	He was the most important apologist for Christianity in his day. Several of his writings are extant, as well as the account of his martyrdom with other Christians.
Saint Irenaeus of Lyons	c. 202	Bishop of Lyons (France); martyr	His greatest work, *Against Heresies*, is an excellent explanation of the errors of Gnosticism.
Saint Cyprian of Carthage	258	Bishop of Carthage (Tunisia); martyr	In addition to his letters and treatises, an account of his martyrdom and the record of a council in Carthage, which he directed, survive.
Saint Dionysius I	c. 264	Pope	He reorganized the Church after the persecution by the emperor Valerian had ended. Fragments of his writings survive.
Saint Methodius of Olympus	311	Bishop of Olympus (Turkey); martyr	Only a handful of his writings have survived, and most are fragmentary. But he was an important theologian during his time and opposed some of Origen's controversial ideas.
Saint Alexander of Alexandria	328	Bishop of Alexandria (Egypt)	His writings explaining the Church conflict with Arius and Arianism show us the nature of the

Name	Year of Death	Description	Notable Contributions
			problematic teachings involved.
Saint Hilary of Poitiers	c. 368	Bishop of Poitiers (France); Doctor of the Church	His greatest work, *On the Trinity*, explains Trinitarian doctrine in response to the arguments proposed by Arianism.
Saint Serapion of Thmuis	c. 370	Bishop of Thmuis (Egypt)	His *Sacramentary* is a prayer book that contains the prayers used by the celebrant for Mass, Baptism, Benediction, ordination, and burial. He was also a supporter of Saint Athanasius against Arianism.
Saint Athanasius of Alexandria	373	Archbishop of Alexandria (Egypt); Doctor of the Church	His many writings explain Catholic teaching in response to the arguments of Arianism.
Saint Ephraem the Syrian	373	Deacon of Nisibus (Syria); Doctor of the Church	His hymns, generally written in response to Gnostic teachings, are his most notable works, but his writings also include homilies.
Saint Basil the Great	379	Bishop of Caesarea (Turkey); monastic founder; Doctor of the Church	His famous work, *On the Holy Spirit*, plus his letters and homilies made him known as a great defender of the Church against Arianism.

(continued)

Name	Year of Death	Description	Notable Contributions
Saint Damasus I	384	Pope	Several of his letters have survived, but he is perhaps best known for asking Saint Jerome to translate the Bible into Latin and for presiding over the Council of Rome in 382, which defined the canon of Scripture.
Saint Cyril of Jerusalem	386	Bishop of Jerusalem (Israel); Doctor of the Church	His *Catechetical Lectures* show us the explanation of the faith that was taught to catechumens in the early days of the Church.
Saint Gregory of Nazianzus	c. 389	Bishop of Nazianzus (Turkey); Doctor of the Church	His many *Orations* made him one of the greatest orators of the day and also showed him to be an excellent theologian.
Saint Gregory of Nyssa	395	Bishop of Nyssa (Turkey)	His many writings explain Church teaching and defend it against various heresies of the day.
Saint Ambrose of Milan	397	Layman when nominated as bishop of Milan (Italy); Doctor of the Church	He wrote many treatises to explain the faith and practice of the Church.
Saint John Chrysostom	407	Patriarch of Constantinople (Turkey); Doctor of the Church	Nicknamed "Chrysostom" (meaning "golden mouthed") after his death for his gift with words, he was the

Name	Year of Death	Description	Notable Contributions
			author of many excellent homilies and widely known as an outstanding preacher.
Saint Jerome of Stridon	c. 420	Priest, scholar, and hermit who died in Bethlehem (Israel); Doctor of the Church	Jerome was more than the famous translator of the entire Bible; he wrote biographies and responded to arguments of the day through several famous treatises.
Saint Augustine of Hippo	430	Bishop of Hippo (Algeria); Doctor of the Church	One of the most prolific and brilliant theologians in the history of the Church, it is difficult to limit his contributions to a short list. However, his *Confessions* and *City of God* are still studied by non-Catholics, and his explanation of the role of grace and free will has been developed for centuries.
Saint John Cassian	c. 435	Monk of Marseilles (France)	His *Conferences* and *Institutes* codify the teachings of the Desert Fathers. Some of his writings were later considered to be Semi-Pelagian, which was a heresy about the role of grace and free will that was later rejected by the Church. He died very soon after this heresy

(*continued*)

Name	Year of Death	Description	Notable Contributions
			became popular and was defined clearly enough to be noted as a problem.
Saint Cyril of Alexandria	444	Patriarch of Alexandria (Egypt); Doctor of the Church	He was a prolific writer on theological matters, and his works include biblical commentaries and responses to the heresies of Nestorianism and Arianism.
Saint Vincent of Lerins	445	Monk and priest of Lerins (France)	Like many Catholics in his time and place, he appears to have sided with Semi-Pelagianism, but his precise standing on this issue is not certain from his writings. He wrote his *Commonitory* as a reference to help him distinguish Catholic truth from falsehood, and it was and still is a helpful guide.
Saint Peter Chrysologus	c. 450	Archbishop of Ravenna (Italy); Doctor of the Church	He was known for his excellent preaching and homilies; some of the homilies still survive.
Saint Leo the Great	461	Pope; Doctor of the Church	He was a strong pope who dealt with multiple heresies and schisms, and his letters and sermons still survive.
Saint Venantius Fortunatus	c. 600	Poet and bishop of Poitiers (France)	He composed Latin hymns and poems that were influential during his lifetime and afterward.

Name	Year of Death	Description	Notable Contributions
Saint Severinus Boethius	524	Philosopher of Rome (Italy); martyr	While in prison awaiting execution, he composed his *Consolation of Philosophy*, a philosophical treatise that was very influential after his death.
Saint Fulgentius of Ruspe	533	Bishop of Ruspe (Tunisia)	Through letters and sermons, he spoke against the errors of Arianism and Pelagianism and was particularly noted for his explanations of grace and free will, following in the tradition of Saint Augustine of Hippo.
Saint Caesarius of Arles	543	Bishop of Arles (France)	He was the most influential bishop in France during his day, and his sermons and letters, along with a biography by his contemporaries, still survive.
Saint Benedict of Nursia	c. 550	Monk, abbot, and founder of a religious order (Italy)	His Rule not only governed his monks at Monte Cassino but also inspired many Benedictine orders, as well as other religious orders.
Saint Gregory of Tours	594	Bishop of Tours (France)	His *History of the Franks* chronicled early French history; his *Life of the Fathers* provides biographies of saintly men of the Church in France.

(continued)

Name	Year of Death	Description	Notable Contributions
Saint Gregory the Great	604	Pope; Doctor of the Church	His many achievements include founder of the medieval papacy; reformer of the sacred liturgy; and influential writer through letters, sermons, *Pastoral Rule* (describing the role of bishops), and *Dialogues* (describing real-life miracles).
Saint Isidore of Seville	636	Archbishop of Seville (Spain); Doctor of the Church	His *Etymologies* was a standard reference book for centuries. He also wrote treatises on Church teaching and the natural world.
Saint Sophronius	639	Patriarch of Jerusalem (Israel)	Though he was a prolific writer, not many of his writings have survived. However, his strong opposition to the Mono-thelite heresy was very influential at the time.
Saint John Climacus	649	Monk of Mount Sinai (Egypt)	His *Ladder of Divine Ascent*, which explains how to draw close to God, was written at the request of his abbot and is still a spiritual classic.
Saint Maximus the Confessor	662	Monk and confessor of Tsageri (Georgia)	He was tortured and mutilated because of his opposition to Monothe-litism; his many writings cover mystical and biblical subjects, as well as theology and responses to Monothelite teachings.

Name	Year of Death	Description	Notable Contributions
Saint Andrew of Crete	740	Bishop of Crete (Greece)	Though he briefly supported the positions of Monothelite leaders, he repented and publicly assented to the orthodox teaching of the Church. His masterpiece is a hymn called the *Great Canon of Repentance*.
Saint John of Damascus	c. 749	Priest and scholar of Damascus (Syria); Doctor of the Church	He was most influential in his opposition to the heresy of iconoclasm. His other writings include responses to heretical teachings, explanations of the Catholic faith, and an explanation of the Assumption of Mary.

The following table lists *ecclesiastical writers* from the early Church.

Name	Year of Death	Description	Notable Contributions
Hermas of Rome	Second century	He was an early Christian but not considered a saint.	His work, *The Shepherd*, contains his purported visions and was written around the year 80. It was considered for inclusion in Scripture but ultimately rejected.
Tatian the Syrian	Second century	Born a pagan, he became a Christian but later founded a heretical sect that forbade	His *Diatesseron* harmonizes the events of the four Gospels. He also wrote *Address to the Greeks* to explain the faults of the Greek religion.

(*continued*)

Name	Year of Death	Description	Notable Contributions
		marriage and the use of alcohol.	
Melito of Sardis	c. 180	Bishop of Sardis (Turkey)	Though he was a prolific author, most of his works have not survived. However, we know about his works because he was widely quoted by early Christian authors.
Clement of Alexandria	215	He was a layman who came to Alexandria after becoming a Christian, eventually serving as the leader of a catechetical school.	Several of his works have survived and cover various topics. Though he was previously acclaimed a saint by the Church, that changed in the seventeenth century because very little is known about his personal life and because he appears to have adhered to some problematic teachings of the early (and controversial) Catholic scholar Origen.
Tertullian of Carthage	c. 220	He was probably a layman though possibly a priest. He left the Church late in his life because he demanded a more rigorous approach to sinners and became a	His many writings include excellent explanations of prayer and the Christian life, as well as Christian defenses against heresies. The Church generally espouses the orthodoxy of his works up to the point in time when he separated from the Church and became a Montanist.

Name	Year of Death	Description	Notable Contributions
		follower of the heresy of Montanism.	
Hippolytus of Rome	236	Priest of Rome who became an anti-pope; reconciled with the Church and died a martyr while in exile	Several of his writings still exist, and they generally explain Catholic teaching in response to heresies and other religions.
Origen of Alexandria	c. 254	He was the leader of a catechetical school in Alexandria (Egypt), later in Palestine (Israel). Though not considered a saint, he was imprisoned and tortured for the faith.	One of the greatest biblical exegetes in the history of the Church, he was also a very prolific scholar. Some of his speculative ideas later led to considerable controversy and were rejected by the Church, which is the reason he is not acclaimed a saint and the reason that many of his writings have not survived.
Lactantius	323	He was born a pagan but became a Christian and teacher. He lived in poverty during the Diocletian persecution. He is not con-sidered a saint.	Several of his writings survive, have a polished style, and explain Christian teaching. However, he is faulted as a Catholic writer for not having a better grasp of Scripture.

(continued)

Name	Year of Death	Description	Notable Contributions
Arnobius	330	Born a pagan, he became a Christian and then Christian apologist. He is not considered a saint.	He wrote a defense of paganism against Christians while a pagan and then wrote a defense of Christianity against the pagans when he became a Christian. The latter writing is faulted for being written shortly after his conversion and therefore is weak in its grasp of Christian doctrine and Scripture.
Eusebius of Caesarea	340	He was bishop of Caesarea in Palestine (Israel); he is not considered a saint.	His major work was *Ecclesiastical History*, but he also wrote apologetic and exegetical works. His attempts to find a compromise with Arianism resulted in questions about his orthodoxy, but he eventually and formally accepted the Nicene Creed.
Didymus the Blind	c. 398	He was a layman-turned-theologian and was blind from childhood. He is not recognized as a saint because of his acceptance of some of Origen's controversial teachings.	Though most of his writings have been lost, some of his biblical commentaries still exist. He was very influential within the Church during his lifetime.

Name	Year of Death	Description	Notable Contributions
Rufinus of Aquileia	410	He was a monk, translator, and theologian of Aquileia (Italy).	His writings include letters between himself and Saint Jerome during their public feud over the controversial opinions of the writer Origen, but he also translated Christian writings into Latin and wrote Scripture commentaries.
Theodoret of Cyrrhus	c. 458	Bishop of Cyrrhus (Turkey)	A highly educated man, he wrote many biblical commentaries. More controversially, he supported the heretic Nestorius' teachings for some time before accepting the teaching of the Church (and rejecting Nestorianism).
Pseudo-Dionysius the Areopagite	Perhaps sixth century	His personal life or real identity is unknown.	Under the name of the early convert Dionysius (Acts 17:34), a Christian theologian composed several works that were highly respected in the medieval world, including *The Divine Names* and *The Celestial Hierarchy*.

Help from the Doctors

Jesus Christ chose twelve men to be His disciples, but He never said anything about Doctors. Why are there thirty-seven Doctors of the Church?

Popes have recognized many great saints in the history of the Church; secular and religious leaders have recognized many great thinkers; among the billions of Catholic men and women who have lived in the past two thousand years, a small number have been recognized as leaders in both holiness and intellectual brilliance.

According to tradition, the Church identifies three conditions for a man or woman to be declared a Doctor of the Church. First, the Church herself must make the proclamation, rather than a single leader or group of devotees or even a bishop. Recognition comes from the universal Church, not by a local decision, because the title acknowledges that the person has something to offer to the universal Church, now and in the future. Second, the person must be recognized as a holy person, that is, a saint. While there have been many profound intellectuals in the Church's past, not all of them have lived lives of holiness suitable for emulation by other Catholics. Third, the person should have left behind a body of Catholic writings and teachings that is considered outstanding. The teachings of Doctors of the Church have provided us with concepts, tools, and explanations of our faith that have profited all the faithful, and that includes even Catholics who have barely learned to read and write.

We can think of a Doctor of the Church as being akin to a Ph.D.— that is, someone with a mastery of an aspect of Catholic theology that he has shared with other Catholics in a very effective way. But we can also think of a Doctor of the Church as a sort of medical doctor for ecclesiastical ailments because his writings often helped bring healing to the Church during a time when the faith was challenged by a heresy or another cultural assault.

Since it would be cumbersome to discuss all thirty-seven Doctors in one chapter, this chapter concludes with a table listing basic details about each one, along with some of his or her notable contributions. While each Doctor has had a profound effect on the Church, there are some specific ways that these men and women have particularly blessed the Church.

Hammer of Heretics

Saint Anthony of Padua (1195–1231) has a nickname: Hammer of Heretics. This is not because he was vindictive or violent but because his Scripture-based arguments in support of Catholic teaching devastated the arguments proposed by followers of Catharism, whom Anthony had been sent to correct.

Catharism was a mixture of teachings from both Catholicism and Manichaeism; Manichaeism was a mixture of teachings from Zoroastrianism, Buddhism, Christianity, and Babylonian folklore. For that reason, the mishmash of theology known as Catharism was more of a separate religion than a heresy. But followers of this religion, the Cathari, thought that *they* were the true followers of Christ. They were quick—and right—to point out the inconsistencies and outright sinfulness in the lives of some Catholics. But an elite group of their own followers, called "the Perfect", were, to them, the epitome of what a follower of Christ should be. The Perfect members fasted, prayed, and vowed to live lives of celibacy. But the reasons that they fasted, prayed, and abstained were very different from the reasons that Catholics do. The Cathari believed that the spiritual world was good and the material world was bad. Therefore, all physical matter was, basically, evil. As Catholics, we fast and do penance for our sins so that we can grow in self-control and so that God will reign in our souls. The Cathari fasted and performed acts of penance because they considered their physical bodies to be essentially bad. Ramifications of that belief included a belief that sexual intercourse is bad, marriage is bad, having children is bad, even life itself is bad, which led to acceptance of suicide and euthanasia, among other immoral ideas.

Surprisingly, this fanatical approach to self-punishment was remarkably popular with members of rich and powerful families, who bragged about the rigorous lives of the Perfect and filled convents with their members. On the surface, the Perfect seemed so holy and penitential. How do you fight a teaching that appears very Christlike but teaches the opposite of what Christ actually taught?

Saint Anthony accomplished this with Scripture. While Anthony may have been the "hammer", the Bible itself provided all the nails he used to put this collection of errors in its coffin. He memorized both Old and New Testaments, quoted from them widely, and used vivid allegories and examples to make his points. But it was not the text of Anthony's sermons alone that brought about conversions in France and Italy. He lived a simple, penitential, and holy life as a poor Franciscan friar. Through his words and example, he led people to the Church and the sacraments, not to himself. Everyone noted his excellent skills as a speaker, yet his speeches were always logical and loving, not bitter or cruel. That turned the tide on Catharism in his day.

Saint Anthony was not the first Doctor of the Church to fight against heresy and falsehood. Many of the Doctors of the Church earned their titles by combating false teachings. For example, Saint Cyril of Alexandria explained the errors of Novatianism and Nestorianism; Saint Augustine of Hippo argued against multiple heresies of his time; Saint Leo the Great discussed the errors of Eutychianism; Saint John of Damascus showed the falsity of iconoclasm; Saints Lawrence of Brindisi, Robert Bellarmine, Francis de Sales, and Peter Canisius debated Protestantism; Saints Athanasius, Hilary of Poitiers, Cyril of Jerusalem, Ambrose of Milan, Basil the Great, Gregory of Nazianzus, and John Chrysostom particularly fought the dangers of Arianism. Since Arianism was the first great heresy raised against the Church and since so many Doctors fought so vigorously against it, it is worthwhile to examine this heresy and their response in detail.

Leading the lost sheep

How can Jesus Christ be both the Son of God and a man? We take this truth for granted today, but in the days of the early Church, it was not obvious to some people how such a thing was possible, much less how to explain it.

In the year 313, the Roman emperor Constantine recognized the Catholic Church as a legal religion in the empire. His personal adherence to Catholicism not only removed the danger of perse-cution faced by Catholics at that time, but it also encouraged many others to consider entering the Church. While Catholic leaders during the previous time of persecution had certainly discussed theo-logical, philosophical, and moral teachings, now they could do so much more publicly. Within a few years, these issues were hotly debated all over the empire. One of these controversies was proposed by a man named Arius (c. 250–336).

Arius was an intelligent man who apparently lived a virtuous life as a Catholic priest in one of the greatest cities of the ancient world, Alexandria, Egypt, and he had developed his own ideas about Jesus Christ. Arius began to preach and teach that Jesus Christ was a creature who had been created by God the Father, a sort of lesser divinity who was certainly important, but not truly God. While it's true that the Church had not yet developed a vocabulary to explain the complicated distinctions of the Trinity, this teaching was clearly a false understanding of the God-Man who had said, "I and the Father are one."[1] Arius refused to accept repeated and gentle corrections from his bishop, Saint Alexander, and instead did his best to win over other bishops to his own ideas. In his ex-planations of his beliefs, he used orthodox terms to explain his het-erodox ideas, which spread even more confusion about what he was teaching. In the year 325, less than ten years after his first public confrontation with Saint Alexander, Arius' teachings were formally condemned by the Church at the Council of Nicaea. That council also approved the statement that we now know—and pray each Sunday—as the Nicene Creed. But sadly, that was not the end of Arianism. Although this heresy continued in various places for cen-turies, the debate over Arius' teachings continued vigorously for about a hundred years.

Why? There were many reasons. Arius was a smooth talker who had won over many powerful people to his side, people who were impressed with his complicated theological explanations and saw him as the underdog in a fight with the Church. It was also simpler to explain Jesus away as a lesser god than to accept the earth-shattering fact that God Himself became a man. Rejecting the Incarnation

[1] Jn 10:30.

makes Christianity a much less demanding and much less personal faith. Jesus becomes a semi-divine example, not our brother and Savior. For those who wanted a more comfortable, less demanding faith, Arianism was the obvious choice.

Some emperors as well as their powerful friends and family and even bishops sided with Arius in the fourth and early fifth centuries. Some of the men now known as Doctors of the Church, including Saints Athanasius, Hilary of Poitiers, Cyril of Jerusalem, Ambrose of Milan, Basil the Great, and Gregory of Nazianzus, refused to give up. They were six different men living in different areas of the ancient world and facing down different emperors. Their personal stories can show us different ways of dealing with false teachings that we can learn from even today.

Saint Athanasius (c. 297–373) succeeded Saint Alexander as bishop of Alexandria; since Arius was a priest of Alexandria, Athanasius was forced to deal personally with Arius and his teachings and was essentially at ground zero of a conflict that spread all over the Roman Empire. When Athanasius continued to write and speak against Arian doctrines and for the Catholic understanding of Christ's nature, even when he knew that the Roman emperors Constantine, Constantius, and Valerian were followers of Arianism and that Julian had completely rejected Christianity, they could not ignore him. Alexandria was one of the greatest cities in the ancient world, and the voice of the bishop of that city was influential. Executing him was too dangerous—it could lead to riots because Athanasius was very popular with the people—so he was sent into exile by four different emperors on five different occasions.

Though inspiring, Athanasius' bravery in surviving the punishment of forced exile, as well as assassination attempts by Arians, is not the reason he was named a Doctor. His many writings included a treatise explaining the Incarnation to respond to Arians, a treatise explaining the Catholic understanding of evil to respond to pagans, multiple documents specifically responding to Arian arguments, a biography of Saint Anthony the Great (whom Athanasius had learned about while living in exile in the desert and who was a great example of a Catholic—not Arian—holy man), and open letters to bishops and the emperor himself explaining his position. Perhaps most famously, he expressed the reason that we must reject

Arianism in a single sentence: "For the Son of God became man so that we might become God."[2]

Saint Hilary (c. 315–c. 368) was bishop of Poitiers, France, when Athanasius was sent into exile. Hilary responded by writing in support of Athanasius and condemning Arius' teachings in the year 355. Unsurprisingly, the emperor sent him into exile as well, choosing a location in the eastern part of the empire called Phrygia (modern Turkey). But that decision backfired; Hilary was so effective in converting the people of the region back to the Catholic understanding of this issue that the local leaders petitioned the emperor to send him back to France. More importantly, he composed his greatest work while in exile, a book titled *On the Trinity*. Although some Christian theological concepts had already been explained in the Greek language, there were no Latin words to explain those concepts. Hilary developed new words in Latin for that purpose. He carefully proved that there *is* a Trinity. He carefully proved that Jesus *is* God. Catholic theologians from Saint Augustine of Hippo to Saint Thomas Aquinas used Hilary's arguments to settle later disputes about the Trinity.

Saint Cyril (c. 315–386) was the bishop of Jerusalem when the controversy of Arianism erupted. Cyril chose a different approach in trying to bring an end to the heresy. Instead of confrontation, he listened to adherents on both sides and wrote explanations that he hoped would bring Arians back into the fold. For that reason, Cyril has been criticized over the centuries for appearing to refuse to stand up to powerful proponents of Arianism. But Cyril's failure to use the controversial word "consubstantial" is not unlike modern attempts by Catholic apologists who sometimes use, or do not use, controversial words when trying to explain Catholic concepts. Such an approach can open hearts, rather than shut down all communication. Regardless of one's opinion about how Cyril chose to explain his belief in Jesus Christ as true God and true man, he was sent into exile three times, proving that his writings were certainly understood by Arians to be opposed to Arianism.

Saint Ambrose (c. 340–397) was the governor of the powerful city of Milan when the city's bishop, who was a follower of Arianism,

---

[2] Athanasius, *De inc.* 54, 3, quoted in the *Catechism of the Catholic Church*, no. 460 (hereafter, the *Catechism* is cited as *CCC*).

died. Since the city was deeply divided over whether the new bishop should be a Catholic or an Arian, Ambrose showed up at the city's cathedral to maintain order. The people, who clearly respected and trusted Ambrose, began shouting his name and calling on him to become their new shepherd. The emperor agreed—over Ambrose's objections that he was not even baptized yet—and Ambrose ultimately became one of the most influential figures of his time.

As bishop of Milan, Ambrose became a trusted advisor to emperors and even convinced an emperor (Gratian) to outlaw Arianism in the western part of the empire. But it was his polished Latin, allegorical style, obedience to the teachings of the Church, and careful explanations of the faith that led the Church to name him a Doctor. His writings against Arianism as well as his letters and treatises on consecrated chastity, the duties of the clergy, and Catholic theology were as influential during his years as bishop as were his personal connections with secular leaders and his personal outreach to the poor.

It is difficult to discuss Saint Basil the Great (c. 329–379) without also discussing his friend Saint Gregory of Nazianzus (c. 329–c. 389). Both were born into Christian families; both were extremely intelligent; both grew up in a region now in Turkey while receiving an education in Athens, Greece, as young men. Basil chose to pursue monastic life and became a bishop. Gregory also became a bishop, poet, and famous orator. Both men opposed Arianism when its arguments and its followers seemed to rule the day.

The Roman emperor Valens was an Arian, and he was tired of the bishop of Caesarea's public opposition to Arianism. He sent a powerful representative to Caesarea to threaten and humiliate the man publicly. But the prefect met his match in Saint Basil the Great, who refused to be cowed into silence. It's said that Basil's letters alone provide a complete picture of the issues involved in the Arian controversy; but Basil also wrote many sermons, a Rule of Life for his monks, and other doctrinal writings that helped Catholics come to a better understanding of what the Church believes.

Gregory responded to a request for help from a small group of faithful Catholics living in Constantinople and became their bishop. Though they were greatly outnumbered by Arians, Gregory wrote and witnessed to the truth about Jesus Christ as their bishop through his sermons; then he simply left town and returned to a quiet life when his efforts had brought most Christians back into the fold of the Church. Gregory was too much of a poet to enjoy the administrative and public demands of the office of bishop, so he resigned soon afterward. But it was precisely through his poetry, letters, and orations that he became known as a great theologian in his own lifetime, a pillar of orthodoxy that faithful Catholics wanted to follow.

In confronting the heresy of Arianism, these and other Catholic leaders faced two great enemies. The first enemy was the theological lie that was being proposed as truth; these men were named Doctors precisely because they were, by God's grace, able to expose the lie and bring hearts and minds to embrace the truth.

The second great enemy they faced was political power. It is not a novelty for Catholics to find themselves governed by leaders who do not share their values, and our modern world is not very different from the ancient world in that respect. What we can learn from the Doctors, however, is that when we are in a battle with secular leaders, we have weapons at our disposal. Those weapons include strictly spiritual ones, such as prayer, humility, and obedience. Remember that all the Doctors were, first and foremost, men who lived holy lives and placed themselves at the service of the Church. But each one also made use of the talents that God had given him, as a great orator or writer or monk or public leader. So, too, the vocations God has called each of us to can become the means by which we face down lies that harm our world today.

Leading others to God through beauty

God leads us to Himself in many ways; beauty is one of His favorite paths. After all, Wisdom 13:3 tells us that God is "the author of beauty". It is not surprising that we enjoy mimicking our Heavenly Father by creating beauty according to our own individual abilities, whether that involves beautifying our homes, dressing ourselves in an appealing way, or planting a garden. For those with greater artistic ability, creating beauty can be done through other mediums, such as painting, music, or poetry.

Saint Ephraem (c. 306–373) was born into a Christian family in the city of Nisibis in modern Syria. He grew up during the time that the Church began to be able to worship freely. But it was not an easy period for the Syrian people because the king of Persia laid siege to Nisibis repeatedly, specifically during the years 338, 346, and 350. When the city was surrendered to the Persians in 363, Ephraem moved south to the city of Edessa, now in Turkey. He lived as a hermit, and some traditions say he was ordained a deacon. Though Ephraem was a prolific writer, his most enduring gift to the Church is his hymnody.

Ephraem was a gifted poet, and he wrote gorgeous lyrics in praise of God. His hymns cover many Catholic themes, but his impetus for putting so much time and effort into writing these hymns was to protect his fellow Catholics from theological error. Poetry may seem an odd way to combat heresy, but in that, he was only following the example of his opponents.

In the previous century, a man named Bardasanes had lived in Syria and promoted his own Gnostic interpretations of Christianity. During Ephraem's lifetime, promoters of these Gnostic heresies moved into Nisibis and spread their teachings in many ways, most particularly through catchy hymns. Gnostics were not the first people to use apparently harmless songs to popularize their own ideas and ridicule the ideas of others, nor will they be the last.

Ephraem was the perfect person to answer this challenge. He simply took the melodies of his Gnostic opponents, wrote Catholic lyrics to replace their lyrics, and trained the women of his church to sing his hymns during the liturgy. Ephraem's hymns were so vastly superior in quality to the Gnostics' hymns that the people voted with their voices; before very long, everyone in the surrounding area was singing Ephraem's hymns, not the Gnostic ones. Although Ephraem's writings also included prose works, homilies, and commentaries (not all of which have been preserved), his hymns almost single-handedly exterminated a heresy.

Beauty in liturgical music is only one kind of beauty. God also teaches us about Himself through the order and beauty of the world He created.[3] Human persons did not first become sensitive to the beauty of nature in the twenty-first century; it started at the beginning of time. God Himself called the created world "good" during

[3] *CCC* 32.

the act of Creation,[4] and the biblical books of the Psalms, Job, and Daniel, among others, show the amazement of the Jewish authors that God has surrounded us with such a remarkable and beautiful world in which to live.

It is therefore no surprise that the Doctors of the Church pointed out the beauty of nature. More than that, they found it fascinating and spent their lives studying aspects of the natural world.

Saint Isidore of Seville (c. 560–636) came from a prominent and devout family in Seville, Spain. He succeeded his older brother, Leander, as bishop of Seville around the year 600 and eventually became known as the most learned man in all of Spain. One of his friends, Saint Braulio, bishop of Saragossa, asked him to put his great knowledge down in writing and send him a copy. Though Isidore never completely finished it, his book, which was called *Origins* or *Etymologies*, covered a wide range of topics: medicine, geography, music, clothing, zoology, warfare, and entertainment, as well as religious subjects. It was the world's first encyclopedia, which is why Isidore is considered the patron saint of the internet.

Saint Albert (c. 1206–1280), also called Albert the Great, was a German Dominican friar, professor at the University of Paris, and bishop of Cologne. Though many know him primarily as the teacher of Saint Thomas Aquinas, he was a groundbreaking thinker in his own right.

Not only did Albert study philosophy and theology, as perhaps might be expected by his decision to enter the Dominican order, but he also studied and wrote about every science imaginable at the time. From the time he was young, he loved to explore the countryside, and he enjoyed hunting and fishing. It is not surprising that his voracious interest started with studies of the natural world—botany, animal life, physics, chemistry, astronomy, mineralogy—and expanded to include medicine, dentistry, and surgery.

The writings of Saints Isidore and Albert are rarely found in print today, but their books were the textbooks used for education and reference in Christendom for centuries. While we know much more about weasels and arctic bears than did Saint Albert, he was the first person to mention them. While modern encyclopedias include many

[4]Gen 1:4, 10, 18, 21, 25, 31.

more topics than Saint Isidore covered, Isidore compiled the first one, by himself and by hand, and summarized his topics in ingenious ways.

These two men are not the only great saints who studied and wrote about the natural world. Saint Hildegard of Bingen (1098–1179), like Isidore and Albert, was fascinated by nature and wrote books about medicine, biology, and cosmology. She will be described in greater detail in subsequent chapters ("A Nation of Saints", "Life in Religious Life", and "Praying like the Saints").

In the lives of these great Doctors, we see that aspects of modern culture that now seem hopelessly alienated from Catholicism—art, literature, and scientific research—are, in fact, "home territory". Great Catholic intellectuals pursued their vocations precisely by creating beautiful works and studying natural beauty, and they became great saints in the process. This can happen again.

Leading others to virtue

In any discussion of the Doctors and virtue, Saint Jerome of Stridon (c. 342–c. 420) is a great place to start. However, that is because one must make an extra effort to recognize virtue in a man who called his opponents names such as "ignorant boor" and "odious".

To be fair, Jerome's story started off in a not uncommon way. He was raised in a Christian household, went off to college, and wandered a bit from his faithful upbringing. Fortunately, Jerome's passions appear to have tended more toward reading great pagan thinkers than engaging in sins of the flesh. Even more fortunately, he experienced a personal conversion to Christ and decided to leave everything behind and live as a hermit. But his hunger for learning and his great intellect led him to leave the wilderness and eventually caused him to become the secretary of the pope. At the pope's death, he retired to live in a cave in the Holy Land as a hermit again. But did Jerome live a virtuous life?

Virtue, according to the glossary of the *Catechism*, is "a habitual and firm disposition to do the good". The theological virtues, which are given to us by God, are faith, hope, and love.

Both Jerome's writings and his personal life easily demonstrate that he had faith and hope in God. If one defines love as a warm fuzzy feeling, Jerome was far from loving toward those who espoused views with which he disagreed. But the Christian definition of love, or charity, is not chumminess. Charity, again according to the glossary of the *Catechism*, is the "virtue by which we love God above all things for his sake, and our neighbor as ourselves for the love of God". By that definition, Jerome was definitely a man of virtue.

Jerome loved God more than the pleasures of food. He famously quipped that it is easy to speak eloquently about fasting—when you have a full stomach. Jerome mortified his diet so radically that he became ill; fortunately, he had the wisdom to recognize the need to modify his diet. Jerome loved God more than the pleasures of sex, but he was as human as any man, describing how he was tempted by fantasies of women while still a young man learning to live as a hermit. Jerome loved God more than the pleasures of human company, choosing isolation rather than the worldly honors that a man of his talents could so easily have been granted in any major city.

Yes, Jerome's struggles with virtue clearly involved not "love of God", but "love of neighbor". His caustic tongue earned him enemies both within and without the Church. But it is important to note that Jerome's verbal battles were not over trivialities. He did not join a fight unless it was over a serious matter involving, you guessed it, our faith in God. For example, Jerome wrote a famous letter in which he ridiculed arguments made by a man named Helvidius, who claimed that the Blessed Mother had children after giving birth to Jesus. Jerome, without benefit of any of the modern Bible tools available to us today, painstakingly showed how wrong Helvidius was through extensive quotations from Scripture. A Christian writer who proposed sloppy arguments about theological issues could expect to be put in his place by Jerome.

Perhaps Jerome's greatest weakness was his sensitivity to any criticism that his opinions might be in opposition to Church teaching. Those who intimated that his positions were doubtful could expect a long, detailed, angry response, which, considering Jerome's intellectual skills, probably felt a bit like being hit by a truck. His friends, including Saint Augustine of Hippo, had to deal tactfully with Jerome on more than one occasion, and his anger cost him an old friend, Rufinus, in one notable controversy. Despite this clear weakness, Jerome clearly earned the title of "saint" through the way he lived his life.

There are few saints who are more completely unlike Saint Jerome than Saint Francis de Sales (1567–1622), but Francis can teach us about Christian virtue too.

Francis was born into a noble French family, and his father had great plans for his oldest son. Those plans did not include the priesthood, which is apparently all that Francis ever wanted. It was not easy to convince his father to accept that God had called his son to the priesthood, and his father was even more upset when Francis accepted a very dangerous assignment: go to the Chablais region of France and preach the Gospel.

Of course, it was much more dangerous than that may sound because Catholics and Protestants were living in a state of war at that time. Twice Francis escaped assassination attempts simply because he was a Catholic priest. Or perhaps because he was such a *good* Catholic priest. But he used his skills as a writer to explain Catholic teaching so effectively that he almost single-handedly brought large numbers of Catholics in the area of the Chablais back to the faith in just a few years. Later he was named bishop of Geneva. One of his most famous works, *Introduction to the Devout Life*, is a spiritual classic, offering wise but simple advice about how to incorporate prayer in daily life, how to face temptations, and how to grow in virtue. Two of the virtues most prominent in Francis' *Introduction to the Devout Life* are prudence and temperance.

According to the *Catechism*, "Prudence is the virtue that disposes practical reason to discern our true good in every circumstance and to choose the right means of achieving it."[5] Francis teaches that "a different exercise of devotion is required of each—the noble, the artisan, the servant, the prince, the maiden and the wife; and furthermore such practice must be modified according to the strength, the calling, and the duties of the individual."[6] In this passage, Francis points out how foolish it would be for a father with a family to spend all day in church instead of working, or for a priest to spend all day on business and never in church. In prayer, as in everything else, each person should work to discern what is truly the greatest good for a given situation.

---

[5] *CCC* 1806.

[6] Frances de Sales, *Introduction to the Devout Life* (San Francisco: Ignatius Press; DeKalb, IL: Lighthouse Catholic Media, 2015), p. 5.

The *Catechism* also states, "Temperance is the moral virtue that moderates the attraction of pleasures and provides balance in the use of created goods."[7] Here is one of Francis' best reminders about being temperate in dealing with our faults.

> One important direction in which to exercise gentleness, is with respect to ourselves, never growing irritated with one's self or one's imperfections; for although it is but reasonable that we should be displeased and grieved at our own faults, yet ought we to guard against a bitter, angry, or peevish feeling about them. Many people fall into the error of being angry because they have been angry, vexed because they have given way to vexation, thus keeping up in a chronic state of irritation, which adds to the evil of what is past, and prepares the way for a fresh fall on the first occasion.[8]

Another Doctor of the Church who can teach us about virtue today is Saint Alphonsus Liguori (1696–1787). A brilliant man from a noble Italian family, Alphonsus had become a lawyer by the time he was only sixteen years old. But he left it all behind to become a priest, founded a religious order of nuns and another order of priests, became a well-known preacher, was ordained a bishop, and wrote innumerable devotional books.

"Justice is the moral virtue that consists in the constant and firm will to give their due to God and neighbor,"[9] as the *Catechism* states. One could say that Alphonsus wrote the book on justice, because he did. His *Moral Theology* examined the moral questions of his day, including everything from the difference between mortal and venial sin, how to obey the commandment to honor God on Sunday when you are a farmer gathering crops, and the practice of giving alms to the poor. Helping people understand the need to be just in our dealings with God and with one another, balanced with mercy, was one of Alphonsus' greatest gifts to the Church.

The *Catechism* teaches that "fortitude is the moral virtue that ensures firmness in difficulties and constancy in the pursuit of the good."[10] In the practice of this virtue, Alphonsus was greatly tempted

---

[7] *CCC* 1809.
[8] De Sales, *Introduction to the Devout Life*, p. 93.
[9] *CCC* 1807.
[10] Ibid., 1808.

near the end of his life. The Italian government had demanded that he make changes to the Rule of Life that was followed by his order of priests. Alphonsus decided what changes he thought were acceptable, but he was unable to see—literally blind—at the time. His assistants— men he thought were his friends—edited the Rule to comply with the government's requests without his knowledge. When the pope found out, he angrily condemned the changes and removed Alphonsus as leader of his own order, thinking that Alphonsus was to blame for the mistake. Alphonsus, a scrupulous man by nature, was devastated by the pope's decision, seeing it as a personal rebuke, and it took time for him to recover his confidence. This test of Alphonsus' fortitude lasted for several years, but he died at peace with God and faithful throughout it all.

The Doctors of the Church were chosen not only for their writings but also for their lived witness as Christians. Sometimes they teach us about virtue through their own personal struggles with scrupulosity, discouragement, oversensitivity, anger, fear, and all the other temptations that beset us as well. In that, they show us that virtue is the work of a lifetime.

Leading others into truth

Pontius Pilate famously asked our Lord, "What is truth?"[11] It is not clear whether Pilate was being sarcastic or simply didn't know. The *Catechism* teaches us that "the Old Testament attests that *God is the source of all truth*."[12] It also says, "In Jesus Christ, the whole of God's truth has been made manifest."[13] Truth comes from God, and Jesus has made truth visible and real to us. Our Lord also said that He was the "light of the world",[14] so anywhere He is allowed to enter—a culture, a home, a human heart—He brings the light of truth to dispel the darkness that covers our fallen world.

During His lifetime, one could literally *see* Truth by watching and listening and learning from Jesus as He walked the streets of

---

[11] Jn 18:38.
[12] *CCC* 2465 (emphasis in original).
[13] Ibid., 2466.
[14] Jn 8:12; 9:5.

Jerusalem. Now we have to *work* to find the truth. We can see this search for truth lived out in many Doctors, including Saint Thomas Aquinas (c. 1225–1274).

Thomas was born into a noble family and became a Dominican friar despite his family, who strongly objected and even kidnapped and held him prisoner for a time. When he was able to return to Dominican life, he lived out his vows to the order—that is, vows of poverty, chastity, and obedience. Fortunately, his superiors recognized Thomas' abilities and ordered him to serve the order as a scholar and to study, among other things, the philosophical and theological issues of the day.

From around the sixth century B.C. to the time of the birth of Christ, a school of philosophy arose in what is now Greece. The ancient Greek philosophers developed ways of examining the world that encompassed many subjects—such as mathematics, biology, political philosophy, and ethics—and the fundamental concepts they discussed and debated were profound and powerful. The collapse of the Roman Empire caused the writings of the Greeks, along with many other writings, to be lost to most of the world for centuries. But when Islam conquered lands where writings about Greek philosophy still existed, some Muslim scholars of the Middle Ages began using and spreading these ideas. In time, Greek philosophy was rediscovered by Christian Europe. But there was a problem with these writings: they were written by pagans.

The fact that the Greek philosophers had lived before the time of Christ and were mostly polytheists was considered a serious impediment to their trustworthiness. Some Christians of the Middle Ages opposed the use of Greek philosophy for a fundamental religious reason: Would it be an offense against God to study the works of pagans? Even if the great Greek philosopher Plato believed in one God, he certainly never knew the Judeo-Christian God.

Thomas Aquinas, following the example of his great teacher, Albert the Great, demonstrated that many of the ideas found in Greek philosophy could be used effectively to answer philosophical and theological questions posed by Christians, both about God and about other ideas. That is, the concepts of Greek philosophy could be excellent tools to help Christians find and explain truth. Thomas' synthesis of thought, bringing together the best of Greek philosophy and Catholic theology, gave Catholics a new way to search for and express truth. He showed not only that the two were compatible but also that the Church's understanding of truth could grow by making use of Greek philosophy.

A Doctor who seems completely unlike Thomas Aquinas but who is also a great teacher of truth is Saint Catherine of Siena (1347–1380). Although Catherine became a Dominican tertiary, she apparently has very little in common with the great Dominican philosopher. After all, Catherine never went to school, never studied under brilliant scholars, and joined a religious order merely as a Third Order member who lived at home. But Catherine prayed.

That was the secret to her "success": she prayed with such great faith that God had no alternative but to grant her what she asked for. For example, later in life, when she was sought out for help by laymen and leaders alike, it became a problem that she had never been taught to read and write. People tried to help her, but she failed each time. So she simply asked Jesus to help her, and—overnight, according to multiple witnesses—she was infused with the ability to read.

During Catherine's time, the pope lived not in Rome but in Avignon. Although that may seem inconsequential to us today, it was not inconsequential to the People of God. Catherine understood the political realities that had forced the pope to move his household from Rome to France, but she also saw that this needed to change. The only thing keeping the pope in France was fear, and, as Catherine knew, perfect love casts out fear. The successor of Saint Peter, who died a martyr like his Lord, should not be afraid of anything, particularly any dangers that were causing division among Christians of different countries and preventing the pope from being the visible head of the Church in the city chosen by the first pope: Rome itself. Though Catherine was an uneducated, poor, apparently simple woman, God gave her incredible wisdom, insight, and patience in dealing with complex negotiations between the pope, religious leaders, secular leaders, warring cities, and warring families. Precisely because she was rooted in Christ through prayer and because she recognized that everything good came from Him, she was able to shame the rich and mighty through her humility, protect the poor through her own selfless example of poverty, and lead ordinary citizens and even popes to truth.

Pope Saint Leo the Great (c. 400–461) had a dilemma. With controversy raging between bishops all over the known world over how to explain the nature of Jesus Christ, someone needed to come up with an explanation of this incredibly complicated and mysterious truth that would settle the matter, not throw fuel on the fire. So he did.

The Tome of Leo was the letter Pope Leo sent to a council of bishops to explain the doctrine of the Incarnation in simple terms that anyone, from a scholar to an illiterate layman, could understand. When *The Tome* was read at the Council of Chalcedon, the bishops as a group exclaimed that "Peter has spoken by Leo!"; the Church has been using his explanation ever since. As Leo explained it:

> For not only is God believed to be both Almighty and the Father, but the Son is shown to be co-eternal with Him, differing in nothing from the Father because He is *God from God*, Almighty from Almighty, and being born from the Eternal one is co-eternal with Him; not later in point of time, not lower in power, not unlike in glory, not divided in essence: but at the same time the only begotten of the eternal Father was born eternal of the Holy Spirit and the Virgin Mary. And this nativity which took place in time took nothing from, and added nothing to that divine and eternal birth, but expended itself wholly on the restoration of man who had been deceived: in order that he might both vanquish death and overthrow by his strength, the Devil who possessed the power of death. For we should not now be able to overcome the author of sin and death unless He took our nature on Him and made it His own, whom neither sin could pollute nor death retain. Doubtless then, He was conceived of the Holy Spirit within the womb of His Virgin Mother, who brought Him forth without the loss of her virginity, even as she conceived Him without its loss.[15]

For these and all the Doctors of the Church, leading others to truth is not something they accomplished by their superior intellects, excellent communication skills, and natural insights, though they all possessed those gifts too. All of the Doctors simply put their

[15] Leo the Great, *Letter* 28, 2, trans. Charles Lett Feltoe, in *Nicene and Post-Nicene Fathers*, 2nd series, vol. 12, ed. Philip Schaff and Henry Wace (Buffalo, NY: Christian Literature Publishing, 1895); emphasis in original. Revised and edited for New Advent by Kevin Knight, NewAdvent.org, 2021, http://www.newadvent.org/fathers/3604028.htm. (*Letter* 28 is better known as *The Tome*.)

God-given gifts in His hands and let Him lead them—and others—to the truth.

Leaders for the future

As long as God calls men and women to live holy lives and teach others how to do so, the Church will continue to name Doctors of the Church. Other men and women besides the thirty-seven who have been named Doctors have been proposed to be added to their ranks. Two relatively recent saints have been popularly recommended as future Doctors, for example, and it is easy to see why.

Saint Teresa Benedicta of the Cross (1891–1942) was born in Germany and known as Edith Stein before she became a Carmelite nun. More than that, she was known as a highly intelligent, popular writer and teacher before her Jewish birth caused her to be shut out of public life by Hitler's anti-Semitic laws. Her writings about philosophy, the role of women, and suffering in the light of Catholic theology are profound and thought-provoking. However, Teresa Benedicta is unlikely to be named a Doctor. She is, after all, a martyr, and the Church considers martyrdom to be the highest example of Christian charity.

Pope John Paul the Great (1920–2005) could be named a Doctor of the Church many times over. His encyclicals alone—which deal with the role of faith and reason, the dignity of human life, social justice, moral teaching, the Eucharist, and other topics—explain Catholic teaching to the modern world and make them new. His decision to release an official catechism for the universal Church, the first one in more than four hundred years, had a profound effect on a world caught up in many contradictory opinions about what the Church taught and why. Perhaps his most personal writing for the Church was his explanation of a new understanding of human relationships and sexuality. It has been suggested that his "Theology of the Body", which he explained in weekly papal audiences for over a year, is a "theological time bomb"[16] that could change the world.

[16] George Weigel, *Witness to Hope* (New York: Cliff Street Books, 2001), p. 342.

Through the Doctors of the Church, Christ's teaching is made new for each generation, to counter new challenges and to bring truth, wisdom, and peace to our fallen world.

Summary

The following table lists all thirty-seven Doctors of the Church, along with a brief summary of each Doctor's notable contribution to the Church.

Name	Dates	Description	Title or Nickname	Notable Contribution
Saint Irenaeus of Lyons	d. c. 202	Bishop of Lyons (France); martyr	Doctor of Unity	Writings explained Church teaching, particularly against heretical teachings of Gnostic sects, leading to apparent martyrdom.
Saint Hilary of Poitiers	c. 315– c. 368	Bishop of Poitiers (France)	Hammer of the Arians; Athanasius of the West; Doctor of the Divinity of Christ	Writings explained Church teaching against the Arian heresy, despite exile and personal danger.
Saint Athanasius of Alexandria	c. 297– 373	Archbishop of Alexandria (Egypt)	Father of Orthodoxy; one of the four Great Greek Fathers of the Church	Writings explained Church teaching against the Arian heresy, despite exile and personal danger.
Saint Ephraem the Syrian	c. 306– 373	Deacon of Nisibus (Syria)	Harp of the Holy Spirit	Wrote hymns, poems, and homilies explaining

(continued)

Name	Dates	Description	Title or Nickname	Notable Contribution
				Church teaching in opposition to Gnosticism.
Saint Basil the Great	c. 329– 379	Monastic founder; bishop of Caesarea (Turkey)	Father of Eastern Monasticism; one of the four Great Greek Fathers of the Church	Contributed influential writings about monastic life and against Arianism.
Saint Cyril of Jerusalem	c. 315– 386	Bishop of Jerusalem (Israel)	Doctor of Catechesis	Opposed Arianism; catechetical writings give us insight into early Church theology.
Saint Gregory of Nazianzus	c. 329– c. 389	Bishop of Nazianzus (Turkey)	The Theologian; one of the four Great Greek Fathers of the Church	Cleared up theological controversies through his poems, letters, and sermons.
Saint Ambrose of Milan	c. 340– 397	Bishop of Milan (Italy)	Patron of the Veneration of Mary; one of the four Great Latin Fathers of the Church	Writings explained Church teaching against the Arian heresy, despite personal danger.
Saint John Chrysostom	c. 347– 407	Patriarch of Constantinople (Turkey)	The Golden-Mouthed; one of the four Great Greek Fathers of the Church	Homilies and letters explained Church teaching against the Arian heresy, despite exile and personal danger.
Saint Jerome of Stridon	c. 342– c. 420	Priest, scholar, and hermit who died in	Father of Biblical Science; one	Defended Church teaching, particularly

Name	Dates	Description	Title or Nickname	Notable Contribution
		Bethlehem (Israel)	of the four Great Latin Fathers of the Church	through letters; translator of Latin Bible used by the Church for over a thousand years.
Saint Augustine of Hippo	354–430	Bishop of Hippo (Algeria)	Doctor of Grace; one of the four Great Latin Fathers of the Church	Contributed innumerable writings on theology and philosophy that affected Church and surrounding culture.
Saint Cyril of Alexandria	c. 376–444	Patriarch of Alexandria (Egypt)	Doctor of the Incarnation	Opposed heresies of Novatian and Nestorius; supported title of Theotokos for the Blessed Virgin Mary.
Saint Peter Chrysologus	c. 406–c. 450	Archbishop of Ravenna (Italy)	The Golden-Worded; Doctor of Homilies	Clear, concise sermons explained Church teaching effectively.
Saint Leo the Great	c. 400–461	Benedictine monk and pope	Doctor of the Unity of the Church	Explained Church teaching, particularly against the heresy of Eutychianism, through numerous sermons and letters.
Saint Gregory the Great	c. 540–604	Pope	Father of Christian Worship; one of the four Great Latin Fathers of the Church	Defended Church teaching through letters and other writings.

(continued)

Name	Dates	Description	Title or Nickname	Notable Contribution
Saint Isidore of Seville	c. 560–636	Archbishop of Seville (Spain)	Schoolmaster of the Middle Ages	Contributed encyclopedic writings on Church teachings and the natural world.
Saint Bede the Venerable	c. 673–735	Benedictine monk and priest of Jarrow (England)	Father of English History	Contributed scriptural commentaries and historical works.
Saint John of Damascus	c. 676–c. 749	Priest and scholar of Damascus (Syria)	The Golden Speaker; Doctor of the Assumption	Wrote poetry, philosophy, and theology, particularly against heresy of iconoclasm.
Saint Gregory of Narek	951–1003	Monk, priest, and theologian of Narek (Turkey)	Author of the *Book of Lamentations*	Contributed commentaries and prayers supporting Catholics against Islam.
Saint Peter Damian	c. 1007–1072	Benedictine monk and cardinal bishop of Ostia (Italy)	Monitor of the Popes; Reformer	Wrote sermons, treatises, letters, and hymns explaining Church teaching, particularly in defense of virtue and monastic life.
Saint Anselm of Canterbury	1033–1109	Benedictine monk and archbishop of Canterbury (England)	Father of Scholasticism	Contributed theological and philosophical writings in defense of Church teaching.
Saint Bernard of Clairvaux	1090–1153	Priest and Cistercian	Mellifluous Doctor	Contributed sermons

Name	Dates	Description	Title or Nickname	Notable Contribution
		abbot of Clairvaux (France)		and treatises explaining theology and virtue.
Saint Hildegard of Bingen	1098– 1179	Benedictine nun and abbess of Bingen (Germany)	Sibyl of the Rhine	Contributed writings including encyclopedia of natural science and works about theology and ethics, as well as letters, songs, and private revelations.
Saint Anthony of Padua	1195– 1231	Franciscan friar of Padua (Italy)	Evangelical Doctor; Miracleworker; Hammer of Heretics	Contributed Scripture-based sermons against Catharism.
Saint Bonaventure	c. 1221– 1274	Franciscan priest and minister general; cardinal bishop of Albano (Italy)	Seraphic Doctor	Contributed theological and philosophical works.
Saint Thomas Aquinas	c. 1225– 1274	Dominican priest and theologian (Italy)	Angelic Doctor	Contributed theological and philosophical works of great depth and quality.
Saint Albert the Great	c. 1206– 1280	Dominican priest and bishop of Cologne (Germany)	Universal Doctor	Contributed theological and philosophical works, as well as writings on natural sciences.

(continued)

Name	Dates	Description	Title or Nickname	Notable Contribution
Saint Catherine of Siena	1347–1380	Third Order Dominican of Siena (Italy)	Seraphic Virgin; Patroness of Europe	Mystical writings and letters were influential in the Church.
Saint John of Avila	1499–1569	Priest (Spain)	Apostle of Andalusia	Contributed sermons, conferences, letters, and treatises on spirituality.
Saint Teresa of Avila (Teresa of Jesus)	1515–1582	Founder and nun of Discalced Carmelite order of Avila (Spain)	Doctor of Prayer	Books and letters explained prayer and the spiritual life.
Saint John of the Cross	1542–1591	Priest and monk of Discalced Carmelite order (Spain)	Mystical Doctor	Contributed mystical works about prayer and the spiritual life.
Saint Peter Canisius	1521–1597	Jesuit priest (Holland; Germany)	Doctor of Catechesis; Apostle of Germany	Contributed theological and apologetic works in defense of the Church against Protestantism.
Saint Lawrence of Brindisi	1559–1619	Capuchin priest (Italy)	Apostolic Doctor	Contributed Scripture-based sermons and apologetic writings against Lutheranism.
Saint Robert Bellarmine	1542–1621	Cardinal priest (Italy)	Prince of Apologists; Patron of Catechists	Contributed catechisms and writings in defense of the faith against Protestantism.

Name	Dates	Description	Title or Nickname	Notable Contribution
Saint Francis de Sales	1567–1622	Founder of the Order of the Visitation (with Saint Jane Frances de Chantal) and bishop of Geneva (Switzerland)	Doctor of Charity	Gave spiritual direction through letters and treatises; defended the faith through pamphlets.
Saint Alphonsus Liguori	1696–1787	Bishop of Saint Agata dei Gotti (Italy) and founder of the Order of Redemptorists	Most Zealous Doctor; Patron of Confessors and Moral Theologians	Contributed innumerable writings about moral theology, as well as ascetical and devotional works and letters.
Saint Thérèse of Lisieux	1873–1897	Discalced Carmelite nun (France)	The Little Flower; Doctor of Merciful Love	Autobiography and letters explained universal call to holiness in her "little way".

Doctors of the Church are particularly noted for their writings; the following table lists representative works that are readily available today.

Name	Title of Work	Availability
Saint Irenaeus of Lyons	*Against Heresies; The Demonstration of the Apostolic Preaching*	In print; some online and at NewAdvent.org
Saint Hilary of Poitiers	*On the Trinity*; homilies	In print; online at NewAdvent.org
Saint Athanasius of Alexandria	*Life of Anthony; Letter to Marcellinus*; treatises	In print; online at NewAdvent.org
Saint Ephraem the Syrian	Hymns; homilies; prose works	In print; some online at NewAdvent.org

(continued)

Name	Title of Work	Availability
Saint Basil the Great	*On the Holy Spirit; Longer Rules; Shorter Rules*; letters; homilies	Some in print; some online at NewAdvent.org
Saint Cyril of Jerusalem	*Catechetical Lectures*	In print; some online at NewAdvent.org; CCEL.org
Saint Gregory of Nazianzus	Poems; orations	Some in print; some online at NewAdvent.org
Saint Ambrose of Milan	Letters; treatises	Some in print; online at NewAdvent.org
Saint John Chrysostom	Homilies; letters	Many online at NewAdvent.org; many in print
Saint Jerome of Stridon	Letters; treatises	Some in print; online at NewAdvent.org
Saint Augustine of Hippo	*Confessions; The City of God; Sermons; Christian Doctrine; The Trinity; Literal Commentary on Genesis; Retractions* (also called *Reconsiderations*); many other writings	In print; some online at NewAdvent.org
Saint Cyril of Alexandria	*Against Those Who Are Unwilling to Confess That the Holy Virgin Is Theotokos*; other treatises and commentaries	In print; some online
Saint Peter Chrysologus	*Sermons and Homilies*	In print
Saint Leo the Great	Sermons; letters	In print; some online at NewAdvent.org
Saint Gregory the Great	*Dialogues; Pastoral Rule; Moralia on Job*; homilies; letters	In print; some online at NewAdvent.org
Saint Isidore of Seville	*Sententiae*	In print; a limited number of writings available online or in print
Saint Bede the Venerable	*Ecclesiastical History of England*; commentaries	*Ecclesiastical History* in print and online at CCEL.org; a few other writings available

Name	Title of Work	Availability
Saint John of Damascus	*Exposition on the Faith*; treatises	In print; some online at NewAdvent.org
Saint Gregory of Narek	*Armenian Prayer Book*; letters	*Prayer Book* available in print
Saint Peter Damian	Letters	In print
Saint Anselm of Canterbury	*Cur Deus Homo*; *Prayers and Meditations*; *Proslogion*	In print; online at CCEL.org
Saint Bernard of Clairvaux	Sermons (particularly those on Song of Songs); letters; treatises	In print; some online at CCEL.org
Saint Hildegard of Bingen	*Scivias*; other writings	*Scivias* and a few other writings in print
Saint Anthony of Padua	*Sermones for Easter*	A few writings in print
Saint Bonaventure	*Soul's Journey into God*; *Tree of Life*; *Life of St. Francis*	In print
Saint Thomas Aquinas	*Summa Theologiae* and many other writings; prayers; commentaries	In print; *Summa* online at NewAdvent.org
Saint Albert the Great	*On Union with God*	In print; a few other writings available
Saint Catherine of Siena	*Dialogues*; letters	In print
Saint John of Avila	*Listen, O Daughter*; letters	In print
Saint Teresa of Avila	*Autobiography*; *Way of Perfection*; *Interior Castle*	In print
Saint John of the Cross	*Dark Night of the Soul*; *Spiritual Canticle*; *Ascent of Mount Carmel*	In print

(continued)

Name	Title of Work	Availability
Saint Peter Canisius	*Catechism*	In print; a few other writings available
Saint Lawrence of Brindisi	*On the Admirability of the Blessed Virgin*	In print; a few other writings available
Saint Robert Bellarmine	*Art of Dying Well*; *Mind's Ascent to God*; *Commentary on the Psalms*	In print; a few other writings available
Saint Francis de Sales	*Introduction to the Devout Life*; *Treatise on the Love of God*; letters	In print
Saint Alphonsus Liguori	*The Glories of Mary*; *The Way of the Cross*; many other writings	In print; a few online
Saint Thérèse of Lisieux	*The Story of a Soul*; letters	In print

Our Family Calendar

All Catholics follow the liturgical calendar of the Church, even those who don't know what that means. That is, Roman Catholics celebrate Christmas, Lent, Easter, and even the Eleventh Sunday of Ordinary Time on the same date all over the world. That calendar varies from year to year, due to leap days, equinoxes, and other details, and the Church has made changes to the liturgical calendar over the centuries.

In some ways, the Church's calendar is like the calendar of a family, for a family calendar also has a "hierarchy" of importance, whether people explicitly acknowledge it or not. For example, while the birthdays of young children may be generally celebrated with the greatest energy and expense, their parents' wedding anniversary came first (God willing) and is in many ways more important because that is the date that two individuals became a family.

The most important date in the Church calendar is so important that it takes more than one day to celebrate: the Paschal Triduum. Holy Thursday, Good Friday, and Easter Sunday are the greatest of all Christian holy days, and all other dates of the calendar revolve around them, like planets around the sun.

Changes to the calendar

But deciding when to celebrate the days from Jesus' Crucifixion to His Resurrection took centuries. Why? Because according to tradition, Jesus arose from the dead on the fourteenth day of Nisan, according to the Jewish calendar used at the time, which (apparently) happened to also be the first Sunday after the vernal equinox. Unfortunately, the positions of the moon and sun do not line up in the same way each year, and the early Christians had to decide whether

91

to celebrate Easter on a particular day of the Jewish calendar *or* celebrate Easter on a particular Sunday. It literally took centuries for everyone to agree that it was more important to celebrate Easter on Sunday than it was to follow the Jewish calendar.

A more recent and dramatic change occurred as a result of the Second Vatican Council. Pope Saint Paul VI issued an apostolic letter in 1969 (*Mysterii Paschalis*) in which he explained proposed revisions to the liturgical calendar. As he wrote:

> It is true that in the course of time the multiplication of feasts, vigils and octaves, as well as the progressive complication of different parts of the liturgical year, have often driven the faithful to particular devotions, in such a way that their minds have been somewhat diverted from the fundamental mysteries of our Redemption.[1]

The pope was gently saying that we were overdue to clean up the Church calendar. If you have a home with a basement, it is easy to understand the pope's point. Every so often, whether we like it or not, we need to clean out the stuff we have accumulated. Many of the revisions that were made to the calendar by Pope Paul VI are those sorts of changes. The feast day of Saint Irenaeus, a bishop and martyr from the early Church, was moved forward a few days so that he wouldn't be perennially overlooked because his feast was too close to the date of the great Saints Peter and Paul. More recent examination of ancient papal records had indicated that Pope Saint Anacletus and Pope Saint Cletus were and are the same person, so two dates from the previous calendar were combined into one. Some saints, such as Saint Vitalis, were removed completely from the calendar because of limited information their lives. An unintended consequence of these changes, however, was that some people falsely began to believe that certain saints were no longer saints because they were no longer in the liturgical calendar. Some saints with a long-standing popular devotion, such as Saints Christopher, Barbara, and Dorothy, seemed to have been ignored.

---

[1] Paul VI, Motu Proprio on Liturgical Year and New General Roman Calendar *Mysterii Paschalis* (February 14, 1969), I, http://www.vatican.va/content/paul-vi/en/motu_proprio /documents/hf_p-vi_motu-proprio_19690214_mysterii-paschalis.html.

Understanding the calendar

To understand better how this happened, it helps to know that the Church helps us recognize the relative importance of different celebrations through their titles in the General Roman Calendar.

Title	Description	Example
Solemnity	Celebration of a person, event, or belief that is of the greatest and universal importance to the Church	Christmas, December 25
Feast	Less important than a solemnity	Saint Stephen, the first martyr; December 26
Memorial	Less important than a feast	Saint Lucy, early Church virgin and martyr; December 13
Optional memorial	Optional liturgical celebration	Saint Thomas á Becket, bishop and martyr; December 29

In your own home, there are certain dates that you simply must celebrate. *Your* birthday, for example. There are others dates that are celebrated because they are part of our culture, such as Halloween. There are also dates that are celebrated because they are important to the nation, such as Independence Day in America.

Solemnities

Over the centuries, the Church has decided that some events must be celebrated by all Catholics, everywhere. Since the Church is, among other things, our teacher in the faith, so is the Church's calendar. Through the solemnities, the Church ensures that our everyday lives are interrupted with celebrations related to Jesus Christ, the other two Persons of the Trinity, and those closest to Him. Consider what these solemnities teach us about our faith.

Person(s)	Solemnity	Date
Jesus Christ	Nativity of the Lord	December 25
	Epiphany; also called the Three Magi	*Moveable date*
	Holy Week: Palm Sunday, Holy Thursday, Good Friday, Holy Saturday; Easter Sunday, followed by Divine Mercy Sunday	*Moveable dates*
	Ascension of the Lord	*Moveable date*
	Body and Blood of Christ; also called Corpus Christi	*Moveable date*
	Most Sacred Heart of Jesus	*Moveable date*
	Christ the King	*Moveable date*
Holy Spirit	Pentecost	*Moveable date*
Holy Trinity	Most Holy Trinity	*Moveable date*
Blessed Virgin Mary	Mary, Mother of God	January 1
	Annunciation	March 25
	Assumption of Mary	August 15
	Immaculate Conception of Mary	December 8
Saints	Saint Joseph, Husband of the Blessed Virgin Mary	March 19
	Birth of Saint John the Baptist	June 24
	Saints Peter and Paul, Apostles	June 29
	All Saints	November 1
The faithful departed	All Souls	November 2

Clearly, the solemnities focus our attention on Jesus' life, death, Resurrection, and Ascension into Heaven. These events, along with reflections on other truths about Him, such as His Presence in the Eucharist, are sprinkled throughout the year. The solemnities of Pentecost and the Most Holy Trinity remind us of that mystery we believe in but can never fully grasp this side of Heaven: our triune God. All the solemnities in which we honor Mary are events that point us back to Christ. Solemnities also remind us of some of the greatest saints and that there are many saints in Heaven, encouraging our desire to intercede for all those we love who have passed from this world.

Feasts

The feast days, of lesser importance than solemnities, are also heavily focused on the life of Jesus Christ, but more dates associated with saints have been added.

Person(s)	Feast	Date
Jesus Christ	Baptism of the Lord	Sunday after Epiphany
	Presentation of the Lord	February 2
	Transfiguration of the Lord	August 6
	Exaltation of the Cross	September 14
Holy Family	Holy Family of Jesus, Mary, and Joseph	*Moveable date*
Blessed Virgin Mary	Visitation	May 31
	Birth of the Virgin Mary	September 8
Saint Peter	Chair of Saint Peter	February 22
Saint Paul	Conversion of Saint Paul	January 25
Other apostles	Saints Philip and James the Lesser	May 3
	Saint Matthias	May 14
	Saint Thomas	July 3
	Saint James the Greater	July 25
	Saint Nathaniel (Bartholomew)	August 24
	Saint Matthew	September 21
	Saints Simon and Jude (Thaddeus)	October 28
	Saint Andrew	November 30
	Saint John	December 27

(continued)

Person(s)	Feast	Date
Evangelists	Saint Mark	April 25
	Saint Luke	October 18
Other	Saint Mary Magdalene	July 22
	Saint Lawrence	August 10
	Saints Michael, Gabriel, and Raphael, Archangels	September 29
	Dedication of the Lateran Basilica	November 9
	Saint Stephen, the First Martyr	December 26
	Holy Innocents	December 28

Unless you attend daily Mass or your parish church is named after one of these saints or events, the feasts may pass you by. Similarly, the memorials and optional memorials of the Church—and there are many of those—celebrate dozens of saints that are not essential to your faith as a Catholic. But you lose something when you are unaware of them, just as your joy might be diminished if you forgot to celebrate the birthday of a particular friend.

A useful question to ask ourselves when we think about these dates is, What would life be like without this solemnity or feast on the Church calendar?

In a world in which many people doubt that Jesus Christ is truly present in the Eucharist, we need an annual reminder that He is. Because we will never truly understand how our God can be "one God in three Persons", we need our priests to do their best to try to explain it to us in their homilies once a year. We also need to be reminded that Jesus' mother, Mary, made an amazing statement of faith when she said yes to God's invitation, and we need to be reminded that she grew in that faith over her lifetime, so that we can try to do likewise.

As for the Church feast days, Jesus' parents obeyed the Jewish Law even though Mary, being sinless, didn't truly need to offer a sacrifice for being unclean (as she did during the event we call the Presentation of the Lord). There are innumerable lessons for us in every feast day.

Person(s)	Feast	Possible Lessons
Jesus Christ	Baptism of the Lord	Reminds us of the necessity of our own Baptism if we wish to be saved.
	Presentation of the Lord	Shows us the importance of humility and obeying just laws.
	Transfiguration of the Lord	Helps us accept that God's glory is not always visible.
	Exaltation of the Cross	Teaches us that our sufferings are both horrible and beautiful, because of Christ's sacrifice.
Holy Family	Holy Family of Jesus, Mary, and Joseph	Shows that it is possible to be a holy family.
Blessed Virgin Mary	Birth of the Virgin Mary	Reminds us that the most perfect follower of Christ lived an ordinary life, just like ours.
	Visitation of Mary to Elizabeth	Encourages us to serve those in need and expect that God will bless us in unusual ways when we do.
Saint Peter	Chair of Saint Peter	Points not toward Peter's perfection (because he was far from that, at least at the beginning) or his successors' power and wealth, but toward his role as teacher of the faith and head of Christ's Mystical Body.
Saint Paul	Conversion of Saint Paul	Reminds us that we all need to be converted and that conversion is possible even for those who hate us.
Other apostles	Saints Philip, James the Lesser, Matthias, Thomas, James the Greater, Bartholomew, Matthew, Simon, Jude, Andrew, and John	Reminds us that each of the apostles left everything behind to follow Christ and lived heroic lives of witness to Him.

(*continued*)

Person(s)	Feast	Possible Lessons
Evangelists	Saints Mark and Luke	Reminds us where we would be without the evangelists, who carefully collected and wrote down Jesus' sayings.
	Saint Lawrence	Teaches us that his behavior during his public martyrdom in the year 258 was so courageous and mysterious that many pagans living in Rome were moved to enter the Church afterward.
	Saints Michael, Gabriel, and Raphael, Archangels	Encourages us to remember that we have angelic protectors all around us.
	Dedication of the Lateran Basilica	Unites the ordinary events of our own parish churches to parish churches all over the world.
	Saint Stephen, the First Martyr	Reminds us about the first—but far from the last—person to die as a martyr for Christ, lest we think that being a Christian is the short route to an easy life.
	Holy Innocents	Reminds us soon after we celebrate Christ's birth into the world about the innocent young boys who were slaughtered at King Herod's command, proving that absolutely no sacrifice is hidden from God.

Why are some saints celebrated with memorials, others with optional memorials, and others not even included in the General Roman Calendar used by the Church worldwide? That will become more obvious in the following chapter when we look at the calendars used by individual nations and regions.

A Nation of Saints

Babies think that they are the center of the universe and that their needs must be met immediately. But they have an excuse: they don't know any better. We adults cannot be excused so easily.

Similarly, Catholic members of any nation can tend to be short-sighted, thinking more highly of saints celebrated in their own country than those of other countries. For Americans, this problem is worsened by the unfortunate circumstance that most modern history curricula for grades K–12 focus much more on George Washington and American history than on the history of the rest of the world. When we do not know where Caesarea was—and that there was more than one region called Caesarea in the ancient world—it is difficult to recognize the saints of Caesarea as relevant.

Each Catholic nation has its own national calendar, for which the General Roman Calendar is modified to add and change particular feasts or memorials. Why? So that the citizens of that nation can remember saints that are of particular importance to them.

Apostles

The most obvious saints for any nation to celebrate are their apostles—that is, the missionary saints who brought the Gospel to that country.

Jesus first called twelve men to be His disciples, and He sent them out to spread the Gospel to all the nations before He ascended into Heaven. Ancient traditions tell us that all these men obeyed and traveled to distant nations to spread the Good News.

Name of Apostle[1]	Nation(s) Evangelized, according to Tradition
Peter	Greece; Italy
Andrew	Bulgaria; Greece
James the Greater (also called James the son of Zebedee)	Spain
John (also called John the son of Zebedee)	Greece; Turkey
Philip	Greece; Turkey
Nathaniel (also called Bartholomew)	Armenia; India
Matthew (also called Levi)	Syria; Ethiopia; Iran
James the Lesser (also called James the son of Alphaeus)	Israel
Thomas	India
Simon the Zealot (also called Simon the Cananaean)	Israel or Iran
Jude (also called Thaddeus and Judas the son of James)	Iran
Matthias	Ethiopia or Israel
Paul[2]	Turkey; Greece; Italy; Spain
Barnabas[3]	Cyprus

Evangelization did not end with the first apostles. Some regions were evangelized by many missionaries over a period of time, and it's often difficult to say that one particular person was the groundbreaking apostle who brought that nation into the Church.

[1] Note that there has been a debate in modern times about the names of some of the Twelve. The traditional view, that "Matthew the tax collector" is also called "Levi" and that "Nathaniel" is also called "Bartholomew" (literally, son of Talmei), is assumed here.

[2] Saint Paul the Apostle, while not one of the Twelve, is generally counted with the original apostles because of his extraordinary witness throughout the Roman Empire.

[3] Like Saint Paul, Saint Barnabas was not one of the original Twelve, but his missionary work appears prominently in the Acts of the Apostles.

But in some countries, there was one holy Catholic man, supported by many other holy Catholic men coming before, after, or with him, who was a living example of Saint Paul's exhortation to "preach the word, be urgent in season and out of season, convince, rebuke, and exhort, be unfailing in patience and in teaching."[4] The following table lists the men who are traditionally considered the apostles of these nations.[5]

Modern Nation	Apostle(s)	Century
Ireland	Saint Patrick	5th
England	Saint Augustine of Canterbury	6th
Germany	Saint Boniface	8th
The Netherlands	Saint Willibrord	8th
Poland, Czech Republic, Croatia, Russia, and others	Saints Cyril and Methodius	9th
Bulgaria	Saint Clement of Okhrida and companions	9th
Denmark	Saint Ansgar	9th
Poland, Czech Republic	Saint Adalbert (Vojtěch) of Prague	10th
Norway	Saint Olaf II	11th
India	Saint Francis Xavier	16th
Japan	Saint Francis Xavier	16th
Brazil	Saint Jose de Anchieta	16th
South America	Saint Louis Bertrand	16th
Guatemala	Saint Peter of Saint Joseph Betancur	17th
Sri Lanka	Saint Joseph Vaz	18th

[4] 2 Tim 4:2.

[5] My apologies in advance for not including apostles for every nation that every reader might think of.

Other evangelizing saints

The liturgical calendar of an individual nation shows the nation's history as well as its character. Saintly Franciscan priests like Junipero Serra did not leave their home countries to live a life of ease in the Americas. They lived in poverty and danger and traveled immense distances out of Christian charity. Some, like the North American martyrs of the seventeenth century, encountered a level of cultural brutality that makes the persecution under the Roman emperor Diocletian—where Christians were at least generally torn apart by animals, not other people—look almost civilized. Perhaps the American stereotype of courage and rugged independence comes as much from early saints as it does from families crossing the prairies in covered wagons.

Some of the saints on a country's liturgical calendar show that the faith can be lost as well as gained. After the Protestant Revolt, many regions of Europe abandoned the faith. Saints such as Francis de Sales and Peter Canisius brought the people of France and Germany back to the Church, one by one, despite threats and violence.

Some countries have been evangelized repeatedly. Saint Matthias the Apostle, according to tradition, evangelized northern Africa, specifically Ethiopia, in the first century. Saint Frumentius was kidnapped and made a slave in Ethiopia in the fourth century, later leaving the country and returning as a missionary bishop to evangelize the people for a second time. But Christianity was brought to the continent of Africa yet again in the fifteenth to the nineteenth centuries. For example, Saint Daniel Comboni served as a missionary priest in Sudan in the nineteenth century for a time and then spent the rest of his life raising funds, founding a religious order, and serving as bishop to regions of Africa. Evangelization was not his only goal; he helped suppress slavery, learned several African dialects so he could communicate with his people, and frequently reminded Europeans to treat African peoples as equals, not children.

Some evangelizing saints are honored both in the nation to which they brought the Gospel, as well as the nation that sent them. For example, both America and Belgium honor Saint Damien de Veuster (1840–1889) for giving his priestly life to the service of lepers on Molokai.

Several countries have a veritable army of saintly citizens in Heaven. These nations received the Catholic faith, though often with some bloodshed, and have populated their liturgical calendar with truly great saints.

France

In the year 496, King Clovis of the Franks was baptized, three years after marrying his Christian queen, Clotilda. The encouragement and personal witness of Saint Clotilda (c. 474–545) and Saint Remigius (438–533), the bishop of Rheims, helped Clovis enter the Church, and with him, the rest of the nation of France.

Almost two centuries previously, a young soldier who had been moved by a vision of Christ[6] to become a Catholic, left the army and his native Hungary to learn about the faith under Hilary, bishop of Tours, France. After living as a monk for some time, he became the bishop of Tours himself and was well known for his charity, mercy, prayerfulness, and simple way of life, which is why he is now known as Saint Martin of Tours (315–397).

Two other French saints celebrated in the Church calendar in the United States include a king and a teacher. King Louis IX (1214–1270) proved that one can be a holy Christian and a powerful man at the same time. He was a good and faithful husband and father, but he was also a merciful and just ruler of his country. For example, when a count captured three children for hunting rabbits on his land and hanged them, people were rightly outraged—and so was the king. Louis ordered the count to be put on trial, not by his noble peers, but by ordinary judges. Judges convicted the count and sentenced him to death. Proving Louis had the wisdom of Solomon,[7] he commuted the death sentence to a very heavy fine and gave all the money to charity. Saint John Baptist de la Salle (1651–1719) revolutionized education in France during his lifetime; he dedicated his life to the

---

[6] In this famous story, Saint Martin passed a shivering old man on a winter day and cut his cloak in half, helping the man out of Christian charity. That night, Jesus Christ appeared to him in a dream and told Martin that he had given his garment to Jesus Himself. Martin had not yet been baptized, but he remedied that situation immediately.

[7] 1 Kings 3:16–28.

unthinkable and lowly task of educating poor children, even going so far as to teach them in the French language, rather than in Latin, which was unsurprisingly much more effective.

There are many more French saints included throughout this book because France experienced such a strong Catholic tradition beginning with the time of King Clovis. But, as will be shown later, France's strong tradition hit a major obstacle: the French Revolution.

Spain

Spain can boast of many great saints: Saint Isidore of Seville, the seventh-century archbishop and scholar who literally wrote encyclopedias (note the plural); Saint Eulogius of Cordoba, a priest and scholar who was martyred by Muslims in the ninth century; Saint Ferdinand III of Castile, the brave and holy king of the thirteenth century who reclaimed parts of Spain from Muslim control for Catholics; Saint Teresa of Avila, the sixteenth-century nun whose mystical and administrative wisdom changed more than just a religious order; Saint Anthony Mary Claret, the nineteenth-century priest who was not only the author of more than a hundred books but also nearly escaped assassination while serving as a missionary bishop in Cuba; and the twentieth-century priest Saint Josemaria Escriva, who founded Opus Dei, an institution of the Church that unites and encourages both laity and clergy to seek holiness in their everyday lives.

Ireland

The liturgical calendar of the saints of Ireland is almost twice the length of that of the United States (not that it's a competition) and includes numerous bishops and abbots and nuns from the fifth century to the ninth. We all know about the great missionary Saint Patrick, but did you know that the faith was spread to the Irish by men they call the Twelve Apostles of Ireland?

As a young man, the future saint Finian studied in Wales for many years, returned to live as a simple monk in his native country, and eventually founded Clonard Abbey. This famous abbey educated many young men and boys, including—you guessed it—twelve men who spread the faith in sixth-century Ireland, primarily through living holy lives as monks and abbots. Other Irish saints not only taught their own people about the faith but also sent out missionaries to the rest of the world for centuries.

On the other hand, when England became a Protestant nation and began a brutal crackdown on the practice of Catholicism in the sixteenth to nineteenth centuries, faithful Catholics in Ireland suffered persecution, and many were martyred. The exact number of Irish Catholic martyrs will never be known, but the heroic example of many, such as Saint Oliver Plunkett (1625–1681), the Catholic archbishop of Armagh and primate of all Ireland, who was tried, convicted, and condemned to death for the crime of being Catholic, is a testimony to the Irish people's great faithfulness during that time.

Poland

Any discussion of saints, holiness, and Poland cannot ignore Pope Saint John Paul II (1920–2005). Born Karol Wojtyla in Wadowice, Poland, he became a living example of Poland's national history. Just as Poland has withstood conquest, war, and oppression many times in the centuries since it formally became a Catholic nation in the tenth century—never losing its Catholic faith—so John Paul experienced great suffering but remained a great witness. For example, he had lost both parents and a brother by the time he was twenty years old; he escaped deportation to Nazi Germany only by becoming a manual laborer; he spent decades of his life under the brutal Nazi government and then the oppressive Communist government; and he almost died from an assassination attempt. But just as Christ's death teaches us how to live, so John Paul's example shows us how to respond to the challenges we face. If the government makes it illegal to study to become a priest, well, study for the priesthood anyway. If you're the bishop of an oppressed country and are under constant surveillance and threats, encourage your flock by your calm example of steadfastness and stand up for your people, even if that means slamming your hand on the table before the Communist leaders sometimes to show that you won't be cowed into submission. Just a few of

John Paul's achievements as pope would be enough to declare him a saint, but there are many of them. He helped defeat Communism in multiple Slavic nations *peacefully*, and he did that so effectively that Communists tried to kill him. He spoke a dozen languages and traveled to more than a hundred countries, truly acting as a universal pastor tending to his flock. He single-handedly developed a theological explanation of human sexuality that could and should provide a Catholic response to the Sexual Revolution. Even in the final years before his death, he taught the world how a Catholic can die at peace with God, despite physical suffering and disability.

Then there are the saints who were raised to the altars during Pope John Paul II's reign. Teaching the world that sanctity is not only for a few chosen souls, he canonized and beatified many holy men and women. Although the saints he canonized came from all over the world, here are a few of the Polish ones who show us so much about how to live as Catholics.

Saint Albert Chmielowski (1845–1916) was a freedom fighter for his country and lost a leg during the war. He studied and became a successful artist before abandoning his career to serve the poor, and his personal example led others to follow him, which resulted in the creation of a religious order of brothers. Blessed Antoni Nowowiejski (1858–1941) was a deeply devout Polish archbishop and was imprisoned in a concentration camp during World War II, along with many of his priests. He was tortured repeatedly and starved to death by the Nazis, never losing his faith in Christ. Saint Ursula Ledóchowska (1865–1939) came from a noble, pious family, entered the Ursuline order, and then founded her own order of Ursuline nuns to educate and serve the poor. She and her nuns served as Catholic missionaries in Russia until they were expelled during the Communist revolution. Blessed Karolina Kózkówny (1898–1914) was born into a large family of farmers and taught the faith to other children. She was only sixteen years old when a Russian soldier killed her during an attempted rape, making her a martyr for purity.

But perhaps John Paul's most famous canonized saint is Saint Faustina Kowalska (1905–1938). Born into a poor family, she had to work when she was a teenager rather than attend school. When she heard God's call to enter religious life, she was turned down by multiple orders, perhaps because of her poverty and lack of education. But she was eventually accepted by one order, became a sister, took the name of Faustina, and served her community as cook, gardener, and doorkeeper. Like so many other great saints, her peaceful, quiet nature hid a profound spiritual life, which we know about only because of her diary. Her visions of Jesus Christ and His message of Divine Mercy have touched the hearts of Catholics and non-Catholics all over the world.

But Poland did not begin giving birth to saints in the twentieth century. Saint Bruno of Querfurt was a Benedictine Camaldolese[8] monk and a missionary archbishop who spread the faith in the late tenth century before being martyred for the faith by pagans. Saint Hedwig was the queen of Poland in the fourteenth century, and her acceptance of an arranged marriage to a non-Christian king led to the king's conversion. The Polish people particularly loved her for her personal charity toward the sick and the poor. Saint John of Kanti[9] (1390–1473) was a brilliant priest and scholar who lived an ascetic life but who earned the deep affection of the laity through his care for those in need. Saint Stanislaus Kostka (1550–1568) was a pious young man from a noble family who had to overcome his family's strong objections to enter the Jesuit order; he died while still a novice. Saint Jan Sarkander (1576–1620) lived during the time of the great violence due to the Protestant Revolt, was married, and was left a widower without children before becoming a Jesuit priest. When Father Sarkander visited the commander of an army of Polish Catholics before an imminent battle, he brought the Blessed Sacrament with him. When no battle resulted, the Catholics took it as a sign of God's protection; this angered a powerful anti-Catholic local leader. He accused Jan of treason, had him arrested and tortured to try to make him give up military details, and then executed him by setting him on fire, making Jan a martyr for the seal of Confession and a saint.

Hungary

Americans tend to know very little about the history of Hungary, so it may be a surprise to learn that Hungary's liturgical calendar includes

---

[8] The Camaldolese order was founded by Saint Romuald in the tenth century and is an offshoot to the Benedictine order.

[9] He is sometimes called Saint John Cantius.

many great native saints. Hungary may lead the world for the number of leaders who have been declared saints of the Catholic Church.

The father of Saint Stephen (969–1038) was a pagan, but he was also the Grand Prince of Hungary. It is not clear whether his decision to become Catholic and baptize his son was for personal or political motives, but his son Stephen's conversion was real. When Stephen succeeded his father and became king of Hungary, he united the Magyar people and defeated attempted revolts by pagan leaders. Stephen of Hungary was also a devout Christian who founded monasteries, encouraged the spread of the faith in his country, and eventually brought peace to his country.

A later Hungarian leader, Saint Ladislaus, was born in Poland in the eleventh century but succeeded his brother to become king of Hungary. Like Saint Stephen, he was a strong leader but also a just Christian ruler who earned the love and respect of his people.

In the thirteenth century, Hungary can boast of not one, but three holy princesses. Saint Elizabeth (1207–1231) was born a princess of Hungary and married the margrave (military governor) of Thuringia (modern Germany). Despite her nobility, she personally cared for the sick and the poor, and after her husband's death, she humbly accepted being forced to leave the castle and work to support her four young children. Saint Kinga (1224–1292) was born a princess of Hungary and married a prince of Poland. However, the couple lived as brother and sister, and she cared for the poor and for lepers before being widowed and retiring to a convent. Saint Margaret (1242–1271) was Kinga's much younger sister and the tenth child of her parents. For that reason, she gave her entire life as a "tithe" to God. She grew up in a convent and loved religious life so much that she refused when her father tried to arrange a marriage for her. Not only did she live a humble, penitential life but multiple miracles resulted through her intercession after her death.

Hungary has produced more than saintly kings and queens. Saint Marko Križevčanin (1589–1619) was a Jesuit priest and missionary when Calvinist soldiers captured, tortured, and executed him for being Catholic. Blessed Ladislaus Batthyany-Strattmann (1870–1931) came from a noble family and became a medical doctor. He married, and he and his wife had thirteen children; they prayed the Rosary as a family daily and attended Mass together. Ladislaus opened his own hospital, which expanded over the years to care for soldiers during World War I, as well as patients who could not afford to pay for their care. He became internationally known as a specialist in eye diseases, yet he took the time to pray over his patients and ask them to pray for him. Blessed Zoltán Lajos Meszlényi (1892–1951) came from a devout family and earned doctorates in theology, canon law, and philosophy before being ordained a priest. He was an auxiliary bishop when he was arrested, imprisoned, tortured, and worked to death by the anti-Catholic Hungarian Communist government.

England, Wales, and Scotland

The liturgical calendar of England and Wales honors many native saints above and beyond those already included in the General Roman Calendar. Some of these additions to the calendar are perfectly understandable. For example, Saint Augustine of Canterbury is credited with the evangelization of the nation of England in the sixth century.

Though Christianity had spread to England much earlier and English bishops had even attended a synod of bishops in France in the year 314, the collapse of the Roman Empire left only pockets of native Christians in England living among native pagans. When Pope Gregory I sent them as missionaries to England, Augustine and his companions feared for their lives and safety, but the people responded to the truth and beauty of the Christian faith.

Other early English saints include Saint Cuthbert, a hermit and monk from the seventh century who became a holy bishop; Saint Etheldreda, a seventh-century princess who asked to be released from her noble marriage to become a nun and whose body was later found to be incorrupt; Saint Dunstan, a tenth-century abbot and bishop who reformed Church practices and served as a minister to multiple English kings; and Saint Richard of Chichester, a brilliant thirteenth-century scholar and bishop who demanded that his clergy live moral, disciplined lives but also protected the Church and clergy from acts of injustice. The English liturgical calendar includes Welsh saints as well, such as Saint David, a sixth-century monk-turned-bishop noted for his ascetic life and now known as the patron saint of Wales, and Saint Winifrid, a seventh-century virgin-martyr.

The protomartyr of the English Church, Saint Alban, lived and died in the third or fourth century when the country was ruled by the Roman Empire. For his faithfulness to Christ, under circumstances that are not certain, he died a martyr and is celebrated on June 20 in England. About a month earlier, English Catholics remember a much larger group of martyrs, all of whom died between the years 1535 and 1681, and all as a result of King Henry VIII's declaration that he, not the pope, was the head of the Church in England. Tens of thousands of Catholic men and women—clergy, monks, nuns, and laymen—died during this period in England, though we will never know the exact total. The most famous martyrs, Saints John Fisher and Thomas More, are typical of these martyrs in some ways. Like the other English martyrs of this time period, they were killed because the government considered their religious beliefs to be acts of treason. Unlike those two high-profile cases, the actual charges made against many Catholic martyrs were vague, unproven, sometimes demonstrably false, and occasionally ridiculous. Helping a priest avoid certain death, for example, could lead to the loss of all your property or your life.

In 1061, an English lady received a vision of the Blessed Mother, who showed her the home of the Holy Family in Nazareth. Inspired, the woman built a replica of what she had seen, and the building became known as Our Lady of Walsingham. Faithful Catholics prayed at the site for centuries. King Henry VIII ordered the church destroyed, along with many other English churches, and many people thought that was the end of Marian devotion. But English devotion to our Lady could not be stopped by something as simple as building demolition, and today there are shrines to the Blessed Mother in England under this title for Catholics, Anglicans, and Orthodox Christians. Additionally, English law in the Middle Ages allowed a husband to set aside part of his estate for his wife to support her in case of his death, which was called a dowry. Because of this long-standing devotion to the Blessed Virgin, the English have come to think of Mary as their particular guardian and of the nation itself as "Mary's Dowry".

It is not certain when Scotland was first evangelized. Some say Pope Victor's missionaries reached the country in the year 203. Some say a Scotsman named Ninian traveled to Rome and brought back the faith in the year 403. Other traditions say that Saint Regulus, bishop of Patras, Greece, brought relics of Saint Andrew to Scotland in the year 347, which is perhaps the reason that the Scottish people have claimed Andrew as their special patron for as long as anyone can remember. But no one debates the timing of Saint Margaret of Scotland (c. 1046–1093), who was born an English princess and became the Scottish queen. In addition to helping her husband, King Malcolm of Scotland, become a better Christian and a true king, she brought a respect for music and the arts, and solid Catholic devotion, to her family, the Scottish court, and Scotland itself.

Austria and Germany

Austria and Germany, as well as Switzerland, share a liturgical calendar in the Church; their calendar contains a lengthy list of saints and blesseds from some of the earliest days of the Church.

This includes two great kings: Saints Henry II and Leopold III. Henry was duke of Bavaria and was crowned Holy Roman Emperor in 1014. He was a strong ruler who encouraged missionaries and built schools and churches, but he was also a man of prayer who had to be dissuaded from giving up his crown because he yearned to become a monk in his later years. Leopold (1073–1136) was margrave of Austria; he was also husband to Agnes, and together they had eighteen (yes, eighteen) children. That alone might be cause for canonization, but Leopold was also a just ruler who defended his country from invasion, founded numerous religious houses—many of which still exist today—and was a pious man.

Two of the earliest German saints have been honored for centuries but were not born there. Saint Severinus was a Roman noble from North Africa who left everything behind to become a hermit in the fifth century. He heard God's call to bring the Gospel to those outside the faith, which led him to evangelize Noricum (a city now in Austria). He cared for those who were seeking refuge in the area after an invasion by Attila the Hun, founded monasteries, and ransomed captives from slavery. But he never stopped living the penitential life of a hermit; he slept on the ground on sackcloth, ate only once a day, and traveled barefoot in every kind of weather. Saint Leonard of

Noblac (France) was a courtier of a pagan king in the sixth century, but he was a Christian. When the queen mockingly told Leonard to pray to his God for help from an invading army, he did—and France won the battle. This miracle helped convert the king, and thousands of Frenchmen followed suit. Leonard left the court to become a monk and then a hermit, and he lived a holy life. After his death, devotion to Leonard spread all over Europe, particularly in Bavaria, where it was said that thousands of favors were granted through his intercession.

As is the case in many European countries, many holy bishops have been recognized as saints, and Germany is no different. Saint Corbinian (670–730) was a hermit and missionary bishop to Bavaria who brought about many conversions as well as miracles. Saint Ulrich of Augsburg (890–973) suffered from bad health as a child but became an excellent scholar and then bishop. He was a strong leader who knew how to enforce the rules and deal gently with his flock, but his personal holiness was the strongest witness to his clergy. Saint Anno II (1010–1075) was a soldier before he became a priest and then archbishop of Cologne, Germany. He was a prayerful man who became highly influential in civil government (though he had some difficulties with the pope, who thought he was a bit too influential), and he founded monasteries and reformed religious life in his diocese.

Some of the greatest German saints are female saints. Saint Odilia (660–720) was born into a noble family but given to a peasant family at a young age because she was born blind. She miraculously regained her sight when she entered a convent as a young girl and eventually became the abbess. Saint Matilda of Saxony (895–968) became a queen when she married King Henry and was mother to many great future leaders. But she was best known during her lifetime for her generosity to the poor, the sick, and prisoners. Saint Hildegard of Bingen was born into a noble family, lived in the twelfth century, and was spiritually gifted from a young age. Though her education was limited, she was a brilliant woman who composed music, wrote theological works, and experienced mystical visions. Popes, kings, and bishops asked her for advice. Not surprisingly, she was named a Doctor of the Church.

However, Martin Luther was also a German, and the number of great German Catholic saints declined precipitously when the nation became Protestant five hundred years ago. But two German men prove that the Catholic faith is an anchor even during the most dangerous times. Blessed Bernard Lichtenberg (1875–1943) was a Catholic priest who lived in Berlin during Hitler's reign. Not only did he publicly criticize Nazi propaganda, but he also organized protests outside concentration camps and filed formal complaints against Nazism's racism. Blessed Nikolaus Gross (1898–1945) was a husband and father who worked as a miner and then a journalist at an underground newspaper that promoted nonviolent opposition to Nazism. Both men were eventually arrested. Blessed Bernard died on the way to a concentration camp; Blessed Nikolaus was executed in prison.

Asia

Many Asian cultures have resisted Christian evangelization, though the evangelization of these countries began only in the past few hundred years for most of them. The cultural traditions, religions, and philosophies of these countries are very ancient, and finding a way to introduce Christian teachings into these cultures has been a challenge even for great saints.

China was first evangelized in the fifth century, with many other attempts in succeeding centuries. Saint Augustine Zhao Rong was a Chinese diocesan priest when he and his companions were martyred for their Catholic faith in 1815. Sporadic persecutions over the centuries produced more martyrs; the Church commemorates many of them together on July 9 each year.

Saint Francis Xavier reached Japan in 1549 with the Good News. Subsequent missionaries, typically from the Jesuit order, like Saint Francis, continued to bring the Gospel to the Japanese people into the seventeenth century. The Japanese government reacted violently against the missionaries and against Europeans many times. In 1597, Saint Paul Miki, a Japanese man who had become a Catholic priest, and twenty-five other Catholics were executed for the crime of spreading the Gospel. Saint Lorenzo Ruiz (d. 1637), a Catholic husband and father who was from the Philippines, died a martyr in Japan while trying to evade a false murder charge, making him the first Filipino martyr.

Korean Catholics endured waves of persecution from the government in the years 1839, 1846, and 1867. More than a hundred martyrs, both missionaries and laypeople, are commemorated together. One of them is Saint Andrew Kim Taegon (d. 1846), who was the first Korean priest to die a martyr.

It is estimated that more than a hundred thousand Christians died for the faith in Vietnam in the seventeenth, eighteenth, and nineteenth centuries. More than a hundred of these Vietnamese martyrs are remembered together on November 24. One of those martyrs was Saint Andrew Dung Lac (1795–1839), who was born into a pagan family but grew up to become a Catholic catechist and then a priest. He was arrested more than once for being a Christian until his final arrest and execution.

Today's news shows that it is still dangerous to be a Christian in many parts of Asia.

Central and South America

When Spain and Portugal colonized regions of Central and South America starting in the late fifteenth century, it is clear that many did so to make a financial profit off the gold and silver resources in the New World. But many faithful Catholics had a much more supernatural goal in mind: to bring the Good News about Jesus Christ to the native peoples who had never heard it before.

The apparition of the Lady of Guadalupe to Saint Juan Diego and her miraculous image on his tilma was a powerful sign to the native peoples of God's love for them, through the Mother of God. The missionary Saint Jose de Anchieta (1534–1597) brought more than the Good News to the people when he left Spain; he is acclaimed the father of Brazilian national literature for his writings, including plays.

Saint Turibius of Mogrovejo (1538–1606) was a brilliant scholar in Spain when he was sent to serve as the bishop of Peru. He used his talents to learn the many languages of his people, traveled throughout his entire large diocese to visit his people, shared their poverty, and rebuked unjust leaders who failed to treat the native peoples with respect.

In the early twentieth century, Mexico was overcome by a bitterly anti-Catholic revolution. Priests like Saint Christopher Magallanes Jara (d. 1927) served the faithful secretly and in great personal danger—until they were captured and executed. Blessed Miguel Pro (1891–1927) was also a priest who was forced into hiding, but he found creative ways to disguise himself and escape capture. When the authorities finally found and arrested him, they brought reporters to attend his death by firing squad, clearly assuming that his final moments would show the weakness of Catholic priests. Instead, the photographer captured him with his arms spread wide, like the Crucified Christ, and proclaiming his final words, "Long live Christ the King!" Within days, his brave witness had inspired Catholics all over Mexico.

North America

In the seventeenth century, the Jesuit order sent missionaries from France to bring the Gospel to the native peoples of North America in the area now known as Canada and the United States. Both nations now share the honor of the courageous witness of these North American martyrs. Eight missionaries in particular, priests and lay brothers,[10] are commemorated on October 19 for their heroic love of the native peoples and for the grace by which God enabled them to remain faithful despite horrific torture and martyrdom.

Only about a decade after the deaths of these brave men and not far away, Saint Kateri Tekakwitha (1656–1680) was born. Orphaned at a young age and disfigured by smallpox, Kateri was raised in a Mohawk village. After she accepted Baptism from a Jesuit missionary, her family shunned her because of her faith and her decision to remain a virgin. She was able to leave her tribe and live among other native converts until her death at a young age, having impressed those around her with her faithfulness and purity.

Many years later, Saint André Bessette (1845–1937) was born into a poor but devout family in nearby Montreal, Canada. Because of his lack of education, he was only grudgingly allowed to enter

---

[10] Technically termed temporal coadjutors, the brothers of the Jesuit order support the priests by performing nonsacramental duties.

the Congregation of Holy Cross and was given the lowliest of tasks. But the many decades he spent at these simple chores gave him the opportunity to receive many visitors—and encourage each of them to pray for the intercession of his favorite saint, Saint Joseph. A million people came to pay their respects at André's funeral and thank God for the miraculous healings that had resulted from his prayers for them.

Other saints celebrated in the liturgical calendar of the United States come from every corner of the country. Saint Junipero Serra was an eighteenth-century Franciscan missionary to the California coast. Saint Elizabeth Ann Seton (1774–1821) founded a religious order of sisters on the East coast. Saint John Nepomucene Neumann was a nineteenth-century priest from the Czech Republic who spent his life serving immigrants (after all, he spoke twelve languages) before becoming bishop of Philadelphia and opening almost a hundred Catholic schools. Saint Damien de Veuster (1840–1889) also left his native Belgium to serve as a priest, but he and Saint Marianne Cope (1838–1918), along with her Sisters of Saint Francis, cared for lepers on the island of Molokai in Hawaii. Saint Rose Philippine Duchesne (1769–1852) survived the French Revolution in her native country and its destruction of religious life to become (again) a religious sister, this time as a missionary. She traveled up the Mississippi River and spent her life caring for and educating the native peoples in Missouri.

The Catholic faith has come only relatively recently to what used to be called "the New World", but that has not stopped our Lord from inspiring men and women with a passion for holiness and service of others.

Saints with more than one homeland

Catholic immigrants have taken their patron saints with them for centuries when they relocate to new countries. Polish and Irish immigrants, for example, did not name their churches after British or Italian saints when they came to America but after great saints of their home countries, such as Stanislaus and Patrick.

Saint Marcellin Champagnat (1789–1840), a French priest, founded the Marist Brothers, a religious order that focused on education of the young; so many Marist Brothers have educated Australian youth that his feast is recognized in their country's liturgical calendar. Saint Teresa of Jesus Journet Ibars (1843–1897) was a nun who founded an order to care for the abandoned elderly in Spain, but the holy example of her nuns who served the needy in Colombia cause Colombians to celebrate her memorial every year.

Some saints are such phenomenal examples of holiness that entire continents claim them in their liturgical calendars. Saint Charles Lwanga and the other martyrs of Uganda in the late nineteenth century are honored for their brave example all over Africa. Saint Peter Claver (1580–1654) ministered to slaves primarily in Colombia, but neighboring South American countries honor him on their calendars as well. The miracle of Our Lady of Guadalupe in 1531, showing Mary's love for all God's people, particularly the poor, is celebrated in North, South, and Central America.

Catholics obviously have a great love for their native sons and daughters who have become saints. Australia and New Zealand honor Saint Mary of the Cross MacKillop (1842–1909), a brave nun who co-founded a religious order to educate children and endured persecution from within the Church herself. Belgian Catholics honor Saint Mucian Marie Wiaux (1841–1917), a simple religious brother who inspired decades of students through his gentle teaching and personal holiness. Saint George Preca was a twentieth-century priest and preacher living in Malta who taught theology to working class people and co-founded a society to catechize the laity. Though that was considered outrageous and dangerous at the time, he was canonized in 2007. The Catholics of Peru (justifiably) love Saints Rose of Lima, a young woman who served her family humbly yet received mystical gifts, and Martin de Porres, a devout Dominican brother who begged and cared for the poor, so much that they are celebrated as solemnities on Peru's calendar.

Our Lord's feast days around the world

As already noted, many days of the General Roman Calendar honor our Savior. The solemnity in honor of Corpus Christi came about through the initial efforts of Saint Juliana of Liege (1192–1258). She was a Norbertine canoness regular and mystic who strongly urged the Church to add a celebration in honor of God's gift to us of the Blessed Sacrament. The Church added Corpus Christi to the universal Church's calendar in 1264.

Since the liturgical days honoring our Lord are generally based on Scripture and therefore have been practiced for many centuries, it is not surprising that few devotions to our Lord have recently become part of the universal calendar of the Church. However, a feast day celebrating Jesus Christ as Priest, celebrated on the first Thursday after Pentecost, was approved in the late twentieth century and has spread to the calendars of Australia, the Czech Republic, England, Poland, Spain, and Wales. Less well known is the fact that a wooden image of Jesus Christ on the Cross, which apparently has turned black from soot over the past few centuries, is celebrated with a feast in Guatemala and is called the Black Christ of Esquipulas.

Our Blessed Mother's feast days around the world

Devotions to our Blessed Mother in local churches are also celebrated throughout the world. While the Marian apparitions at Guadalupe, Lourdes, and Fatima are rightly famous and approved by the Church, many long-standing regional devotions to Mary are not the result of apparitions. We tend to think only of the holy lives of Saints Juan Diego, Bernadette, and Jacinto and Francisco Marto (the seers of those respective visions), but we forget that not everyone who receives a vision also receives and accepts the call to live a saintly life. Also, not every vision is approved by the Church, with such visionaries often falling somewhere on a spectrum of "a bit confused" to "more attached to their vision than to Christ and His Church" to "only interested in the money and popularity associated with being a visionary". Perhaps a less dramatic but less subjective devotion to Mary can be seen in Marian images.

It is a fact that any person is more likely to be moved by a photograph of a beloved family member than a photograph of a complete stranger. It is also a fact that beautiful images will more generally evoke an emotional response than ugly ones. Art critics notwithstanding, a portrait by Leonardo da Vinci would win the attention and long-standing affection of more people than would an abstract portrait by a more modern artist.

It is not surprising that a well-executed image of a loving mother and child would stir up our own natural affections and memories of childhood. If that image depicts something *super*natural and true as well, such as a lovely Virgin with her Son, the God-Man, then such an image will supernaturally educate, encourage, heal, and strengthen the viewer. After all, God the Father made us to be both body and spirit, and He knows how to reach our souls through the physical world in which He has placed us. Catholics all over the world have been encouraged in devotion by inspiring images of the Blessed Mother. For the sake of brevity, the following table lists only one such image per region of the world.

Title	Description of the Image	Original Region and Date	Origin of the Image	Current Location	Feast Date
Our Lady of Good Counsel	Painted fresco image of Mary and Jesus	Europe; discovered in 1467	Some say the image was miraculously transported from another church; some say it was part of a larger fresco and was revealed during church restorations.	Genezzano, Italy	April 26
Our Lady of Czestochowa	Painted wooden icon with jewels depicting Mary and Jesus	Eastern Europe; fourteenth century	Legend says it was painted by Saint Luke the Evangelist on a table from the home of the Holy	Czestochowa, Poland	August 26

(*continued*)

Title	Description of the Image	Original Region and Date	Origin of the Image	Current Location	Feast Date
			Family; art historians say it was painted in the sixth to ninth centuries and brought to the monastery in the fourteenth century.		
Our Lady of Guadalupe	Image of Mary on cactus fiber cloak	Americas; 1531	The image was imprinted in an unknown way and has inexplicably survived almost four hundred years and a bomb blast.	Mexico City, Mexico	December 12
Our Lady of Lebanon (besides many sites in the Holy Land)	Bronze statue of Mary, painted white	Middle East; 1907	Since the statue was installed, it has become a pilgrimage site for not only Catholics but also Muslims in the area.	Harissa, Lebanon	First Sunday of May
Our Lady of Africa	Dark bronze statue of Mary	Africa; 1872	The statue was housed in a Trappist	Mbuya, Uganda	April 30

Title	Description of the Image	Original Region and Date	Origin of the Image	Current Location	Feast Date
			monastery before being placed in a magnificent basilica, where it is venerated by both Catholics and Muslims.		
Our Lady of Perpetual Help	Byzantine-style icon of Mary and Jesus	Asia; 1906	The image, originally from Germany, follows the tradition of a fifteenth-century icon currently in Rome.	Manilla, Philippines	June 27

All these images—and many Marian statues, paintings, and icons like them all over the world—are more than just lovely pictures. They help us draw close to "our tainted nature's solitary boast", as William Wordsworth (a Protestant) described it. Mary is a human being, like each of us, but she never said no to God's will, unlike each of us. As such, she is what all Christians should want to be: selfless, compassionate, always ready to listen, and encouraging to sinners and saints alike.

Each Marian image that has become an object of devotion over time can teach us something about God. The image of Our Lady of Good Counsel shows us a tender, beautiful woman holding her wise Child.[11] Because of His wisdom, she can counsel us in the right direction. Our Lady of Czestochowa and her Son are shown royally dressed, but their serious faces—and the slashes across her face, made

[11] Photos of all the Marian images described here can be found online.

by Hussites who tried unsuccessfully to steal the icon—show us that they know all about suffering and pain.[12] The innumerable symbolic messages in the image of Our Lady of Guadalupe showed the native peoples who first saw it that the Blessed Virgin was greater than any of their gods of the sun, moon, or stars.[13] The statues of Our Lady of Lebanon[14] and Our Lady of Africa[15] have done the seemingly impossible: they have brought Catholics and Muslims together to pray for help and healing. In the icon of Our Lady of Perpetual Help,[16] Mary seems to comfort her Child as angels show Him (and us) the instruments of the Crucifixion.

But all these images have one more thing in common: miracles. Jesus performed miracles, and He promised that those who believe in Him would perform even greater ones. When people come to His Mother, asking her to intercede with Jesus for conversion for a wayward child, health for a sick spouse, food for a hungry family, or the ability to forgive personal injury, she listens. After all, it is not the pigment or the bronze material that we venerate and speak to; we pray for help from a human woman who has successfully fought the war against sin and is now in Heaven, hoping that we will join her.

But it's not all good news

The Church's liturgical calendar of saints is one of the greatest proofs of the catholicity of our faith: there are saints on the calendar from practically every corner of the globe. Unfortunately, the liturgical calendar also indicates regions where the faith is generally weakened or particularly threatened.

---

[12] See image on Wikipedia's website at https://en.wikipedia.org/wiki/Black_Madonna_of_Cz%C4%99stochowa#/media/File:Czestochowska.jpg.

[13] See image on *Wikipedia*'s website at https://en.wikipedia.org/wiki/Our_Lady_of_Guadalupe#/media/File:Virgen_de_guadalupe1.jpg.

[14] See image on *Wikipedia*'s website at https://en.wikipedia.org/wiki/Our_Lady_of_Lebanon#/media/File:Ladylebanon.JPG.

[15] See image on WordPress.com at https://ivarfjeld.files.wordpress.com/2011/11/pray-muslims.jpg?w=900.

[16] See image on *Wikipedia*'s website at https://en.wikipedia.org/wiki/Our_Lady_of_Perpetual_Help#/media/File:Desprestaur.jpg.

The Nordic countries—Norway, Denmark, and Sweden—were evangelized in the Middle Ages and converted from paganism to Christianity through missionary saints like Blessed Theodgar (an eleventh-century German priest) and great kings like Saint Olaf II (995–1030). Though there are other recognized saints from this region, these nations fell away from Catholicism during the Protestant Revolt. Today Norway is the most Catholic of these countries, with Catholics comprising only 5 percent of the population.

Some countries have added dates to their liturgical calendars that are not festive dates. South Korea commemorates large groups of Christian martyrs in their calendar, as well as a Day of Prayer for Reconciliation and Unity of the Korean People, who have been separated into two nations for decades. Japanese Catholics similarly honor a group of 188 martyrs on July 1, including Blessed Peter Kibe (1587–1639), who traveled thousands of miles from Japan to Europe on foot to become a Jesuit priest and then went straight back to his homeland, where he quickly—but bravely—became a martyr. Another feast day on September 10 honors more than 200 Japanese martyrs, all of whom died for the faith in the seventeenth century.

Sometimes the liturgical calendar is downright puzzling—due to what's *not* there. The Greeks were one of the first peoples to be evangelized. Saint Paul himself preached in the Areopagus, though he apparently made only one convert, the man now known as Saint Dionysius the Areopagite.[17] There have been many holy Greek Christians since then, but, because of the schism between the Catholic Church and the Orthodox churches in 1054, Catholic presence has diminished in that country. Similarly, Catholics living in Russia and Slavic nations often entered the Orthodox churches, for various reasons and not always willingly, after that schism. On the other hand, only God knows how many millions of Catholic and Orthodox faithful died or suffered lifelong persecution under Communist rule for remaining faithful to Christ.

By the second century after the death of Christ, the people living in the region now known as France had begun to embrace Christianity. From the earliest days of the Church, France produced great saints: Saint Hilary, the fourth-century bishop of Poitiers; Saint Genevieve,

[17]Acts 17:34.

a holy nun who saved the city of Paris in the fifth century; and Saint Remigius, a bishop who converted the king in the late fifth century. The Middle Ages saw a plethora of holy French bishops and laymen who were recognized as saints by their countrymen. However, the French Revolution, Napoleon Bonaparte, Modernism, and world wars have all battered the Church in France.

But bad news was meant to be restored by the Good News. During the Boxer Rebellion in China, which occurred during the years 1899–1901, the small village of Donglu was attacked by a large army. This town was largely inhabited by Catholics. According to the Chinese Catholics who were present, the Blessed Mother miraculously appeared to them, dressed in white. A horseman, commonly thought to be Saint Michael the Archangel, then chased away the attacking army. In thanksgiving for her protection, the local priest had an image painted, with Mother and Child dressed in the golden robes of Chinese emperors. Since 1949 when the Communist government gained control of China, the Christians of China have been bitterly persecuted, with that persecution intensifying dramatically in the past several years. May Our Lady of China come again, and soon, to protect the faithful Christians living in the modern-day catacombs of China—and elsewhere—today.

Shepherd Saints

The holy men who have served God as priests, deacons, and bishops throughout the centuries are the greatest antidote to the poisonous attitude that our modern culture has toward the ministers of the Church. That is, where our culture sees only bad priests, male dominance, and unrealistic attitudes about sexuality in Catholic teaching, the saints show us a completely different picture of Catholic teaching and how to live it out. The beautiful example of those men who have received and lived out the Sacrament of Holy Orders in a holy way is not just an encouragement to priests; it is a lesson for us all.

What is a priest?

The *Catholic Bible Dictionary* says that "a priest is an authorized mediator who offers sacrifice to God on behalf of others."[1] Ancient civilizations in India, Greece, Rome, Ireland, Germany, China, Japan, Egypt, and the Middle East would not quibble much over that definition. They, too, had male and female priests who performed sacred rituals for the sake of members of their religions. Their priests may have offered sacrifice in the forest or in temples, may have been appointed to or inherited their positions, may have worshiped one God or many gods, and may have had complex or simple rites, but all performed rites and sacrifices for the sake of their people.

But God placed specific limits on the role of the priest when He revealed Himself to His Chosen People. From the patriarch Abraham through the prophet Moses, God commanded His people to serve Him only[2] and gave detailed instructions about how to offer

---

[1] Scott Hahn, ed., *Catholic Bible Dictionary* (New York: Doubleday, 2009), p. 725.
[2] Ex 20:3.

sacrifices to Him.[3] Jewish priests were initially the fathers of families, such as Abraham, Isaac, and Jacob,[4] but later the tribe of Levi became the family of priests that served the entire nation.[5] The Pharisees who appear in the Gospels were not priests; it was still primarily the members of the tribe of Levi who offered the lambs in the Temple in Jerusalem during Jesus' last Passover.

Fifteen hundred years later, Protestant Christians denied that priests were needed anymore. After all, Hebrews 7:27 says, "[Jesus] has no need, like those high priests, to offer sacrifices daily, first for his own sins and then for those of the people; he did this once for all when he offered up himself." According to them, there is no need for us to offer sacrifices to God because Jesus Christ offered His sacrifice for all of humanity. But they forget something very important. More precisely, they forget twelve very important men.

Jesus did not choose twelve Levitical priests, seven women, or a thousand people of all ages and races to be His disciples. He chose twelve men, and He did much more than give them an explicit command to preach the Gospel to all nations before He ascended into Heaven:[6] He trained them to be priests.

When Jesus asked those men to be His disciples, He did not establish branch offices so He could come back to their towns and visit them. He asked His followers to leave their families, friends, jobs, and all their possessions behind, in an act of personal abandonment, and place their trust completely in Him.[7] Jesus prayed over and healed many people, and He expected His disciples to do the same.[8] He instituted sacraments and taught them to do it.[9] He acted as a compassionate, caring shepherd for those who followed Him, and He carefully led them to think the same way about serving His people.[10]

---

[3] See particularly the book of Leviticus.

[4] Gen 22:13; 26:25; 31:54.

[5] Ex 32:26.

[6] Mt 28:19–20.

[7] Mt 4:19–20; Mk 1:17–18; Lk 5:10–11.

[8] Mk 9:28–29.

[9] Key New Testament scriptural references for the sacraments are the following: Baptism: Mt 28:19; Jn 4:1–2; Eucharist: Mt 26:26–29; Mk 14:22–25; Lk 22:17–19; Confirmation: Acts 8:14–22; Reconciliation: Jn 20:21–23; Anointing of the Sick: Mk 6:7, 12–13; Matrimony: Mt 19:6; Holy Orders: Acts 6:3–6.

[10] Mk 6:34–38.

He revealed God's truth to His listeners, and He trained His disciples to go out and preach as well.[11]

The men who receive the Sacrament of Holy Orders today do the same thing. They make a radical gift of themselves to serve Christ and His people, and they live out that gift by offering the sacraments, teaching sound doctrine, and shepherding the people they are assigned to serve. But being a holy priest is not as easy as it might seem.

Two pillars of the priesthood

Catholics tend to gravitate toward Saint Peter as a model leader. After all, Peter is mentioned first in every list of the Twelve Apostles in the Gospels,[12] gave the first homily in the history of the Church,[13] and was told by Christ that He would build His Church on Peter, after renaming him "Rock".[14] Protestants tend to focus on Saint Paul as a model leader. After all, Paul's letters in the New Testament far outnumber the number of letters in Sacred Scripture written by anyone else, and who could deny the timeless brilliance in Paul's explanations of complicated theological issues that great minds have spent millennia trying to understand?[15] But the two men, individually and together, are perfect models for Catholics and for priests.

One of the most striking and overlooked characteristics of the entire Bible is the willingness of the authors of each book to confront the reality of human weakness. Far from being shown as perfect men at the beginning of their ministries, both Peter and Paul clearly had problems. Peter had to be shown that a carpenter was a better fisherman than he was,[16] and Paul had to be struck physically blind to recognize that he had been blind to the truth about the Resurrected Christ.[17] Both were hotheaded.[18] Both needed to be taught.[19]

[11] Lk 9:1–2.
[12] Mt 10:2; Mk 3:16–18; Lk 6:14–16.
[13] Acts 2:14–36.
[14] Mt 16:18.
[15] The eighth chapter of his Letter to the Romans is one example.
[16] Lk 5:5–6.
[17] Acts 9:1–9.
[18] Jn 18:10; Acts 23:3.
[19] Mt 16:23; Acts 9:17–19.

Both made mistakes.[20] But both recognized that they needed a savior to be free from their sinfulness, and they recognized Jesus Christ as that Savior.

Both were, by the grace of God, highly effective as evangelists. Peter brought more than three thousand people into the Church (though perhaps not single-handedly) in one day.[21] Paul traveled all over the Roman Empire to bring the Gospel to those who had never heard it, enduring and surviving beatings and imprisonment.[22] Both men completely gave themselves over to the service of Christ and His Church to the point of martyrdom.

The lives of Saints Peter and Paul thus sum up what it means to be a priest. That is, Christ calls imperfect men to this very important task, but He is ready to provide the healing and grace that they need. He gives them great opportunities to lead people to Himself, but those opportunities often require turning to others for help and even more often involve great personal sacrifice.

A priest may therefore find himself stuck in seemingly hopeless situations, limited by his own weaknesses, and overwhelmed by opposition. In such cases, he is merely following in the footsteps of Saints Peter and Paul and needs only to humble himself, as they did.

Parish priests

Saint John Vianney (1786–1859) is the patron saint of priests. Most Catholics are aware that John served as the parish priest of a small village in France for his whole life. The dramatic aspects of his life are also commonly known: he spent many hours every day hearing confessions, could read the consciences of at least some of his penitents (knowing what they had done wrong whether they told him or not), allowed himself only a few hours of sleep each night, and fought battles (somehow) with the devil.

John Vianney lived only a few centuries ago, and few people would dispute the details of his life, as might happen when discussing

---

[20] Jn 18:25–27; Acts 9:1–2.
[21] Acts 2:41.
[22] Acts 11:23–28.

the miraculous events attributed to some earlier saints. For that reason, one of the most surprising things about Saint John is that the laity would hold him up as the kind of priest they would like to see in their own parish.

After all, there is a lot more to the story of John's life. Not only was John a poor student in general, but he was lousy at Latin, which was a significant problem since Mass was celebrated in Latin. He was perhaps the worst student in his class—so bad that his superiors sent him to the tiny town of Ars, clearly thinking that he couldn't do too much damage or cause too many complaints to the bishop since there were only about two hundred people living there.

As soon as he arrived, John did several astonishing things. First, he willingly undertook a severely penitential way of life. He fasted frequently; one report states that he ate only one potato a day by the end of his life. Nothing else. He prayed fervently and for hours, which was, after all, the reason the devil showed up and pestered him so often, physically beating John on occasion. But his stated reason for these seemingly extreme and unusual penances was simple: he wanted his people to be holy. He offered up all his sacrifices explicitly for them.

Another astonishing thing that John did would never be considered "pastoral" in today's world. He confronted his congregation with certain cultural practices that he did not believe were in keeping with the Christian life. He told them to stop holding dances. Why? He was particularly worried about the sort of behavior that often occurred when men and women got together for a good time late at night. He also told them to stop working on Sundays. Since his parishioners were largely farmers, the temptation to do unnecessary labor on Sunday was a serious one. He also told them to stop wearing immodest clothing, a correction that was almost certainly aimed at women. When we try to imagine how bad their dances, clothing styles, and excessive work could possibly have been— compared to our own culture—we have to wonder what Saint John would say to us today.

But John Vianney was not the first holy priest to bravely confront women who were wearing provocative clothing. For example, Saint John of San Facundo, also called John Sahagún (1419–1479), was a Spanish priest and Augustinian Canon Regular living in Salamanca when he preached against the extravagance of the clothing styles he saw. How did the people react? Women literally threw stones at him.

John Vianney was not the first or last priest to spend hours in the confessional. A modern holy priest, commonly known as Padre Pio, became famous for the same reason. Catholics flocked to Pietrelcina, Italy, to confess their sins to the gruff but beloved Saint Pio (1887–1968). Saint John Nepomucene (1330–1383), on the other hand, literally laid down his life for the sacrament. John was a preacher and counselor to the king of Bohemia (today's Czech Republic), and when the king suspected his innocent queen of adultery, he demanded that John reveal the queen's confession to him. John refused and was executed, becoming a martyr. A less dramatic but life-changing event happened to Saint Vincent de Paul (1581–1660) through this sacrament. He was a young Frenchman only hoping for a comfortable life as a priest when he was called upon to hear a peasant's confession. The uneducated man later said that his soul would have been lost if Father Vincent hadn't helped him understand his sinful state; the event showed Father Vincent his lifelong vocation to serve the poor through all the sacraments, as well as through material help.

During the nineteenth century—the century in which Saint John Vianney lived—there was an explosion of holy priests who established groups to serve the needy. Saint Vincent Pallotti (1795–1850) was a parish priest of Rome who was a wonder-worker with condemned prisoners and people who were close to death. He also founded the Society of the Catholic Apostolate, which brought together priests, brothers, and the laity to serve the needy and draw people to the Church and Jesus Christ. How many poor, young boys in nineteenth-century Italy—which was struggling with political upheaval and unemployment—avoided falling into lives of crime and violence because of the homes for boys founded by Saint John Bosco (1815–1888)? Like Saint Vincent Pallotti, Saint John Bosco was known for his spiritual depth and the purity and devotion he displayed even when a young boy.

Priests are obviously concerned about the spiritual growth of their flocks. Blessed Columba Marmion (1858–1923) was probably best remembered by his fellow Benedictines in Belgium as an excellent spiritual director and professor, but he also wrote books that are still considered spiritual classics. Sodalities such as the one founded by Blessed William Chaminade (1761–1850) of France formed clergy and laity into communities of faith to support one another. Saint Philip Neri (1515–1595) of Rome was such a cheerful, outgoing young man that he could start conversations with strangers on street corners and convince them to join him at praying in churches and serving the sick. But he was also so joyful and deeply contemplative that he had the opposite problem of most of us: he had to distract himself from thinking too deeply about God during Mass or he would fall into a long ecstasy. Saint Anthony Zaccaria (1502–1539) of Milan became a doctor before recognizing God's call to religious life. He established religious congregations for men and women, but he became best known for promoting a greater love for Communion among the laity through the celebration of Forty Hours' Devotion.[23]

Even non-Christians celebrate Saint Valentine's feast day, but how many remember that he was a martyr precisely because he was a Catholic priest? According to tradition, he disobeyed an imperial order that prohibited soldiers from marrying and married young couples anyway. Saint John de Britto (1647–1693) was a Portuguese priest sent to India to bring the faith to the people there; he was executed for that reason. Saint Claude de la Colombiere (1641–1682) was a French priest serving in anti-Catholic England; he was so successful at bringing people back to the Catholic faith that he was put in prison. Imprisonment ruined his health, and he died soon after being released. Like many other English men during the centuries of Catholic persecution, Saint Robert Southwell (1561–1595) left England to study for the priesthood in Europe; he returned secretly to serve the Catholics living there but was ultimately found, tortured, and executed for being a priest.

Although Saint John Vianney did not die a martyr, one can imagine that it might have looked possible when he confronted his parishioners about their seemingly benign customs. If your pastor gave a homily about the eternal consequences of not honoring Sunday as a day of rest, as well as the consequences of sexual immorality and immodesty, how would your congregation respond? Would they give him a standing ovation or write letters to the bishop? John was too humble to want the former and too holy to care about the latter. He wanted his people to get to Heaven, first and foremost.

[23] The devotion typically consists of forty consecutive hours of Exposition of the Blessed Sacrament.

Saint John did not just give his people "thou shalt not" dictums. He told them what was poisoning their relationship with God and one another, explaining why and then inviting them to participate in something much more beautiful and exciting than social events and increased revenue. He invited them to follow him into the spiritual beauty of the Mass, the peace of praying Vespers as a community, the comfort of shared devotions to saints, and the mercy of God shown through the regular practice of the Sacrament of Reconciliation.

Did the residents of Ars complain about long confession lines populated by a bunch of out-of-towners? Scowl when a special stop was added to the train line to help even more visitors reach their tiny town? Or did they take comfort in the jewel of a pastor that they knew cared for them personally and only wanted them to get to Heaven?

Today, many Catholics complain about their priests. Specifically, they tend to complain that their priest doesn't support *their* favorite parish group, give the kinds of homilies *they* want to hear, or spend money however *they* think it should be spent (or not spent). Before we complain that our priests today aren't nearly as holy as the great Saint John Vianney or any of these other holy men, we must remember that there are two sides to every relationship, even the one between a priest and his flock. Saint John Vianney's congregation obeyed. That is, they followed his advice, began practicing their faith more fervently, and sought holiness. Perhaps God gave them the holy pastor they deserved.

The greatest preachers and missionaries

Although God calls all Christians to share the Gospel with other people, priests are uniquely called to this vocation. Over the centuries, many priests have become famous for their God-given ability to share the Good News. Through their efforts, innumerable lukewarm Catholics have been set on fire for the faith and those who have never heard of Jesus Christ have embraced Him and His Church.

This amazing phenomenon has happened since the earliest days. Saint Peter, with the help of other apostles present at Pentecost, managed to bring three thousand souls into the newly founded Church during his first homily.[24] According to the most ancient traditions, the

[24] Acts 2:14–41.

other eleven apostles[25] were so effective at preaching the Gospel that various governments tried to kill them to make them stop. (Tradition also says the opponents of Christianity were successful in making martyrs of all the Twelve Apostles except for Saint John.) Although some of Saint Paul's contemporaries complained that his speaking style was less than impressive,[26] he clearly brought many people to the faith in person, as well as through his letters. But the Twelve Apostles *knew* Jesus Christ, and Saint Paul received a vision of Him. How have subsequent preachers managed to bring about conversions without those advantages?

It is helpful first to distinguish the characteristics that do *not* necessarily make a man a great evangelizer for Christ. For example, simply having the natural ability to speak in front of a crowd is not sufficient. The great Franciscan preacher Saint Anthony of Padua (d. 1231) was noted for having a voice that carried well in a crowd, as well as a charismatic personality, but his exceptional knowledge of Scripture was what allowed him to cut the positions of his opponents to shreds.

Great preachers also do not preach only for the theologians, way over the heads of most of their listeners. Saint Peter Chrysologus (c. 406–c. 450) was considered an excellent homilist, so much so that his collected sermons allowed him to be named a Doctor of the Church. However, Peter made a point of keeping his talks brief and to the point. After all, he wanted the faithful to understand and live out what they had heard, not merely be impressed by his words. Saint John Chrysostom (c. 347–407) had been a hermit, deacon, and priest before he became the patriarch of Constantinople. As patriarch, John wrote commentaries on the Bible and many letters, but it was his insightful and practical homilies that won over his listeners. Pope Saint Leo the Great (c. 400–461) somehow found the time to deal with Attila the Hun, the Eutychian heresy, and the social upheaval caused by Gothic invasions to preach at churches all over the city of Rome, leaving behind ninety-six excellent sermons for us to read.

Some great preachers are best remembered for the way they addressed a specific spiritual topic. Saint Bernardine of Siena (1380–1444) was a

---

[25] That is, the other eleven disciples, with the addition of Saint Matthias and without the traitor, Judas Iscariot.

[26] 2 Cor 10:10.

Franciscan friar whose homilies often focused on one subject: the Holy Name of Jesus. Bernardine encouraged his listeners to call on the name of Jesus frequently and ask for His help at all times. Saint Paul of the Cross (1694–1775) preached and founded an order of priests dedicated to a different but just as important topic: the Passion of Jesus Christ. Saint John Eudes (1601–1680) and Saint Louis de Montfort (1673–1716) were both French priests who sought to free their Catholic listeners from the depressing heresy of Jansenism, which was common in France at the time. Saint John encouraged Catholics to foster a devotion to what we would call the Sacred Heart of Jesus and the Immaculate Heart of Mary and Saint Louis encouraged Catholics to consecrate ourselves as slaves of the Blessed Virgin.

Sometimes great preachers became widely known because of their effectiveness in answering objections to the Catholic faith. Saint Dominic de Guzman (1170–1221) preached (and sent his spiritual sons—the Dominicans—to preach) against Catharism, a dualistic religion that pretended to be Christian and was widespread in Europe, particularly in France, at the time. Saint Peter Canisius (1521–1597) not only defended the Catholic faith in writing but also preached and participated in debates to respond to claims of the Protestant reformers while living at the epicenter of the debate, Germany itself.

No one would have guessed that Saint John of Capistrano (1386–1456) would become a Franciscan priest, much less an internationally known preacher, when he was a young man. His achievements early in life—as an Italian knight, a lawyer, a governor, and a married man—seemed to destine him for a prominent secular career. But after being captured as a prisoner of war, his priorities changed. He entered the Franciscans—apparently his marriage was annulled—and counted two other canonized Franciscan saints as friends: Saints James of the Marches and Bernardine of Siena. John spent many years traveling throughout Austria, Germany, Hungary, Italy, Poland, and Russia inspiring and preaching to Christians. When the Ottoman Turks (Muslims led by Sultan Mehmed II) conquered the city of Constantinople in 1453, it was clear that their next goal was the invasion of Europe through Hungary. Saint John was commissioned by Pope Callistus II as the spiritual leader of an army of seventy thousand European men to fight off the invasion, though he was seventy years old at the time. John's rousing preaching, prayers, and brave example at the

Battle of Belgrade were later given as the reason for the success of the Christian army, though John himself died shortly after the battle.

When the Dominican priest Saint Vincent Ferrer (c. 1350–1419) preached, miracles occurred. Born in Spain to a noble father, he traveled to England, France, Ireland, Italy, Scotland, and Switzerland to preach the Good News; modern biographers doubt the claim that Vincent had a supernatural gift of tongues that allowed him to be understood by his listeners in so many different lands, but they can't explain how he could've been so effective in so many languages without some help from above. However, Vincent is generally known today for another reason. During his lifetime, there was a period when three different men claimed to be the true pope. Initially, Vincent was convinced that the man we now consider the true pope, Urban VI, was not the valid pope, and he supported his friend Pedro Cardinal de Luna when de Luna took the step of proclaiming himself Pope Benedict XIII. However, as the presence of three claimants to the papacy caused tension and violence within Christendom, Vincent repeatedly tried to convince his friend to step down for the good of the Church. When Pedro de Luna refused, Vincent had to take the deeply painful step of abandoning a friend and encouraging civil leaders to do the same. Only when a widely acclaimed and respected preacher took a public stand over such a controversial issue was it possible for peoples from many nations to unite and to bring an end to a terribly divisive period in Church history.

When the founder of the Jesuit order, Saint Ignatius of Loyola, sent his priests out to bring the Gospel to all nations in the sixteenth century, one of those priests was Saint Francis Xavier (1506–1552). Francis had been born in Spain but met Ignatius while studying at the University of Paris, becoming one of the first members of the new Jesuit order. Francis left for Goa (modern India) in 1540, later traveled to Japan, and died on his way to China in 1552. During those short twelve years, he became one of the greatest evangelizers the Church has ever known. He brought people into the Church by teaching them the truths of the faith, even putting the teachings in songs so that people could learn them more easily, adapting his manner and style of dress to appeal better to each culture, and sharing the poverty of those he came to serve. And he preached. It is said that forty thousand people became Catholic through Francis' evangelization.

For some of these great preachers, we have written records of their sermons and writings. However, the hallmark of a great preacher is generally not his words on the printed page but the power of his words spoken to his audience—that is, the profound effect that these words had on real human hearts. Since all the above saints died long before any modern technology could record them in action, we can't imagine what it would have been like to listen to them preach. Or can we?

Venerable Fulton Sheen (1895–1979) was born on a farm in Illinois. A brilliant student with a talent for public speaking, he could have been successful in just about any career he chose. He chose to become a priest. He also chose to be a particular kind of priest: the kind who explains to his Catholic flock how to live out their faith every day, but in a memorable and intellectually convincing manner.

What did he preach about? When many Western intellectuals found Communism fascinating, Fulton was not afraid to point out its errors and dangers. After being complimented for a particularly brilliant explanation of a complicated theological concept and realizing that his adoring listeners did not really understand what he'd said, he vowed never to do such a thing again. Instead, he dedicated himself to making the faith explicable to ordinary Catholics—and even non-Catholics—which he did weekly on a national television show for more than a decade, also writing more than seventy books. In time, he became a theology professor, bishop, archbishop, media personality, and director for the Society for the Propagation of the Faith, raising millions of dollars for missions all over the world.

We cannot watch videos of Saint Peter or Saint John Chrysostom preaching a sermon. But we can watch Fulton Sheen and make some guesses about what makes for a great Christian preacher. Fulton used humor—sometimes self-deprecating humor—to draw his audience to his message. He did not deliver off-the-cuff, half-researched, sloppy sermons that he awkwardly read from notes. He put time and effort into making his talks effective, memorizing them and delivering them with warmth, friendliness, and professionalism. He was no "ivory tower" thinker who lived far from the everyday lives of laypeople; he had many friends, he spent time with them, and he used the news of the day to introduce timeless truths. He even personally brought many high-profile figures into the Church. But he also famously spent an hour a day, every single day of his long priestly life, with the One who gave him his vocation in the first place. In his autobiography, *Treasure in Clay*, he devoted an entire chapter explaining his dedication to making a daily Holy Hour—and why every Catholic should try to do the same. This passionate love for our Lord, combined with natural and supernatural gifts that were daily placed at God's service, is the key to understanding the great Catholic preachers throughout history. And as good sheep, we should follow their example.

Deacons

In the second through fifth chapters of the Acts of the Apostles, we see the apostles boldly proclaiming the truth about Jesus Christ,[27] attracting many new believers,[28] performing miraculous healings,[29] and facing down the very leaders who maneuvered to make the Romans execute Jesus in the first place.[30] This exciting narrative of miracles in word and deed in the early Church is brought to a full stop by that all-too-human experience of parish and community life: complaining.

The sixth chapter of Acts shows us that the early Church living in Jerusalem was generally composed of two groups of people: Jews and "Hellenists". In the Jewish capital of the world, almost everyone who lived there was a Jewish believer, but some of those Jews had been born in lands where Greek was spoken, rather than Hebrew and Aramaic. Greek-speaking Jews had established their own synagogues in Jewish cities so that they could worship and communicate in the language that they spoke and understood. The early Church embraced all those who accepted Christ as their Savior, whatever language they spoke, so both groups became members of the early Church when they were baptized into the new Catholic faith. But as always happens when there is a majority and a minority in a population, extra effort must be made to ensure that members of the minority are not

27 Acts 2:14–36.
28 Acts 2:41.
29 Acts 3:6–7.
30 Acts 4:19–20; 5:29.

overlooked. That was not happening. Greek-speaking Jews who had
become followers of Christ had a good reason to complain; the entire
Christian community was donating to serve the poor among them,
including a daily distribution of food or goods to support poor widows, but that support was reaching only Jewish widows, not non-
Jewish ones.

The Twelve Apostles called a meeting of the Christian disciples.
They asked the Greek-speaking community to name "seven men of
good repute"[31] who were also Spirit-filled and wise. Those men
would be their "boots on the ground", ensuring that the community members were being served equitably, while the apostles could
devote their time to prayer and preaching. Importantly, we are told
that the apostles "laid their hands"[32] on the selected men—a sign of
what Catholics now call ordination.

Those first seven men[33] were named: Stephen, Philip, Prochorus,
Nicanor, Timon, Parmenas, and Nicolaus. The Church claims to
know very little about the latter five men, except that they must have
been good men to have been so chosen and that they spent their lives
serving as deacons. The Church honors them as saints together on
July 28 in her liturgical calendar.

Most Catholics know that Saint Stephen was the first Christian
to be martyred; after all, the Church has ordered his feast day to
be celebrated on the day after Christmas. The sixth and seventh
chapters of Acts paint an inspiring portrait of Stephen. From the
long speech he gives during his trial before the high priest in this
passage, he articulately explains the history of the Jewish faith and
Jewish people, clearly trying to lead his listeners to see the continu-
ity between Jewish faith and faith in Jesus Christ. But for whatever
reason—there are many possibilities—he interrupts his speech by
confronting his listeners that they are resisting the Holy Spirit Himself when they reject Jesus Christ. As they respond angrily, Stephen
is apparently given a vision of Christ in Heaven because he begins
to describe it. That is too much for the crowd, and they drag him

[31] Acts 6:3.
[32] Acts 6:6.
[33] There is debate about whether these seven men were specifically named as deacons at this
time or whether the diaconate arose more gradually. This book assumes the more traditional
interpretation: that they were the first deacons.

out of the city to stone him. He forgives them as he is dying, just as the Lord had done.

From this episode, we learn that deacons did not just deliver food to the poor. They also defended and explained the Catholic faith to nonbelievers; it was Stephen's effectiveness as an apologist that had made him enemies.

In the next chapter of Acts, we meet the deacon Philip (not to be confused with Saint Philip the Apostle). Although the persecution that followed the death of Stephen forced many Christians to scatter and leave Jerusalem, Saint Philip used every opportunity he was given to God's advantage. As he traveled, he continued to proclaim the Good News. He exorcized demons in the name of Christ. He healed the sick. He made converts to the faith, including a minister to the queen of the Ethiopians. Tradition says that he died a martyr in Phrygia (modern Turkey).

In the year 258, the Roman emperor Valerian decided to rid himself and the Roman Empire of those annoying Christians by sending guards to execute Pope Sixtus II while he was celebrating Mass in the catacombs. He gave Sixtus' deacon three days to turn in all the treasures possessed by the Church to the authorities. He probably thought that was an easy request, but he did not know Deacon Lawrence. On August 10, Lawrence presented himself to the prefect of Rome, surrounded by the poor people whom the Church supported. The poor, Lawrence explained, were the true treasure of the Church. The prefect was not converted or amused; he ordered Lawrence to be tortured by being slowly burned on a great gridiron. Surely, he thought, such a long, painful torture would cause the deacon to apostatize, give up, or be humiliated. Instead, Lawrence made jokes about being ready, like a piece of meat, to be turned over and cooked on the other side. The witness—in life and in death—of Lawrence the Deacon not only caused him to be named a saint of the Church but also caused a wave of conversions to the faith. His bravery during a public trial led many Roman men and women to want to know more about that mysterious group called the Catholic Church.

Other deacons have followed in Lawrence's footsteps. Saint Agathopedes was a deacon in Thessalonica (Greece) who was ordered to give up the Church's copies of Sacred Scripture to be burned. He refused and was martyred by drowning in the year 303. A year later, a deacon in Spain was arrested because he was a Catholic; Saint Vincent of Saragossa initially survived brutal torture with iron hooks but died a martyr in prison soon afterward. Saint Benjamin was a deacon in Persia (modern Iran) in the fifth century. He was imprisoned, released, and then arrested and executed for preaching in the streets about Jesus Christ.

Although the diaconate has developed over the centuries and is no longer generally considered a pathway to other Holy Orders, quite a few holy men have been deacons before rising to higher positions in the Church. Popes Zachary, Leo IX, Boniface IV, Eleutherius, Symmachus, Hormisdas, Callistus I, Siricius, and Damasus I were all deacons before they were elected to the papacy and are now considered saints. Several deacons have become Doctors of the Church as well as saints: Athanasius (also bishop of Alexandria), Peter Chrysologus (also archbishop of Ravenna), Gregory I (also pope), John Chrysostom (also patriarch of Constantinople), Leo I (also pope and Doctor of the Church), and Ephraem of Syria. Although it has been a long time since becoming a deacon was a common career path before becoming pope, that does not mean that becoming a deacon isn't an excellent path to holiness.

Bishops

Just as the development of the diaconate over the centuries shows us its purpose within the Body of Christ, so, too, with the role of bishop. There is an obvious lesson in the etymology of the name of the office; the modern word "bishop" comes from the Greek word for "overseer". It has certainly been true throughout the centuries that the bishop serves as an administrator and guide for the spiritual, moral, and even material health of those under his care. But what does it mean to be a Christian overseer, or a bishop, as the Church understands it?

Perhaps the most famous bishop in the history of the Church is the one who evangelized his former captors. Though he miraculously escaped from slavery among the pagan Irish, Saint Patrick (c. 385–461) could not escape something more powerful: God's inner call to return and bring the Good News of Jesus Christ to those same people. After being ordained to the priesthood, Patrick went back to Ireland, preached the Gospel, and planted the seeds of faith all over Ireland, which would bear fruit in innumerable Christian communities, churches, and monasteries. It is commonly said that Ireland is the only country that was evangelized without any martyrs. Whether that is technically true—the Druids did not give up without a fight—it is certainly true that the Irish people were remarkably open to the Gospel. Saint Patrick of Ireland became the first and greatest bishop of that country not just because he taught them about Jesus Christ but also because he knew how to form his converts into Christian disciples who spread that message to others.

Today, people typically think of Saint John Fisher (1469–1535) only as the companion of fellow-martyr Saint Thomas More or as one of the many Catholics who died during the reign of the English king Henry VIII. While laying down your life for your faith in God certainly makes you an imitator of Jesus Christ Himself, there were many other reasons John Fisher could have been canonized as a saint even if he had not died as a martyr.

For example, John was not only a priest; he was also a highly effective preacher and debater. He was not only a professor, but he was also a scholar, theologian, and a promoter of classical education. He lived an upright and ascetic personal life, even while he traveled in the circles of the rich and powerful. His self-discipline may have saved his life; some say Queen Anne Boleyn was responsible for a meal that sickened his household staff and killed two members on one occasion. He escaped death only because he did not eat the poisoned porridge.

But Saint John's virtue and honesty ultimately cost him his life. He is best remembered for being the only Catholic bishop in England brave enough to stand up to King Henry when he demanded the right to divorce his wife and marry his mistress. All those bishops who capitulated out of fear and greed—who remembers their names now?

Saint Anthelm of Belley (1107–1178) was the prior at a Carthusian monastery in France when the pope decided to make him a bishop. While many men sought out higher positions in the Church out of greed or a desire for power, Anthelm strongly resisted the offer for some time, preferring to live the later years of his life as a simple Carthusian monk. But the pope was persistent, and Anthelm eventually became the bishop of Belley.

Problems with clerical celibacy did not begin in the modern age; Anthelm soon discovered that some of his priests were not even trying to obey the vow of chastity that they had made when they were ordained. For a few years after becoming their bishop, he tried to persuade those priests gently to change their ways. Proving that there is indeed a way to solve this problem besides ignoring it, he then deprived the guilty priests of their incomes. And what did this holy man do during his leisure time? He personally cared for lepers and visited Carthusian monasteries.

Saint Charles Borromeo (1538–1584) came from a powerful and wealthy family in Italy, and, in an obvious abuse of power now known as nepotism, he was made a cardinal at the young age of twenty-two when his uncle became pope. But Charles proved that it is possible to be given an inordinate amount of authority and money and to use it wisely—if you are a holy man. When the Council of Trent got bogged down in internal squabbling and Church leaders vacillated about how to respond to the arguments of the Protestant reformers, Charles used his diplomatic skills and influence to coax them all into working together. He supervised the writing of the Catechism of the Council of Trent and reformed liturgical books. He renounced his family's wealth as soon as it was possible, and when he was made archbishop of Milan, he showed that he was serious about the reforms prescribed in the Council of Trent by enforcing them in his own archdiocese. He did such a good job as a reformer that someone tried to kill him. He died of health problems when he was only forty-six years old.

Even if Karol Wojtyla had never become Pope John Paul II, his actions as a Polish bishop living under oppressive Communist rule would have made him a credible candidate for canonization. He wrote pastoral letters to his people, but since, of course, the government would never let them be printed or safely mailed to Catholics, he had them typed, copied by nuns, and secretly distributed. When the government made it extremely difficult for new parishes or church buildings to be established, he organized priests to go door-to-door for months or years until they'd gathered so many parishioners that the new parish virtually already existed by the time they asked for permission. His creative but unflinching willingness to stand up for Christ and His Church strengthened Polish Catholics, but it also showed the world that capitulation was not the only possible response to oppressive Communist rule.

Saints Patrick, John Fisher, Anthelm, Charles Borromeo, John Paul II, and all the other holy bishops in the history of the Church were overseers of their people; but they weren't overseers like the cruel Egyptian ones who forced the Israelites to make bricks, as described in the book of Exodus. They were overseers in the same way that Jesus Christ was the overseer of His apostles and followers. Or to use the words of Christ Himself, each one sought to be a "good shepherd",[34] the kind of shepherd who cares for the wounds of his sheep, feeds his sheep, and even lays down his life for his sheep.

[34]Jn 10:11, 14.

Leaving the World Behind

Even non-Catholics know Saint Francis of Assisi; he is the holy man whose statue can be found in many backyards, with real birds and stone birds around him. As a result, many people seem to think he's the saint who cared for animals.

Well, yes, he did, but that was not his primary charism, and the Franciscan order does not just feed the birds. God inspires some men and women with the knowledge of a unique way to meet Jesus Christ, and, because they ask, He gives them the tools and abilities to help others find their way to Him too.

Most often, the founder is troubled by something in the surrounding culture that kept him, and still keeps others, from seeking Christ. Saint Francis renounced his father's name, home, and wealth because he saw that material possessions were separating him from God. Twelfth-century Europeans, even those who had left their families to live only for God, had become somewhat financially comfortable, and they needed to be made *less* comfortable.

Saint Peter Julian Eymard (1811–1868) was a priest in one religious order when he decided to establish his own. Why? Because it saddened him that there was no religious congregation in the entire Church specifically dedicated to the worship of Jesus' Presence in the Blessed Sacrament. Blessed Francesco Faà di Bruno (1825–1888) founded a religious order of nuns whose vocation was to care for women in need. Who were the women in need? Women without families or skills to support themselves, repentant prostitutes, and single moms—the same group of women who unfortunately need Christian charity in every culture and every time and place.

In each religious congregation, individual members focus their lives on the charism of the order. (Note that within the Church, the terms "order", "congregation", and "institute" have developed specific meanings over the centuries but will be used interchangeably here.) The unique charism of each order forms the lives of those who follow it, just as the constant demands of being a medical doctor affects the way he lives every day of his life or the sensitive nature of an artist causes him to see daily living in a unique way.

When the rich young man now known as Saint Anthony the Great (251–356) decided to leave the world behind and live alone for God in the desert, he was thinking about only his own salvation. But his example—and the example of the other early monks whom we call the Desert Fathers—inspired thousands of men and women to do the same during his lifetime, and countless Christian communities have arisen over the centuries in their wake. All have had the same goal of attaining holiness in God's sight, but with many variations in location, size of community, emphasis in devotion, practical rules for daily living, permission or prohibition of private ownership, the taking of vows or not, and many other factors.

The greatest religious orders of the Church

While some religious congregations have come and gone, some have had a lasting impact on the Body of Christ, as well as the surrounding world, over the centuries. The following summaries can help us recognize how religious orders developed over time and affected other religious orders.

Note that this is not an exhaustive list of all the religious orders of the Church, and some orders have multiple names and multiple branches. For example, Saint Silvester Gozzolini (1177–1267) based his religious congregation on the Benedictine Rule, so members of his order are sometimes called Silvestrines, and other times they are called Silvestrine Benedictines. See also the end of this chapter for a table describing each of the founders of these orders.

Augustinian Canons	
What is the name of the order?	The order is also called the Canons Regular of the Order of Saint Augustine, with other branch orders.

(continued)

Augustinian Canons	
What is the origin of the order?	Saint Augustine of Hippo established a religious community in the fourth century and described its Rule of Life in a short document. By the eleventh century, that general rule had been adapted, used, and developed by many religious communities.
What is its unique charism?	Initially very similar to monks—because they took vows to hold property in common and stay in one place—canons became a different entity because their vows later included poverty, chastity, and obedience. Canons are similar to monks because they live in community and take vows but are also similar to secular clergy in that they are often attached to and serve at a specific church.
Who were some saints of the order?	Saint Augustine himself, who enthusiastically promoted this way of life, was the first saint to live it out. But the congregational calendar of the Augustinian Canons is full of saints and blesseds who found this way of life helpful in growing in sanctity. Perhaps the most famous example is Saint Rita of Cascia, who was a wife, mother, and widow before entering the order.
Has it offered any other gifts to the Church?	In addition to supporting one another to grow in holiness, canons minister to the faithful through education and care for the sick and needy living in the community nearby. Augustinian *friars* arose at the same time as other mendicant orders (see below). As friars, they take vows of corporate poverty but do not take vows of stability so that they can engage in apostolic activity, such as preaching.

Basilians	
What is the name of the order?	The order is also called the Order of Saint Basil the Great, with two main branch orders.
What is the origin of the order?	Saint Basil the Great led other monks in forming some of the earliest monastic communities and left behind a description of his way of life. This general collection of rules has been enriched by many subsequent councils and regulations proposed by Basilian abbots, particularly the *Constitutions* created by Saint Theodore the Studite.

What is its unique charism?	The Rule of Saint Basil emphasizes poverty, obedience, self-denial, and renunciation.
Who were some saints of the order?	Many monks have become known as saints and holy men besides Saint Basil the Great himself. Saint Procopius was a Bohemian priest and wonder-worker who lived in the tenth century and founded a Basilian monastery. Saint Josaphat Kuntsevych was a famous priest, preacher, and archbishop of modern Ukraine who attempted to reconcile the Orthodox and Catholic believers in his area, leading to his martyrdom.
Has it offered any other gifts to the Church?	At present, there are two kinds of Basilian monasteries for priests, monks, and nuns: those generally in the East and those generally in the West.
	Monks began following the Rule of Saint Basil in the fourth century, and many monasteries arose and followed this way of life for centuries. Following the Great Schism in 1054, Eastern Orthodox churches continued to follow the Basilian Rule. Some Eastern Catholic communities also follow the Basilian Rule.
	A daughter order following the Rule of Saint Basil arose in the late eighteenth century in France in response to the French Revolution.

Benedictines	
What is the name of the order?	The order is also called the Order of Saint Benedict, with many branch orders.
What is the origin of the order?	Through personal trial and error, Saint Benedict of Nursia developed a Rule of Life for monastic life in community that has benefited innumerable religious communities since the sixth century.
What is its unique charism?	Benedict's Rule of Life is often summarized as "pray and work", meaning that his monks attempt to keep both prayer and labor in balance in their daily lives. Benedictine monks also take vows of stability, fidelity, and obedience.

(continued)

Benedictines	
Who were some saints of the order?	Many popes have been Benedictines, including Saint Celestine V. The first six abbots of the famous Benedictine Abbey of Cluny (France) were Saints Berno, Odo, Aymard, Majolus, Odilo, and Hugh. Saint Hildegard of Bingen (now also a Doctor of the Church) was a Benedictine nun and abbess. Saint Boniface, who brought the Gospel to Germany, was a Benedictine.
Has it offered any other gifts to the Church?	The Benedictine order achieved perhaps its finest moment during the twelfth century, when the Benedictine Abbey of Cluny became the model of monastic life and the instigator of Church reform for all of Christendom. Many future orders of the Church were based on the Benedictine Rule, including the Cistercians.

Carthusians	
What is the name of the order?	The order is also called the Order of Saint Bruno or the Order of the Chartreuse.
What is the origin of the order?	Saint Bruno, the bishop of Cologne, established an order of hermits in 1084; the order's Rule of Life is unique in that the members are hermits who also live in community.
What is its unique charism?	Each monk spends most of his time in prayer, silence, and solitude but also performs manual labor that supports the community. Communal life is also lived through weekly recreation with one another.
Who were some saints of the order?	Carthusians prefer solitude to publicity, so few members have been canonized. However, the founder of the order, Bruno, is considered a saint by the Church. Denis van Leeuwen (1402–1471) became widely known as a theological writer, and Guigo II (d. c. 1188) was a Carthusian prior and writer of classic works on prayer. Both are commonly, if not officially, considered saints.
Has it offered any other gifts to the Church?	The simplicity and silence of Carthusian life is widely respected, even in the secular world. Unlike many other great orders, it is said that the Carthusian order's rule is so excellent that the order has never needed to be reformed. The order includes both Carthusian monks and nuns.

Cistercians	
What is the name of the order?	The order is also called the Order of Cistercians, with two main branch orders: Common Observance and Strict Observance.
What is the origin of the order?	Saints Robert of Molesme, Alberic of Citeaux, and Stephen Harding established the first house at Citeaux, France, in 1098, as part of a general reform of monastic life that swept Europe at the time.
What is its unique charism?	Though the order is based on the Rule of Saint Benedict and therefore balances prayer and work in the lives of the monks, there is also an emphasis on evangelical poverty and simple communal life.
Who were some saints of the order?	In addition to the saintly founders, the order boasts two of the greatest saints in the history of the Church: Saint Bernard of Clairvaux, abbot and Doctor of the Church, and Saint Peter Damian, bishop and Doctor of the Church.
Has it offered any other gifts to the Church?	This order, based on the Benedictine Rule, revived simple monastic life in Christendom through its emphasis on poverty and simplicity. The order includes both monks and nuns. The Trappists, formally known as the Order of the Cistercians of the Strict Observance, are a relatively recent daughter order.

Carmelites	
What is the name of the order?	The order is also called the Order of the Brothers of the Blessed Virgin Mary of Mount Carmel, with Discalced Carmelite branch order.
What is the origin of the order?	According to tradition, early Christian hermits lived on Mount Carmel, the mountain best known as the home of the prophet Elijah. These hermits originally followed a simple rule described by Saint Albert of Jerusalem. When unrest in the Holy Land caused these men to return to Europe around the twelfth century, the order was reformed into a mendicant order (see the Franciscans and Dominicans below) living in community.

(continued)

Carmelites	
What is its unique charism?	The Carmelite vocation is centered on prayer, community life, and acts of service. Since its reformation, members live in community but as a mendicant order. The spirituality of the order is strongly focused on the Blessed Virgin and contemplative prayer.
Who were some saints of the order?	Saint Albert, patriarch of Jerusalem, is credited with the first rule of the order, and Saint Simon Stock was inspired to reform the order into a mendicant order in the thirteenth century. In the sixteenth century, Saints Teresa of Avila and John of the Cross, spiritual giants and now Doctors of the Church, established the Discalced Carmelites, refocusing the emphasis on poverty, prayer, and smaller communities. Saint Thérèse of Lisieux was named a Doctor of the Church for her profound explanation of the "little way" to holiness.
Has it offered any other gifts to the Church?	The explanations of prayer described by great Carmelite saints, as well as the simple, prayerful lives of its members, have been great gifts to the Church. The order of Discalced Carmelites, a major reform of the order, was created in the sixteenth century. Carmelites include friars, nuns, and laypeople, each in separate orders.

Franciscans	
What is the name of the order?	The order is also called the Order of Friars Minor, with many branch orders.
What is the origin of the order?	Saint Francis of Assisi inspired men to follow his way of life, which became a religious order in the Church in 1209.
What is its unique charism?	Emulating the poverty of Jesus Christ, Franciscans are a mendicant order; they beg for their food and do not accumulate property. They also travel to preach the Gospel.

Franciscans	
Who were some saints of the order?	Many priests have found the Franciscan way of life a path to sainthood: Saints Anthony of Padua, Bernardine of Siena, Bonaventure, Lawrence of Brindisi, and Pio of Pietrelcina. Female saints include Saints Clare of Assisi (Second Order) and Elizabeth of Hungary (Third Order and queen).
Has it offered any other gifts to the Church?	The Franciscan emphasis on material poverty and itinerant preaching dramatically changed religious life because many religious houses at the time had become wealthy and insulated.
	First Order Franciscans are called friars; women comprise the members of the Second Order and are also called Poor Clares. Laity can become members of their Third Order.
	Over time, two distinct branches of the order developed: Capuchin Franciscans and Conventual Franciscans.

Dominicans	
What is the name of the order?	The order is also called the Order of Preachers, with many branch orders.
What is the origin of the order?	Saint Dominic de Guzman was an Augustinian Canon when he traveled with his bishop to evangelize a region of France troubled by heresy. Based on that experience, he founded an order in 1216 to preach the Gospel and combat heresy all over the world.
What is its unique charism?	Dominicans are most noted for their intellectual dedication to spreading the Gospel and for service, and they emphasize Gospel poverty and simplicity but do not remain bound to a specific location. This is called "stability" in religious life.
Who were some saints of the order?	Famous Dominicans include Saints Thomas Aquinas (Doctor of the Church), Albert the Great (Doctor of the Church), Catherine of Siena (Doctor of the Church),

(continued)

Dominicans	
	and Pius V (pope). The order has also inspired preachers such as Saints Vincent Ferrer and Louis de Montfort, as well as laymen, such as Rose of Lima, to great personal holiness and sainthood.
Has it offered any other gifts to the Church?	The Dominican order has given the Church an extraordinary number of canonized saints of remarkable intellectual depth.
	As with the Franciscan order, friars, nuns, and laypeople are members of the three orders within the Dominicans.

Jesuits	
What is the name of the order?	The order is also called the Society of Jesus.
What is the origin of the order?	Saint Ignatius of Loyola founded this order in 1534. Members take vows of poverty, chastity, and obedience, with a special vow of obedience to the pope.
What is its unique charism?	Jesuits particularly serve in evangelization and apostolic ministry, going wherever the pope sends them, particularly to bring the Gospel.
Who were some saints of the order?	In addition to the founder, one of the founding members of the order, Peter Faber, is also acclaimed a saint, and Saint Francis Xavier is considered one of the greatest evangelizers in the history of the Church, second only to Saint Paul the Apostle. Saint Robert Bellarmine was named a Doctor of the Church for his influential writings, and Saint Peter Claver was named a saint for his dedication to service of slaves.
Has it offered any other gifts to the Church?	Ignatius' personal emphasis on spiritual discernment is a hallmark of the order and its spirituality. The Jesuit emphasis on intellectual gifts has benefited the world in many ways, including education. The example of Jesuit martyrs has also been a powerful witness to the faith. Priests and brothers (formerly called temporal coadjutors) serve within the Jesuit order.

Martyrs of the religious orders

Every one of these religious orders has fostered not only holiness but also the heroic sacrifice of martyrdom:

- A group of Augustinian missionaries, most from Spain, traveled to Japan in the seventeenth century, brought about many conversions, and were brutally killed during a government crackdown against Christianity.
- Saint Hildebert of Ghent, a Benedictine abbot, was martyred in the eighth century for supporting the use of icons in prayer during the iconoclastic heresy.
- The Carthusian monks of London, along with the rest of England, were ordered to accept King Henry VIII as head of the Church in the sixteenth century. Many refused and were variously starved to death or hanged and disemboweled.
- Many of the nuns living in the city of Orange, France, who were martyred together during the French Revolution and are now acclaimed as blesseds were members of the Cistercian order.
- Saint Titus Brandsma was a Dutch Carmelite priest and an internationally known speaker who spoke out against Nazi anti-Jewish propaganda before World War II. He was arrested and sent to Dachau concentration camp, where he was executed after being made the subject of medical experiments by the Nazis.
- Many Franciscan missionaries to China, including priests, friars, nuns, and laypeople, were martyred during the anti-Christian, anti-foreigner Boxer Rebellion in the early twentieth century.
- Saint Peter of Verona was brought up to believe in the heresy of Catharism but converted to Catholicism, became a Dominican, and went back to his native land to bring the truth to his countrymen. He was brutally killed on a roadside in 1252 because of his faith.
- Saints John de Brébeuf, Isaac Jogues, and other Jesuits were martyred in extremely brutal ways by North American tribes during the seventeenth century while attempting to bring the Gospel to the native people.

But that's not all

The largest orders in the Church are not the only ones. Many other orders have also had a profound influence on the Church and were founded in response to the needs of the Church and the surrounding culture at a given point in time.

Saint Norbert of Xanten founded the Premonstratensian order, sometimes called the Norbertine order, in 1120 at Premontre, France. He used the Rule of Saint Augustine to govern his order, which is why members are sometimes called Premonstratensian Canons, but he also used some aspects of the Cistercian order. There were hundreds of Norbertine houses in the Middle Ages, and it was very influential in the conversion of Germanic peoples at the time.

Military orders arose in twelfth-century Europe. Though the history of these orders is occasionally spotty, they were established for a just cause: to protect Christian nations from invasion by Muslim forces and to allow Christians to travel safely to, as well as live in, the Holy Land.[1]

The Trinitarian order, which was founded in the late twelfth century, and the Mercedarian order, which was founded in the early thirteenth century, were established to ransom Christians who had been captured and enslaved by marauding Muslims, a common occurrence at the time. Members of the orders raised money in Christian lands and then traveled in person and at great personal risk to Muslim countries to buy back Christians and return them to freedom. It is estimated that these orders ransomed ninety thousand Christians from slavery during the three hundred years of greatest activity.

In the thirteenth century, seven devout men were living in the city of Florence, Italy. They had founded a confraternity of laymen;[2] they were praying together on the Feast of the Assumption when the Blessed Mother startled them by appearing to all seven men in a vision. In the vision, Mary encouraged these men to leave the world behind and focus on eternal things. Buonfiglio Monaldi, Bartholomew degli Amidei, John Buonaguinta, Benedict dell'Antela,

---

[1] The military orders include regular orders such as the Knights Templar and Knights of Malta, as well as secular orders. See the entry for "Military Orders" in the *Catholic Encyclopedia*, available at NewAdvent.org, for more information.

[2] A confraternity is a group of laymen devoted to a particular service of charity or religion.

Geraldino Sostegni, Ricovero Uguccione, and Alexis Falconieri all obeyed the vision; they eventually founded a religious order in 1233 and became saints of the Church. They called themselves Servants of Mary, or Servites, and members today include priests, brothers, sisters, nuns, and laypeople, all devoted to growing in holiness, preaching the Gospel, and encouraging devotion to the Blessed Mother.

The Theatine order was founded in 1524 with the goal of encouraging both the laity and their fellow clergy to live lives of evangelical perfection. Though a small order, they raised the standard for their fellow priests through their austere way of life and strong intellectual bent.

Numerous religious orders were founded specifically to serve those in need. Saint Vincent de Paul founded many organizations to care for the needy during his lifetime in seventeenth-century France, leading Blessed Frederic Ozanam (1813–1853) to establish one of the best-known groups still serving the poor: the Society of Saint Vincent de Paul. Saint John of God (1550–1630) founded the Brothers Hospitallers[3] in 1572 in Spain to serve the sick. Saint Joseph Calasanz (1556–1648) founded the Order of Poor Clerics Regular of the Mother of God of the Pious Schools (Piarists) in 1617 in Italy to teach poor children. Saint John Bosco founded the Society of Saint Francis de Sales in 1859 in Italy to educate young people and foster vocations to the priesthood. All these institutions still exist and are still serving the needy all over the world.

Some orders were formed to evangelize with an emphasis on a specific devotion. For example, Saint Paul of the Cross established the Passionists in 1720 to foster an awareness of the Passion of our Lord, and Saint Alphonsus Liguori founded the Redemptorist order in 1732 to focus on the mission of our Redeemer, Jesus Christ.

In summary, what do we—that is, all Christians—learn about how to live a holy life from the religious orders of the Church?

We tend to think of monastic life as a life of complete isolation. But men and women who have chosen to leave the world behind for God generally realize rather quickly that they, too, need the support—emotional, material, and spiritual—of other people. Saint Antony of

---

[3] The Brothers Hospitallers did not formally become a religious order until after Saint John's death.

Kiev, who lived in the eleventh century, tried to live like a hermit when he was a young man but soon recognized that any way of life, including monastic life, requires training and direction. He traveled to a monastery to learn how to be a hermit from another hermit. It is notable that women, who tend to be more social than men, tend to be more attracted to orders that serve others, rather than, say, the Carthusians, which have developed a form of sign language to communicate so as to live in more complete silence. The balance between solitude and community life will be different for a layperson than a monk or nun, but the point is that there must be a balance.

Some of the developments in religious life over the centuries simply make sense in retrospect. With the growth of both the priesthood and monastic life in cultures that were being influenced by the widespread acceptance of the Catholic faith, *of course* the canons regular would arise as a bridge, to bring the best of both vocations together. *Of course* those who leave the world behind for God's sake would want to devote considerable time to prayer, but they would need to engage in some work to sustain themselves and avoid laziness and pride. *Of course* it would be a temptation to leave one monastery if you didn't like your superior (or the food or the work or your cell or ...) and find a better one, so taking a vow of stability would keep you from rejecting ordinary, real-life difficulties. *Of course* some people are better suited to preaching than others and would more easily accept the trials of constant travel and perhaps rejection. One lesson that we laypeople can take from all these developments is that monastic life has real-life challenges that keep it from being the blissful experience we might expect it to be.

Because our culture is so secular, it is hard for us to imagine how a monastery could be rich. But in a truly Christian culture, families would want all their children to consider a religious vocation and support them if God called one or more to pursue such a way of life. In a truly Christian culture, Christians would want to support the "professionals" financially to pray for healing for sick family members, pray for wisdom for difficult personal decisions, and pray in thanksgiving when blessed with success. In a truly Christian culture, Christians would be ashamed if they spent more money making their homes gorgeous for dinner parties than making their parish church beautiful for God. While the mendicant orders' attempts to restore Christlike poverty to religious life in the Middle Ages was certainly necessary, one could argue that at least some of the wealth in monasteries should put us to shame, because much of it came from ordinary, poor Catholics who made true financial sacrifices out of love of God.

Men and women, being created so differently by God, have found different paths in their efforts to devote their lives to Him. The separation of male and female communities from one another is a good idea not only to avoid the temptations of the flesh; we think and act in such completely different ways that it avoids a great deal of confusion.

Each religious community has a focus, or a lens by which members see the world and live out their vocation. As laypeople, we can spiritually benefit by adapting that lens to our own lives. Many laypeople have chosen to follow the spiritual focus of a religious order, whether formally a member or not, and grown in holiness as a result. We, too, can benefit spiritually by studying the spirituality of religious orders. If you want to deepen your prayer life, start by reading the works of holy Carmelites. If you want to understand better the teachings of our faith, study the works of saintly Dominicans. If you want to serve the needy in your community more effectively, look at the Christlike examples of old and new orders that teach, feed, and heal those in need. The wealth of the religious orders of the Church is not in dollar bills but in their words and witness over the centuries.

Founders of religious orders

The following table explains the role of each of the founders of major religious orders in establishing that order.

Name	Dates	Religious Order	Role as Founder
Saint Augustine of Hippo	354–430	Augustinian Canons Regular	Augustine established a monastery and described its basic rule of life. But the order's rule was very general for many centuries; Augustine can very generally only be called the founder.

(continued)

Name	Dates	Religious Order	Role as Founder
Saint Benedict of Nursia	c. 480–547	Benedictines	He developed a Rule of Life based on his personal experience as a monk and abbot over different communities.
Saint Bruno of Cologne	c. 1030–1101	Carthusians	He developed a Rule of Life based on his personal experience as a hermit and abbot.
Saint Robert of Molesme	1027–1111	Cistercians	He was a Benedictine monk before becoming a hermit and helping to establish a new order.
Saint Alberic of Citeaux	d. 1109	Cistercians	He was a hermit who joined Saint Robert in establishing a new order.
Saint Stephen Harding	d. 1134	Cistercians	He was a hermit who joined Saint Robert in establishing a new order.
Saint Albert of Jerusalem	1149–1214	Carmelites	As patriarch of Jerusalem, he wrote a brief description of the way of life of hermits living on nearby Mount Carmel. In this, he was more of a legislator for the order than a founder.
Saint Francis of Assisi	1181–1226	Franciscans	Francis developed a way of living the Gospel; he is a founder in the sense that many other men and women wanted to follow him in the way of life he established.
Saint Dominic de Guzman	1170–1221	Dominicans	As a priest and Augustinian Canon, he developed a religious order to meet the needs of his culture, focusing on preaching and theology.

Name	Dates	Religious Order	Role as Founder
Saint Ignatius of Loyola	1491–1556	Jesuits	He established a religious order based on a small group of his followers.

Defunct religious orders

Not every religious order in the history of the Church still exists. Some orders—such as those described previously in this chapter—have demonstrated an amazing longevity over the centuries. Their resiliency despite war, famine, persecution, and cultural change is impressive, as well as being an encouraging sign of the presence of God. But it is worthwhile to examine briefly some orders that no longer exist.

Over time, some religious orders have simply merged into other religious orders. This could happen if two orders have very similar missions, if one order is unable to continue on its own, or for other reasons. For example, many small female religious orders originating in the nineteenth century merged into larger orders in the middle or late twentieth century, often following Vatican Council II.

Sometimes a religious order has made the decision to disband or has been forcibly disbanded by a secular or higher ecclesiastical authority. For example, the Gilbertine order, which was founded in the year 1130 in England and was a contemplative monastic order including nuns, sisters, brothers, and canons regular, was completely dissolved by King Henry VIII in 1539 during his persecution of the Catholic Church. The Livonian order was originally an order of crusading knights; founded in 1237, it lasted until 1561 after some scandals involving the use of force in conversions. The Haudriettes were a French order of nuns, which was founded in the early fourteenth century and underwent various internal reforms until the time of the French Revolution. The order was dissolved at that time and never restored.

Reformers and second founders

Some saints provided such strong leadership to their religious orders that they are sometimes called second founders or reformers of the order. For example, the founders of the Carthusian and Cistercian orders established new orders, largely based on the Rule of Life of the Benedictine order, to reform the less-than-perfect practices they saw there.

Name	Dates	Religious Order	Role
Saint Benedict of Aniane	750–821	Benedictines	He reformed the practice of the order, in part by incorporating aspects of the Rule of Saint Pachomius and the Rule of Saint Basil the Great.
Saint John Gualbert	985–1073	Benedictines	He established the Vallombrosan order within the Benedictine congregation to live a more austere way of life than was lived at the time in other Benedictine houses.
Saint Bernard of Clairvaux	1090–1153	Cistercians	Though he joined the order soon after its founding, his influence on the order and on all of Europe cannot be underestimated; he was personally involved in the founding of sixty-eight monasteries.
Saint Silvester Gozzolini	1177–1267	Benedictines	He established the Silvestrine order within the Benedictine congregation, with an emphasis on poverty and silence.
Saint Clare of Assisi	1193–1253	Franciscans	She is considered the founder of the order of Franciscan nuns since she drew up its Rule of Life.
Saint Bonaventure	c. 1221–1274	Franciscans	He resolved important issues caused by factions in the order that developed soon after its founding.

Name	Dates	Religious Order	Role
Blessed Raymond of Capua	1330– 1399	Dominicans	He restored discipline to the order soon after its founding.
Saint Colette of Corbie	1381– 1447	Franciscans	She reformed the practice of religious life among Poor Clare nuns.
Saint Teresa of Avila	1515– 1582	Carmelites	She established the Discalced Carmelite order to return Carmelite practice to a simpler, stricter way of life.
Saint John of the Cross	1542– 1591	Carmelites	He helped establish the Discalced Carmelite order to return Carmelite practice to a simpler, stricter way of life.

Life in Religious Life

About a hundred years ago, in an America that was Christian but far from Catholic, Saint Frances Xavier Cabrini (1850–1917) died. She was born a premature baby into a large family of Italian farmers and repeatedly faced health problems as a child, which is the reason that two religious congregations refused to let her join. However, this amazing and holy woman came to America with six other sisters to serve Catholic immigrants from Italy, eventually founding a religious order for women called the Missionary Sisters of the Sacred Heart of Jesus. At the time of her death, she had established sixty-seven institutions including schools, hospitals, and orphanages to serve people in need. Her death was mourned not only by her sisters and by pious Catholics all over America but also by (so the story goes) the inmates of Alcatraz prison, some of whom had benefited from her generosity in serving the poor but had not, apparently, learned as much from her personal life of virtue.

A hundred years ago, no one needed to explain "religious life" because Catholic sisters and brothers of various religious orders were much more common, at least in many parts of the United States. Today, however, due to the decimation of religious orders since the Second Vatican Council, many Catholics encounter religious women and men—outside of priests and deacons—very rarely.

Therefore, most people's knowledge of religious life begins and ends with *The Sound of Music*, leaving the typical American with very fundamental questions about religious life. For example, why would anyone choose such a life in the first place? Saint Anthony the Great (251–356) can teach us the answer to that question, particularly through *The Life of Anthony*, an early biography written by the saint and Doctor of the Church Athanasius of Alexandria (c. 297–373).

Why enter religious life?

According to Athanasius, Anthony was a young man living in a city on the bank of the Nile River in Egypt when his parents died. His parents were a pious couple who had raised him in a Catholic but very wealthy home. At the time of their unexpected deaths, Anthony became a very rich teenage boy whose closest relative was a younger sister. History, both modern and ancient, is littered with the scandalous way that some teenagers have responded to being suddenly given great wealth without any parental supervision, but Anthony was not that sort of teenager. Instead, he went to Mass.

That is, to better understand what God was calling him to do with his life, Anthony prayed, asked God to show him his vocation, and listened. God answered.

The Gospel reading at Mass that day was the story of the rich young man who asked Jesus about how to enter eternal life but who walked away sad when Jesus invited him to give up his possessions and follow him.[1] Anthony was cut to the heart by this passage. Certainly, Anthony had a great deal in common with that rich young man in the Gospel. It is also true that *every* Christian at any age and in any place should be able to recognize a personal invitation from Christ in this exchange. Each Christian—priest, monk, nun, or layman—could take Matthew 19:21 as a command from Jesus repeatedly and seriously to evaluate what possessions are separating him or her from God's call to perfection. As the Second Vatican Council taught us, "All the faithful of Christ of whatever rank or status are called to the fullness of the Christian life and to the perfection of charity."[2] But Anthony recognized that God was asking even more from him than that.

As a wealthy man, Anthony had many good and virtuous vocational options available to him. He could have used his wealth to become a businessman, marry and have children, become better educated, or travel around the world. Instead, he realized that God was personally calling him to a more radical way of following Christ and

[1] Mt 19:16–22.

[2] Vatican Council II, Dogmatic Constitution on the Church *Lumen Gentium* (November 21, 1964), no. 40, http://www.vatican.va/archive/hist_councils/ii_vatican_council/documents/vat-ii_const_19641121_lumen-gentium_en.html.

that that way involved literally giving up his material possessions. So he did.

Shortly afterward, another Gospel reading convinced him that merely selling most of his wealth and giving it to the poor was not enough. Anthony obediently sold what was left, placed his younger sister in a nunnery (one of the earliest records we have for a monastery for women), and lived a very simple life on his own. Soon afterward, he began seeking out other holy men for advice about how to live this new way of life. As pious men and women have discovered throughout the ages, just as you need instruction from someone with greater experience if you want to become a blacksmith, a chemist, or a banker, so you need training to learn how to live a solitary, penitential life.

Anthony learned what he could from other Christians and left his village to live alone in the desert. Living in the Egyptian desert, then and now, is not an easy choice if you are bothered by the physical discomforts of heat and cold, lack of food and water, wild animals and annoying pests, and all the other reasons that individuals do not typically choose to live in the desert. Social isolation may sound tempting to everyone from time to time, but there is a reason that solitary confinement is one of the worst punishments inflicted upon prisoners; people get lonely. But Athanasius' description of Anthony's temptations primarily focuses on the spiritual trials, rather than physical or emotional trials, that he faced.

Just as marathon runners today will undergo a difficult regimen involving food, sleep, and exercise to prepare themselves to win a race, so Anthony disciplined his body to win the greatest possible prize—holiness—and his regimen lasted not for months but for a lifetime. Not because our bodies are evil or because he wanted to brag about his results, but because of his personal awareness of his own concupiscence, Anthony chose not to indulge his body's desires for comfort. He wanted his body to obey God, not his every whim. This attempt at physical self-discipline, along with the intervention of the devil, led to severe sexual temptations. Athanasius says these temptations lasted for twenty years. Again, Anthony fought—and won—this battle not because he hated his body but because he loved Jesus Christ.

In later years—and it should be remembered that Anthony died at the age of 105—he faced other temptations. The many men who chose to follow him as monks needed to be fed, clothed, protected, and taught. Visitors—some pious and some merely curious—constantly sought him out. The dangers of wild animals and desert life almost never left him because he almost never left the desert. Even the power of his prayers to bring about miracles could have led him to pride, if he had ever forgotten that the power to heal came from God, not himself.

The most important lesson Anthony's life story teaches us is that the why of religious life can have only one right answer: because God asked. Anthony chose to leave his former life behind because God spoke to him in his heart and invited him to do so. In the same way, God spoke to Saint Clare of Assisi (c. 1193–1253) to leave her home and become the first female follower of Saint Francis' way of life. Countless other men and women, like Anthony, have taken the time to ask God's advice about their vocations and then listened to His answer. But the importance of respecting God's invitation is not the only lesson we find in Anthony's biography.

For example, it is important to notice how God called Anthony. The Bible story of the rich young man was perfectly timed and tailor-made for a rich young man on a Sunday morning in Egypt. Even today, God's call is personally directed to each individual and his circumstances, not a cattle call offered blindly to a group.

Also, we tend to think of each saint as he lived at the time of death, not appreciating the fact that there were many previous and perhaps less-than-perfect stages that the saint passed through beforehand. This makes it easy to forget that as a young man, Anthony was inexperienced enough to need the advice of others but humble enough to ask for help in his spiritual growth.

Finally, discerning God's call is a lifelong process. Every man and woman who has embarked upon any sort of religious life had to listen continually to God's voice at each step. For Anthony, this involved not just learning from others how to live in the desert but also discerning how to lead and teach his followers, how to face increasingly violent and physical assaults of the devil, and how to console and correct laypeople who were suffering or causing suffering in others.

Anthony was not the first or only Christian to live in the desert, but he was certainly one of the greatest. His life shows us one path for those who want to live as Christ did; are there others?

The development of religious life

Like Saint Anthony the Great, Saints Pachomius, Basil the Great, Jerome of Stridon, and many others chose to leave the world behind and live in deserted places in the early centuries of the Church. It is commonly said that this way of life developed after the Roman Empire stopped persecuting Christians. It is certainly true that when the powerful witness of martyrdom was no longer a threat—or a challenging option for those who had past sins on their consciences or an abundance of zeal—Christians began to consider other radical ways of following Christ. But Anthony left for the desert long before the persecution of Christians first ended in the year 313, and while a few Christians aggressively sought martyrdom, most (rather reasonably) only accepted it when the only other option was unfaithfulness.

Our Lord Himself was the one who encouraged Christians to consider complete abandonment in a penitential life. After all, He began His ministry by going into the wilderness to pray, fast, and face temptations,[3] He asked His disciples to leave the world behind and follow Him,[4] and He left cities, towns, and friends behind repeatedly to go pray in solitude.[5] The Desert Fathers were not espousing a completely new idea so much as they were imitating their Master. Unfortunately, as often happens in the Christian life, doing what the Master did was not as easy as it might sound.

While our Savior was apparently able to give up the comforts of food, civilization, and human comfort for forty days straight the first time He tried it, most of us would find that a daunting task. Setting aside the issue of how to fast in a way that is penitential but not suicidal, even the decision of *what* to eat has caused problems for saints. Saint Hilarion of Cyprus (d. 371) tried to live on a diet of fifteen figs a day until he recognized something that a modern dietician could have told him: it was making him sick. In a letter he wrote around the year 392, Saint Jerome also described his own bout with what we could call Vitamin A deficiency, as well as how he resolved it by changing his diet.

[3] Mt 4:1–11; Mk 1:12–13; Lk 4:1–13.
[4] Mt 4:19; Mk 1:17; Lk 5:27; Jn 1:37, 43.
[5] Mt 4:23; 26:36; Mk 1:35; 6:46; 14:32; Lk 5:16; 9:18, 28; 11:1; 22:41.

Living safely in isolation requires more than good food choices. After all, the food you eat has to come from somewhere. When Saint Benedict of Nursia (c. 480–c. 550) first began to live as a hermit in a cave, he relied on a friend from a nearby monastery to bring him bread to eat. How long can that last?

Yet Saint Benedict, the founder of Western monasticism, eventually left us a wealth of time-tested experience about how to balance the desire for a solitary life with the blessings of community life, penitential practices with reason and safety, and the practical aspects of community stability with the human need to work for our daily bread. His experience also teaches us that such experimentation is not without dangers: some of his monks tried to kill him on one occasion, apparently because the way of life he had imposed as abbot was too demanding for them. Benedict realized he had been too severe with his monks, so he left them and started again elsewhere with a revised plan of life. Proving that he learned from both his successes and his mistakes, the Benedictine Rule of Life he left behind at his death has been one of the most enduring in the history of the Church, inspiring and being adapted by many subsequent religious orders. For example, Saint Romuald was a young Italian noble who had repented of his wild life when he showed up at a Benedictine monastery. He eventually founded the Camaldolese[6] Benedictines around the year 1012.

However, just because an idea, plan, or device is highly effective or even divinely inspired, that does not mean it cannot change, over time, into something much less effective or even broken. If Alexander Graham Bell could have foreseen modern robocalls, for example, he might have reconsidered his decision to develop the telephone.

Centuries after the death of Saint Benedict, the cultural situation had changed. Rather than existing in a partially pagan culture, Benedictine abbeys in Europe were situated in deeply Catholic communities. Not only were the abbeys agriculturally self-sufficient, but these religious communities were supported by the rich, the poor, and everyone in between. Powerful leaders gave the abbeys land and other gifts—sometimes this was for pious motives; sometimes this was for self-aggrandizing ones. People from all walks of life, but particularly wealthier families with more sons than land to give them,

---

[6] Camaldoli was the location of his first monastery.

sent their children to be educated or to become members of those religious communities.

Modern descriptions of religious life tend to depict the monks of the Middle Ages as scandalously wealthy, awash in gold decorations and fancy food, while the ordinary people starved. It is certainly true that not every monk of the time period was living a chaste, simple life—that's why the Hildebrandine reform of the eleventh century (see below) was so important—but that overlooks some important facts. First, giving generously to the Church so that the church in which one worships is beautiful and brings glory to God is a virtuous act that was encouraged by all Christians until practically yesterday. Second, the monasteries and churches of the medieval world served God through hospitality, as well as their worship. Those who were poor and in need, as well as entire communities during times of plague and famine, went to the monks for food and necessities. In a world without welfare, ordinary people did not fill out government forms to get help; they relied on the Christian charity of men and women who had already sacrificed their lives to serve God and His people. A simple case study proves the value of monastic life. When King Henry VIII destroyed Catholic religious life in England in the sixteenth century, he also destroyed this monastic safety net for the poor. Although the Industrial Revolution also bears much of the blame for the horrible living conditions of the poor that Charles Dickens depicted so vividly in his nineteenth-century novels, the rejection of Catholic monastic life certainly helped foster grinding poverty in England.

But back in the Middle Ages, feudal life put a considerable amount of power in the hands of the ruling class. Those feudal leaders, though Christian, tended to think and behave along the lines of the secular, rather than biblical, Golden Rule; that is, he who has the gold makes the rules. Kings and the leaders under them thought they had the right to choose those who would govern cities and monasteries as bishops and abbots. Those positions were both influential and generally financially comfortable, so of course they thought their own family members and friends should enjoy them. The fact that some of their candidates were laymen, not clergy, and often had no personal interest in living a penitential, celibate life was irrelevant. These irresponsible appointments of unfit candidates to positions of authority in the Church caused scandal as well as real harm, as the appointed men and women used their influence as abbots, abbesses, and bishops to pursue their own personal whims and desires. But what could the Church do to stop the scandalous decisions of such powerful men?

In the year 1073, a man named Hildebrand was elected pope, and he knew what to do about it. Though he took the name of Gregory VII when he became pope, the changes he introduced have become known to history as the Hildebrandine reform, and they literally changed Christendom.

Pope Gregory VII told kings that only he, the pope, could name bishops and abbots. When Holy Roman Emperor Henry IV tried to name bishops and abbots himself, Gregory excommunicated him. Three times. Gregory also faced down an anti-pope, propped up by the angry Henry, and otherwise exerted his authority, as pope, to make important decisions for the Church, without asking permission from civil leaders. The related problem of simony—in which a candidate bribed his way into important positions in the Church—was also opposed and acted upon by Gregory.

Gregory also did not ignore the fact that many clergymen were not practicing celibacy, which had unfortunately been the case for quite some time; instead, he acted. First, he wrote an encyclical in which he told the Christian people that they were absolved of their obligation to obey any bishops who allowed married priests in their dioceses. Next, he deprived married priests of their income. Gregory's enforcement of clerical celibacy was a serious attempt to remedy a public and widespread scandal.

In the tenth century, a duke had founded an abbey in Cluny, France. In the eleventh century, this abbey paved the way for monastic reform long before Gregory became pope, specifically through its strong and saintly leaders. The abbot of Cluny, Saint Odo (879–942), came from a noble family and was a highly educated man when he decided to enter Cluny as a mere monk, bringing his library of a hundred books with him. His personal holiness and strong leadership revitalized the abbey. Saint Odilo (962–1049) served as abbot of Cluny for fifty years, during which time he made his abbey into a model of holy life and service of the poor. He famously developed the "Truce of God", in which he somehow managed to convince feudal leaders to cease their military hostilities for holy days, allowing ordinary people to be able to survive the constant fighting of the times. Saint Hugh (1024–1109) was another great abbot of Cluny who spoke out against simony and lay investiture, but who also focused his monks on their greatest work: prayer and worship. Blessed Peter the Venerable (1092–1156) became abbot when Cluny had already become the model of monastic life in Europe; his strong leadership and literary output—commentaries, sermons, poems, and even a Latin translation of the Koran to assist Catholic missionaries—were a powerful influence on the Church. The effect of this one monastery was so widespread that it is often called the Cluniac reform.

Other saints tried to revive the devout practice of religious life in other ways. From the tenth century to the twelfth century, new orders arose, generally using the Rule of Life practiced by the Benedictine order as a foundation. The Camaldolese, Carthusian, Cistercian, and Norbertine orders all had unique charisms specific to their founders' vision of how to reform monastic life based on the challenges of the surrounding culture.[7] When Saints Francis of Assisi and Dominic de Guzman later established their mendicant orders in the thirteenth century, one of their most important—and controversial—decisions was to address the problem of wealth and power head-on by requiring their followers to take a vow of poverty.

In the sixteenth century, leaders of Protestantism publicly ridiculed the practice of religious life, not without cause in the case of individuals who were failing to live out their vows. The official response from the Church to their valid (and invalid) complaints—though a long time in coming—came through the documents of the Council of Trent (1545–1563). In the meantime, the Holy Spirit provided another response to their arguments through the saints.

While Saint Teresa of Avila (1515–1582) did not establish the Discalced Carmelites as a direct response to Martin Luther, her recognition that a simpler, more prayerful, and poorer way of life would bring greater sanctity to the women and men who followed it was a powerful rediscovery of a truth that had been lost in some religious houses. At the same time when Teresa was facing incredible social pressure for daring to reform the Carmelite order in Spain, Saint Philip Neri (1515–1595) was transforming the city of Rome with the Oratorians,

[7] See the previous chapter on religious orders, "Leaving the World Behind".

a congregation of priests and lay brothers who were not bound by vows—except the bond of charity—but who inspired Catholics to personal conversion through spiritual conferences and lived example.

On the other side of the world, the discovery of the New World had revealed a new continent of people who had never heard the Good News of Jesus Christ, as well as opened doors to the known but previously almost inaccessible continent of Asia. In addition to inspiring established religious orders such as the Franciscans to evangelize these peoples, the Holy Spirit raised up a new order to help with this task. Unlike religious houses focused primarily on serving in a particular location, the Jesuit order was formed by Saint Ignatius of Loyola (1491–1556) with an important difference. In addition to the usual vows of poverty, chastity, and obedience, he added a fourth vow to go wherever the pope should decide the Jesuits were needed. And they were needed all over the globe.

In the sixteenth and seventeenth centuries, another innovation arose: clerks regular. Responding to the needs of the times, groups of priests gathered together to live and serve specifically as priests, not as monks or itinerant friars. Saint Cajetan (1480–1547), for example, was an Italian priest from a noble family. When Protestant reformers made public criticisms about the weak practice of the faith, particularly by the clergy, he established the Theatine Clerks Regular, using the lifestyle of the apostles as a basis for their way of life. The devotion, preaching, and intellectual rigor that his Theatine priests modeled to Catholics not only inspired greater fervor among the laity but also inspired greater discipline among the priests.

Clearly, developments in religious life have occurred as a direct response to the needs of the culture and time in which those people lived. It remains to be seen how the Holy Spirit will redirect the practice of religious life to meet modern and future challenges.

Taking vows

To understand the basics of religious life, it might help to think about a popular bumper sticker saying: Practice random acts of kindness.[8]

---

[8] Yes, bumper stickers are very brief and can be interpreted many ways. Two obvious interpretations are used in the example.

Imagine yourself in your car, stuck in stopped traffic on a highway, facing a car with this bumper sticker. You decide to practice a random act of kindness by letting a merging car enter into the lane in front of you. So far, assuming the action was legal and safe, that could be considered an act of Christian charity. But, thirty seconds later, as another car attempts to merge into your lane, you decide to emphasize the word "random" in that statement, saying no to this car by cutting him off.

Believe it or not, this pedestrian example demonstrates why the Catholic Church allows and encourages men and women to take vows concerning religious life, contrary to Protestant arguments about the lack of necessity for religious vows. Left to our own (fallen) natures, we will be only as charitable as we feel like being at a given moment. On the other hand, when we have taken a formal vow, signed a contract, or performed some other public, sincere, or significant decision to do (or not do) something, we hold ourselves to a much higher standard. Even if we encounter a cantankerous, grumpy religious who fails completely in his behavior to act in a charitable manner, at least that difficult person is like a marathon runner trying to reach a high goal, rather than like a jellyfish, moved to and fro by emotions and random events.

The first two vows of religious life are clearly given by Christ Himself: poverty and chastity. While He could have been born into luxury, He lived the first thirty years of His life in a small village working at simple manual labor.[9] When He called His disciples to follow Him, it was to follow Him in a life where food was sometimes scarce,[10] people were not always welcoming,[11] and clothing and other property was limited.[12] His most famous failure was Judas, who became a thief[13] perhaps because he was unsettled by this uncomfortable way of life.

Our Lord was just as clearly and counterculturally chaste. Although there were some communities of Jewish men and women living apart from other people during Jesus' lifetime, they were not common.

[9]Lk 3:23.
[10]Mk 8:1.
[11]Lk 4:29.
[12]Mk 6:8–9.
[13]Jn 12:6.

Jewish people, then and now, assume that the normal, God-approved vocation for men and women is married life. Ludicrous modern fiction notwithstanding, it is clear from the Bible that Jesus never married—precisely because there are zero references to Him ever having a wife, and it would have been unremarkable and easy for the biblical authors to mention this if He had. On the contrary, in His own Person, He showed us that living a celibate life, though possible only with God's grace, is a gift that a person can freely choose to give to God.

That, after all, is the key ingredient to any sort of religious life. Men and women accept God's call to set aside good, natural desires for married life and financial responsibility to make their lives into gifts to God. Without God's call and a willing yes, religious life is not possible.

Another important vow for religious life is the vow of obedience. This vow to obey orders from one's superior is not completely countercultural, since members of the armed forces, the police, and even elected officials generally take some sort of oath that they will discharge their office according to given rules. Promising to obey orders may sound like a limitation on one's personal freedom, but few people would argue that it helps a team of soldiers work together more efficiently in difficult circumstances. In religious life, this vow of obedience helps the entire community work together toward their common goals, and it also teaches humility. That is, the monk who has vowed to obey his superiors has recognized that he trusts his order or community and those in the hierarchy above him to make good decisions about his physical, mental, and spiritual life, and he has chosen to let go of making those decisions for himself. The fact that he trusts his superiors, however, doesn't mean that obedience is always easy.

Sometimes the humility that comes with such holy obedience can be a trial in itself. Innumerable saints have been blessed with a knowledge of their own limitations and have humbly declined when offered a more important or powerful position. Saints Ambrose of Milan (340–397), Chad of Mercia (seventh century), and Raymund of Peñafort (1175–1275) were not lazy or practicing false modesty when they resisted being promoted to the office of bishop. They were aware of their own weaknesses and were afraid that they would serve God poorly if they were given greater responsibility. But each one of these men accepted, under obedience, the call of the Church to more demanding service, and they brought their trust in God, not pride in their own abilities, to their new positions.

The life of Saint Euphrasia (380–420) gives us an example of obedience that can be more easily applied to daily life. According to tradition, Euphrasia was born into the family of the Roman emperor, and her father died when she was young. Her mother took Euphrasia with her when she decided to live a solitary life as a widow near a convent in Egypt. When she was old enough, Euphrasia herself decided to become a nun, even asking her relative the emperor to give away the property she had inherited. At first, she was very happy in this life, but in time, she began to wonder about the comfortable life she had turned down. Her imaginings became a temptation. Fortunately, her abbess was a very wise woman. She ordered Euphrasia to move a pile of rocks from one corner of the convent to the other. When that was completed, the abbess told her to move the rocks back. This happened thirty times. By humbling herself to accept a ridiculous order out of obedience to her superior, Euphrasia learned the freedom and joy that come from accepting obedience to authority. When we have to perform the modern equivalent of pointless, annoying tasks, all out of obedience to our superiors, we can ask Saint Euphrasia to help us do that as promptly and cheerfully as she moved piles of rocks.

As is shown by the example of Saint Euphrasia, the decision to enter religious life needs to be affirmed again and again, just as married couples have to remind themselves repeatedly about their marriage vows during the ups and downs of ordinary life. A man and a woman considering marriage should spend time getting to know each other and seriously consider whether they are ready to marry this person at this time. Similarly, entering religious life requires time and consideration.

Another common vow of religious life for some orders, the vow of stability, may seem odd to modern sensibilities. After all, globalization and the internet make it easy for any layperson to assume that the next job offer might come from the other side of the world and a major relocation may be necessary. But when a monk (or nun) makes a vow of stability, he is promising to remain in a given location, within a particular community of individuals, following specific rules, for the rest of his life. Making such a decision means that he is personally committed to that way of life, and it should be done precisely because he recognizes that he's "home", that is, in the exact place that God wants him to be. In addition to the positive benefits for the monk, who can experience this decision as a joy and a relief, there are benefits for the community. If a monk was not asked to take a vow of stability, it would be easy for him to move repeatedly from monastery to monastery, always trying to find a "more perfect" community, proving that those in religious life are just as tempted by "the grass is always greener on the other side of the fence" mentality as the rest of us.

On the other hand, stability is meant to be a means by which a person grows in holiness, not an absolute good to be obeyed at all costs. Saint John Gualbert (d. 1073) left his Benedictine monastery with a few other monks, apparently because of a scandal over the election of a new abbot. His decision to leave his monastery bore fruit when he established a new house of monks and a new order now known as the Vallombrosan[14] Benedictines.

However, taking a vow of stability places a limit on some activities, and the founders of the mendicant orders sought to avoid those limits when they established their orders in the thirteenth century and omitted the vow of stability. The great Italian Saint Francis of Assisi famously experienced a great awakening to the joy of total dependency on God when he gave away everything he had down to every bit of his clothing. His decision to renounce wealth also opened his eyes to the blessings of poverty, which allowed him to travel the countryside to preach the Gospel and even to foreign lands as a peacemaker and evangelist to Muslims. Saint Dominic de Guzman of Spain similarly set aside the benefits of the vow of stability in his Dominican order to pursue evangelical poverty better and to be better able to teach and preach the Gospel wherever it was needed.

Similarly, Saint Ignatius of Loyola saw that the way God was calling him and his Society of Jesus to serve the Church required a different approach. Rather than preaching the Gospel within the existing churches and dioceses of the sixteenth century, Ignatius saw that his Jesuits, with the proper training, could go wherever the

---

[14] Vallombrosa was the location of the first monastery.

Church—according to the decision of the pope—needed them. Jesuit Saint Francis Xavier (1506–1552) brought the Gospel to India, Japan, and almost to China. Another Jesuit, Saint Peter Faber (1506–1546), stayed closer to home, preaching and bringing people back to the Church from Lutheranism in Spain, France, Germany, and Portugal. Many priests trying to bring the teachings of the Church to a bitterly anti-Catholic England during the sixteenth and seventeenth centuries entered the Jesuit order, including martyr-saints Edmund Campion and Henry Morse. Some Catholic priests went through the training to become Jesuits while they were in prison, proving that the Gospel can be shared anywhere.

Agnes Bojaxhiu (1910–1997) had already become a teaching sister and was living in India when God called her to do more. We know her now as Saint Teresa of Calcutta, and she added a fourth vow to the vows of the order she founded. The sisters, brothers, and priests of the Missionaries of Charity now take a vow to "serve the poorest of the poor" every day of their lives.

Thus, every order establishes vows and guidelines designed to better serve their primary mission within the Body of Christ. An order's foundational rules are like guideposts to help the order's members remain faithful to the specific charism of their order.

Choosing the road less traveled

While we tend to think of "priest" and "monk" as the only vocations available for men who want to serve God, "brother" is another option.

The term "friar" comes from the French word for "brother", and many holy men have been called by that title without becoming priests. Besides Saint Francis of Assisi, who famously refused to become a priest out of humility, Blessed John of Fiesole (1387–1455) remained a mere friar during his life. But he is better known today to the secular world as Fra Angelico, a great Italian painter of the Renaissance who used his artistic skills to serve God while living a holy life as a Dominican friar.

Saint John of God (b. 1495) had lived a rootless life as a shepherd and soldier—narrowly escaping death for dereliction of duty on one occasion—when he tried to settle down and live a more faithful life in Granada, Spain. His deep repentance over his past sins led him to become a servant of the sick in the hospital, and he eventually founded an order of brothers to serve sick people, an order that spread all over the world.

Saint Michael Febres Cordero (1854–1910) was educated by a religious order, the Brothers of the Christian Schools, and he decided to join that order and become a teacher as an adult, despite his family's opposition. In his native Ecuador and later in Spain, he became a prolific writer about evangelization and educational methods. Years after his death by pneumonia, his body was found to be incorrupt, and two miraculous healings resulting from his intercession caused him to be named a saint.

All these men emphatically chose to become brothers, not priests, precisely because they heard God calling them to serve in that way. Similarly, God has called women to renounce the more common path of marriage and motherhood to become "brides of Christ" and to serve Him in a very countercultural and unexpected manner.

Saint Brigid of Ireland (435–c. 525) is justifiably famous for becoming a nun, inspiring many other women to follow her into religious life, and serving as abbess over the many convents she founded. Ireland had only recently come to the Catholic faith, largely as a result of the evangelizing work of the great bishop Saint Patrick of Ireland (385–461). But Brigid did not start out with such a promising future. Yes, her father was a pagan king, but her mother was a Christian slave who belonged to him, and since her mother was sold before Brigid's birth, Brigid was later returned to her father because he was also her owner. The life of a female slave in an Ireland that was still partly Christian and partly pagan could have been a tragedy. But Brigid seems to have been deeply devout and fervently Catholic almost from birth. She was precociously tenderhearted and extremely generous with the poor. Her sweet disposition may have inspired her father to free her from slavery, and, according to tradition, God rewarded her sacrificial giving to the poor by miraculously blessing the success of her mother's dairy business. This eventually allowed Brigid's mother to purchase her own freedom. Her father, the king, even offered to arrange a marriage for Brigid, but she had already fallen in love with the King of Kings.

Saint Katharine Drexel (1858–1955) came from a completely different time, place, and family. Her culture—nineteenth-century Philadelphia—was solidly Christian, and her family was very wealthy.

Her parents were devout Catholics who lived out their faith, both through financial support of the needy and hands-on service of the poor in their community. Katharine was acquainted with many powerful leaders, in the world and in the Church. She asked for a favor for one of them, the bishop of Wyoming, from the pope himself when she was invited to a papal audience in 1887. She begged the pope to send missionaries to help Native Americans, but the pope responded by challenging her to become a missionary herself. Katharine recognized God's call in the pope's words, so she became a sister, founded an order of sisters to teach and serve Native Americans and black Americans, and poured her entire fortune into making it happen.

Many men and women have become holy men and women by leaving the world behind and entering religious orders as brothers, sisters, and nuns. However, from the lives of the saints, we can see that it is not always easy, possible, or perhaps necessary to leave one's family behind to serve God and grow in holiness.

When Saint Francis of Assisi founded his order of Friars Minor, he may never have expected that women would want to follow the same way of life. But, following in the footsteps of Saint Clare of Assisi, they did; those two orders are sometimes known as First Order Franciscans (for men) and Second Order Franciscans (for women). In time, laymen decided that they wanted to live their daily lives according to Francis' spirituality too, and they became known as Third Order Franciscans or tertiaries. This nomenclature became more common, and several religious orders now offer this third way for laymen to join in the spiritual life of the order.

Saint Catherine of Siena is perhaps the most famous tertiary saint in the history of the Church, but she is certainly not the only one. Saint Rose of Lima (1586–1617) lived a deeply devout and penitential life as a Dominican tertiary in Peru, yet she lived with her family, not in a convent, and had a profound effect on the spiritual life of her neighbors and community. Saint Angela of Foligno (1248–1309) lived a life that was far from devout before the deaths of her husband and children; after a profound conversion, she became a Franciscan tertiary in Italy and became known as a mystic and spiritual writer. Blessed Anna Maria Taigi (1769–1837) was similarly an ordinary married woman with children before she underwent a spiritual conversion and became a Trinitarian tertiary in Rome. Not only did she experience mystical visions and give advice to popes and bishops, but she also helped her own family members become more virtuous and devout, an accomplishment perhaps just as miraculous. Not all tertiaries became canonized saints through mystical experiences though. Some tertiaries from Japan, Vietnam, and England earned that title by dying as martyrs for their faithfulness as members of the underground Church.

Becoming religious

Every religious order or religious house in the history of the Church has a process, more formal or less formal, by which it allows new members to join. In today's world, a prospective member is commonly called a postulant. A postulant who has convinced both himself and his superiors that he may have a vocation to such a life becomes a novice. After completing the novitiate, the person is accepted into the order and becomes a full-fledged member.[15]

Considering the precipitous drop in religious vocations at the end of the twentieth century, one might suppose that this process of entering a religious order has been shortened or made easier to encourage more men and women to join. But religious orders are no more interested in having unsuitable, unhappy, lifelong members than businesses are interested in having unsuitable, unhappy, short-term employees. This caution in accepting candidates can occur for many reasons. Saint Eustochia Calafato (1434–1491) was turned down at first when she tried to enter a Poor Clares convent because her brothers threatened to burn it down if she tried to become a nun. In time, she calmed them down and was accepted. Saint Rita of Cascia (1381–1457) was turned down repeatedly because she was a widow, and they accepted only virgins. She prayed, persevered, and eventually won them over. Saint Antoninus of Florence (d. 1459) wanted to become a Dominican, but the abbot clearly thought he was too young or uneducated. He told Antoninus to go study a specific Latin document, probably assuming that the young man would tire of it

---

[15] Different orders sometimes use different terms and often have different lengths of time and criteria for each stage.

and go away. A year later, Antoninus returned, having memorized the entire thing. The abbot immediately changed his mind.

But for some saints, being refused turned out to be a good decision and a great blessing. If Saints Louis and Zelie Martin had not been refused when they tried to enter religious life in nineteenth-century France, they wouldn't have married and given the world five saintly daughters, including Saint Thérèse of Lisieux. Saint Joseph of Cupertino (1603–1663) was refused by not one but two religious houses; when he was allowed to become a mere servant at a third religious house, it seems to have helped him grow in spiritual maturity and humility. He was finally accepted as a Conventual Franciscan and became a priest with great spiritual gifts. More humorously, Saint Rose of Viterbo (1234–1253) tried repeatedly to enter a nearby convent but was always refused. When she died a holy death, revered as a saint by those around her, the pope gave her justice and ordered that same convent to bury her in their cemetery.

A final example proves that being unable to enter religious life is no barrier to great sanctity. Saint Benedict Labre (1748–1783) was rejected by three strict religious orders. God inspired him to become a lifelong pilgrim instead. To some, he appeared to be nothing but a smelly, homeless man as he traveled all over Europe, praying in churches with an intense devotion to our Lord in the Blessed Sacrament. The number of miracles that happened during his lifetime—cures, levitation, and multiplication of food—was exceeded only by the number (more than a hundred) that occurred soon after his death.

But there is more to be said about religious life, and it can be examined through the example of religious women.[16]

Wise virgins

In Matthew 25:1–13, Jesus tells a parable of ten maidens on their way to a wedding feast. Five prepare for the coming of the bridegroom; five do not. When the bridegroom arrives, only the former five are ready for him. Jesus concludes the parable by saying, "Watch therefore, for you know neither the day nor the hour."

---

[16] Note the difference between religious sisters and nuns, as described in the table describing the terms used in religious life in the following section.

In a modern wedding, the bridesmaids rejoice with the bride over her engagement, talk over the details of her wedding plans, prepare for the great day by adjusting their schedules and getting fitted for their dresses, and make sure they are ready for the big day when it comes. Every Christian should do the same; we should rejoice over the Good News that Christ has come to save us, talk with Him frequently about our daily plans, prepare to meet Him by pursuing a life of virtue, and make sure we are ready for the eventual day when He arrives—either at death or when Christ comes in glory for the second time to judge the world.

Since the earliest days of the Church, wise women have taken that parable as a description of their vocation and chosen some sort of life of consecrated virginity, living in this state "for the sake of the kingdom of Heaven".[17]

On the surface, the most obvious female saints to consider as "wise virgins" would be those whose wisdom was respected even by powerful contemporaries. Saint Catherine of Siena (1347–1380) famously counseled multiple popes, even though she complained privately that the smell of sin hanging around the papal Curia was so strong that it made her ill. Saint Teresa of Avila (1515–1582) was actually feared by some civil and religious leaders, one of whom privately said that he would rather discuss theological matters with any number of learned men than debate with her. (Why? Because she asked questions that he couldn't answer.) Saint Hildegard of Bingen (1098–1179) did more than describe her mystical visions and write hymns; she wrote works about science, medicine, and Church doctrine, and she was even sent on preaching tours around Germany to explain the faith. All these saintly women were greatly respected for their wisdom.

But the parable of the wise virgins does not teach us that it is important to be thought wise by powerful men or that wisdom comes from being rich and powerful. Those are the lies of our modern world: that being a woman means trying to be like a man and that being a *successful* woman is rooted in having power over others. On the contrary, many saintly women show us that the power and wisdom of God becomes manifest in our lives precisely when we accept our calling as sons and daughters of God, however He calls us.

---

[17] Mt 19:12; see also *CCC* 922.

Saint Bertilla Boscardin (1888–1922) became a member of the Sisters of Saint Dorothy in Italy as a young woman. She came from a peasant family, so she had little education and was initially given various tasks around the convent. Though her superiors did not always recognize her true vocation, Bertilla did. That is, she recognized that her true vocation lay in being a nursing sister. Her patients, particularly children, adored her for her kindness and devotion. She was an anchor of strength to those around her during World War I, as she cheerfully performed her duties and prayed her Rosary even when bombs were dropping outside the hospital. She suffered from a painful sickness for twelve years, but she bore it with incredible peace. Crowds of people, many of whom had personally been cared for by the holy sister, came to her grave, where multiple miracles occurred.

Many people recognize Saint Catherine Laboure (1806–1876) as the nun who received a vision of the Blessed Mother and whom Mary instructed to make and distribute a medal with her image on it. Many people also know that this medal is now called the Miraculous Medal because so many miracles have occurred as a result of men and women choosing to wear the medal out of devotion. While the most famous miracle resulting from wearing the medal was the complete conversion of a skeptical Jewish man who later became a priest, there have been multiple other inexplicable cures, healings, and conversions. However, Catherine Laboure is not *Saint* Catherine Laboure because she saw a vision. She is considered a saint because she lived a holy, simple life as a sister in her community and obeyed her superiors, which involved caring for the elderly and answering the door of the convent to admit visitors. Rather than letting the heavenly gift of visions of the Blessed Mother become an occasion of pride, she told her superior about her visions only a few months before her death. The sisters in her convent knew nothing of her relationship to the Miraculous Medal and thought she was no one special. Precisely because she was too humble to profit personally from a worldwide spiritual phenomenon, she showed that she understood the virtue of simply doing her duty to God without fanfare.

Saint Teresa Couderc (1805–1885) became the superior of a new religious order of sisters when she was only twenty-three years old. She and her sisters had the innovative mission of organizing retreats for women in southeastern France. When a financial setback to the order occurred, she blamed herself; the bishop apparently blamed her too because he replaced her as superior with a wealthy widow who had only recently joined the order. For the rest of her life, Teresa was a simple sister in the order, working in the background and generally forgotten as the foundress. On one occasion, a cardinal came to visit. He recognized holiness in Teresa's face; when he did not see her later among the other sisters, he had to ask where the sister who'd been left out was. But Teresa had spent her life praying and making sacrifices for the success of the order—so that other women would be spiritually blessed and strengthened through the sisters' work—and that was enough for her.

Our Lord Jesus Christ, though by far the wisest man on earth during His lifetime, was not invited to advise great rulers, give lectures to great thinkers, or lead mighty armies. The wisdom of Christ was shown in His acceptance of the Cross, not in receiving worldly honors. It would be ridiculous to believe that His followers should not be just as humble.

Saint Teresa Benedicta of the Cross (1891–1942) was a brilliant philosopher and teacher before becoming a Catholic nun and dying as a martyr in Auschwitz. In one of her essays on the role of women, she wrote:

Only the person blinded by the passion of controversy could deny that woman in soul and body is formed for a particular purpose. The clear and irrevocable word of Scripture declares what daily experience teaches from the beginning of the world: woman is destined to be both wife and mother.[18]

Those might seem to be startling words since they come from a woman who never married or had children. But as Saint Teresa Benedicta and all the "wise virgins" mentioned above would agree, one's vocation does not change one's biology. Or to use a more common phrase, grace builds on nature.

A Catholic woman who marries and has children has a God-given vocation to love and serve God and to love and serve her husband and children. That is, she daily looks for ways to care for and build up the members of her family and community, much as is described in the thirty-first chapter of the book of Proverbs, through ordinary activities.

[18] Edith Stein, *Essays on Woman*, 2nd ed., rev. (Washington, DC: ICS Publications, 1996), p. 45.

That may include bargain-hunting, making meals to please (at least some) of her family members, listening to their problems, praying with and for them, and actively planning ways to help them become the people God calls them to be.

A Catholic woman who accepts God's call to religious life takes Jesus Christ as her Bridegroom. She puts Him first in her heart, abandoning all others. Her "family" consists of those people that her way of life has placed before her. Generally, that includes other members of her order and community, but those are not her only "spiritual children". Saint Bertilla poured her heart into the sick and dying children in her ward. Saint Catherine Laboure showed compassion for the needy and suffering people who came to her convent for support. Saint Teresa Couderc did not allow the ridicule of other sisters—who'd been told lies about her and her role in the order—to make her bitter, but instead treated them all with charity. As for Saint Teresa Benedicta, she explicitly accepted her arrest and execution by the Nazis because of her Jewish ancestry as a suffering she offered for the entire Jewish people. Witnesses later said that on the crowded train that took her to the concentration camp, some mothers were so distraught and hopeless that they sat in shock and ignored their own children. Teresa cared for those children with the compassion of a mother, just as one would expect from a wise virgin on her way to meet her Bridegroom.

Terms used in religious life

The following terms are commonly used in aspects of religious life. Religious life is also described in the *Catechism of the Catholic Church*.[19]

What Is the Person Called?	Description
Postulant	Postulancy is typically the first stage for a prospective member of a religious order. The amount of time spent as a postulant varies based on the order.

---

[19] CCC 914–33.

What Is the Person Called?	Description
Novice	A novice is a person who has completed the stage of postulancy. Typically, the novice is clothed in a modified form of the order's habit. The amount of time spent as a novice varies based on the order.
Brother	A brother, also called a lay brother, is a member of a religious order or community who has taken solemn vows. Saint André Bessette was a religious brother of the Congregation of the Holy Cross in Canada and died in 1937.
Nun	A nun typically takes solemn vows and lives in a cloistered community. Saint Elizabeth of the Trinity was a twentieth-century Carmelite nun.
Sister	A sister typically takes simple vows and serves outside her convent. Saint Joan de Lestonnac was a religious sister of the Sisters of the Company of Mary who died in the seventeenth century in France.
Canon	A canon is a member of a group of clerics living according to a Rule of Life. Saint Hugh of Grenoble was an Augustinian Canon before becoming a bishop in the eleventh century,
Hermit	A hermit (male or female) lives a simple life away from others, typically supporting himself through manual labor. Saint Peter Orseolo was a political leader in Venice, Italy, in the tenth century before he became a hermit.
Anchorite	An anchorite lives a more radical form of hermitic life. Saint Pachomius the Great was an anchorite during the fourth century in Egypt.
Cenobite	A cenobite is a monk or nun who lives in a religious community. Saint John Cassian is one of the earliest and most famous cenobites.
Friar or mendicant	A friar or mendicant is a member of a religious order that involves a more rigorous life of poverty. Saint Simon Stock helped turn the Carmelite order into a mendicant order in the thirteenth century in England.

(continued)

What Is the Person Called?	Description
Prior or prioress	A prior is a superior in a monastic order; the female form of the name is prioress. Saint John de Sahagun was a prior in fifteenth-century Spain.

Other Terms Associated with Religious Life	Description
Religious order or religious institute[20]	The members of a religious order traditionally take vows of stability, poverty, chastity, and obedience.
Second Order	The feminine counterpart to a religious order is sometimes called a Second Order.
Third Order	An association of laypeople within a religious order is often called a Third Order or tertiary.
Rule of Life	The Rule of Life is the plan of life followed by a religious order.
Constitution	A constitution is the fundamental code followed by the members of a religious order.
Solemn vows	Members of a religious order may take solemn vows, which are absolute and irrevocable; ownership of property is prohibited, as well as marriage.
Simple vows	Members of a religious order may take simple vows temporarily or perpetually; ownership of personal property is allowed.

Institutes of consecrated life

For many centuries, most religious orders would be classified as what are currently known as religious institutes, that is, communities where

[20] In the past, canon law distinguished between religious orders and religious congregations, based on whether members took solemn vows or simple vows. At present, "institute", "order", and "congregation" are terms that can be used interchangeably to refer to all such groups.

most or all members take vows. In recent centuries, the Church began to recognize communities of people who do not take vows when they join, which are called secular institutes and societies of apostolic life.

For example, the priests, nuns, and laypeople who are members of the Franciscan orders are members of a religious institute. Secular institutes include the Company of Saint Ursula, founded by Saint Angela Merici in the sixteenth century in Brescia, Italy, as well as the Schoenstatt Apostolic Movement, founded by a German priest in 1914. The Daughters of Charity of Saint Vincent de Paul are members of a society of apostolic life.

The following chart shows how these terms are currently used by the Church, as defined by the Congregation for Institutes of Consecrated Life and Societies of Apostolic Life.[21]

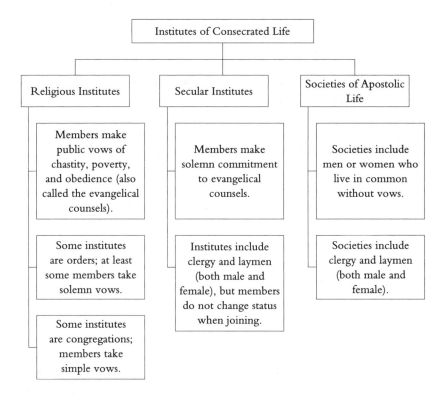

Institutes of Consecrated Life		
Religious Institutes	Secular Institutes	Societies of Apostolic Life
Members make public vows of chastity, poverty, and obedience (also called the evangelical counsels).	Members make solemn commitment to evangelical counsels.	Societies include men or women who live in common without vows.
Some institutes are orders; at least some members take solemn vows.	Institutes include clergy and laymen (both male and female), but members do not change status when joining.	Societies include clergy and laymen (both male and female).
Some institutes are congregations; members take simple vows.		

[21] See the document on the Vatican's website at http://www.vatican.va/roman_curia /congregations/ccscrlife/documents/rc_con_ccscrlife_profile_en.html.

Marriage and Sanctity

There is one thing that most of the greatest saints of the Catholic Church have in common: they were not married. While the call to celibacy is one of the greatest vocations in the Church, that does not mean that the call to married life is a consolation prize for those who lack spiritual depth. Particularly in light of modern cultural misunderstandings of the meaning and purpose of marriage, it is helpful to begin an examination of married saints with an examination of Catholic marriage.

The Sacrament of Matrimony

The *Catechism of the Catholic Church* begins its excellent explanation of the Sacrament of Matrimony[1] by pointing out that God Himself created marriage and that the love between the man and the woman He created was meant to be an image of His unfailing love for them. Adam and Eve were supposed to love each other as God loved them. But from the moment sin entered into their hearts and into the world around them, it became easier for a human person to love self more than spouse. That selfishness inevitably leads to conflict.

Fortunately, God had a plan to repair all the damage due to man's sinfulness: Jesus Christ, who made a new and everlasting covenant with all of redeemed humanity. On the Cross on Calvary, Jesus laid down His life for His Bride—which is both the entire Church and each individual Christian—showing us the way out of a life dominated by sin. More than that, He showed us that marriage was redeemable too.

> On the threshold of his public life Jesus performs his first sign—at his mother's request—during a wedding feast (cf. Jn 2:1–11). The Church

[1] *CCC* 1601–66.

188

attaches great importance to Jesus' presence at the wedding at Cana. She sees in it the confirmation of the goodness of marriage and the proclamation that thenceforth marriage will be an efficacious sign of Christ's presence.[2]

Marriage is *good*. It is now possible for a man and a woman, both born under original sin, to remain sacramentally married for life. This is precisely because Christ Himself has restored creation and is ready to give one sinful person the strength and grace required to be married to another sinful person, which is no small feat.

While almost everyone lives in a family at some point during life, it is the saintly married couples who most clearly show us the power of the sacrament to conquer evil in our world, foster the good of both spouses, and nurture any children with whom they are blessed. And that is no consolation prize in our fallen world.

Living witnesses

Saint Macrina, her husband, and children were Christians living in Pontus (modern Turkey). When the Roman emperor[3] renewed the persecution of Christians in the early fourth century, both parents understood the danger. If they were discovered, they and their children would be arrested and threatened with torture and execution. What should a Christian parent do in such circumstances?

Macrina and her husband chose to run away from the city with their children and live in secret in the mountains near the Black Sea along the boundaries of the Roman Empire. This may sound like the Johann Wyss novel *The Swiss Family Robinson*, but the reality was far from idyllic fiction. Imagine taking your own family into the woods to live off the land in a deserted place and to be subject to arrest if found. The family almost starved to death more than once, lived in great isolation and poverty, and remained in hiding for seven years.

---

[2] *CCC* 1613.

[3] Sources differ on whether the persecution occurred during the reign of Diocletian, Maximian, or Galerius. Diocletian and Maximian were co-emperors and reigned at the same time over different regions; Galerius reigned after them. Christians were persecuted during the time periods covered by both reigns, which includes the years 284–311.

But through their perseverance and faith in Jesus Christ, they survived to see the end of the persecution of Christians.

Saint Macrina the Elder, as she is now known, had at least one son. He is known to us as Saint Basil the Elder; that man grew up to become a lawyer, marry a devout woman (now known as Saint Emmelia), and become the father of nine children. Of those nine children, five are considered to be saints of the Church: Basil the Great, Gregory of Nyssa, Peter of Sebaste, Naucratius, and Macrina the Younger. As was written by Saint Gregory of Nazianzus,[4] a great friend of Basil the Great who gave Basil's funeral oration, when so many children in a family grow up to be holy men and women, it's clear that one must give credit to the parents.

Almost a thousand years later, Blessed Louis of Thuringia and Saint Elizabeth of Hungary lived and reigned in what is now Germany. Both were born into nobility in the thirteenth century and agreed to an arranged marriage. Both were deeply devout Christians as well. Elizabeth is a canonized saint because of the heroic level to which she cared for the sick and poor, despite her wealth and position, even putting sick people into her own bed to care for them. Louis was a devout man who—unlike some other husbands of saintly women—encouraged his wife's generosity and was faithful both to her and to God. Louis chose to become one of the leaders on a crusade to the Holy Land, though he died of a fever before he was able to leave Europe. Louis' brother then took over the throne of Thuringia and evicted Elizabeth, though she accepted rejection with great humility and trust in God, dying only a few years later.

The children of these two couples did not need weekly CCD classes or youth retreats to learn how to live as adult Christians; their parents had already made profound, life-changing sacrifices in front of their very eyes. Those children knew the reality of poverty and grief, but because of their parents' Christian witness, they knew that true riches and joy come from living for God.

---

[4] Gregory of Nazianzus, *Oration* 43, 28, trans. Charles Gordon Browne and James Edward Swallow, in *Nicene and Post-Nicene Fathers*, 2nd series, vol. 7, ed. Philip Schaff and Henry Wace (Buffalo, NY: Christian Literature Publishing, 1894). Revised and edited for New Advent by Kevin Knight, NewAdvent.org, 2021, http://www.newadvent.org/fathers/310243.htm. Some brief descriptions of Macrina can also be found in Saint Basil the Great's *Letter* 204 and Saint Gregory of Nyssa's "Life of Saint Macrina", which focuses on the death of Saint Macrina the Younger.

Living the Gospel

All Christians are called to live the Gospel in their daily lives; unfortunately, only the saints do that well. But married saints are great examples of how to bring Christ's teachings to everyday life.

Saints Isidore and Mary were a married couple living in the late eleventh century in Madrid, Spain. Isidore was a peasant farmer working in the service of a wealthy landowner, and Mary was his wife. Though she bore him a son, the child died. The couple then mutually decided to live chastely, as brother and sister, for the rest of their lives.

Neighboring farmers in Madrid mocked Isidore for spending so much time praying and for being so generous with the poor when he was only a poor peasant himself. In time, their ridicule turned to puzzlement. Why did Isidore's fields produce more abundant crops than his neighbors' fields? In hindsight, we find it puzzling that they should be so surprised to find that God rewards those who make personal sacrifices out of love for Him. The people of Madrid later also acclaimed the wife of Saint Isidore the Farmer to be a saint when prayers for her intercession were miraculously answered during a drought. This resulted in her being given an unusual title: Saint Mary of the Head, because the relic of her head was processed through the town.

In 1347, Giacomo and Lapa di Benincasa became the parents of twin daughters in their home in Siena, Italy. One of the daughters died, but the other one—thanks be to God—survived and grew up to become one of the greatest saints of the Church, Saint Catherine of Siena.

Though the exact number sometimes varies in Saint Catherine's biographies, it appears that Lapa was a mother to twenty-five children, and, as was the case with the birth of those twins, about half of her children died while young. While death in childhood was a much more common occurrence in every age prior to the discovery of antibiotics, it cannot ever be easy for parents to lose a child. Add the noise, confusion, financial demands, and ordinary infighting of a family of more than ten children, and it is easy to see that the gift of fruitfulness in Giacomo and Lapa's marriage came at a price. Yet the many charming stories about Saint Catherine's childhood shows, indirectly, a family that lived and practiced their faith. Catherine had visions of Jesus Christ starting when she was five years old. Who taught her about Him? She said a prayer on each step of the staircase as she came down to breakfast. Who taught her to pray? She made a personal vow to consecrate her virginity to Christ when she was seven. How did she know such a practice existed for adults?

In the early twentieth century, Luigi Quattrocchi married Maria Corsini, and they made their home in Rome. He was a lawyer, and together they had four children. They both had successful careers; Luigi held various important positions in the government, and Maria was a professor and writer. Yet they prayed the Rosary daily as a family; attended daily Mass; served their community in many ways, such as sheltering refugees during World War II; encouraged their children in their vocations (three of them entered religious life); and gave their children the great gift of a joyful, happy home. For all these reasons and more, the Church acclaimed them as saints.

Although Giacomo and Lapa have not been declared saints of the Church, all three of these couples give us insights into how parents can live the Gospel in their families. During his homily at their beatification, Pope Saint John Paul II described Saints Luigi and Maria as having lived "an ordinary life in an extraordinary way".[5] By caring for the poor and needy in their communities, practicing their faith as a family, placing their fruitfulness in God's hands, accepting the crosses of daily living, and teaching their children about Christ and His Church, all Christian families can do likewise.

Gifts of the Holy Spirit

As has already been described in the previous chapter, Zelie Martin (1831–1877) and Louis Martin (1823–1894) were the parents of the great Saint Thérèse of Lisieux. They were also the first Catholic couple to be canonized at the same time in the history of the Church. One might be tempted to think that they were canonized simply

---

[5]John Paul II, Homily on the Beatification of the Servants of God Luigi Beltrame Quattrocchi and Maria Corsini, Married Couple (October 21, 2001), http://w2.vatican.va /content/john-paul-ii/en/homilies/2001/documents/hf_jp-ii_hom_20011021_beltrame -quattrocchi.html.

because their daughter was so holy. That would be wrong because there are many details in the lives of this holy couple that show the presence of the Holy Spirit in their lives, details that can benefit parents today.

One of the many ways that the Holy Spirit helps an individual Christian is through discernment. If we are docile to His promptings, the Spirit of God moves us in gentle, sometimes incomprehensible ways toward the goals that God Himself has set for us. Both Louis and Zelie were deeply devout when they were young and were open to potential religious vocations. Both actively pursued that option and asked to be accepted into religious life. Both were refused point-blank. Rather than becoming bitter over that rejection—note that they did not know each other yet—they simply turned their attention to a different moral obligation: finding employment. Louis became a watchmaker; Zelie became a lacemaker. One day, they passed each other on a bridge, and the Holy Spirit took over. They were married in 1858.

Zelie had grown up with an overbearing father and a distant mother. Although she wanted children, she lived in a culture so unlike our own that she apparently was not clear about how one went about the process of begetting children. Louis and Zelie initially came to the mutual decision that they would live as brother and sister after their marriage. Fortunately, a priest encouraged them to think otherwise about married life (the Holy Spirit must have again been present for such a delicate conversation to have taken place), and the couple eventually had nine children.

Zelie adored being a mother, and Louis was adored by his daughters. It cannot have been a trivial matter to such devoted parents that four of their nine children died young. One child, Helene, died at the age of five. Two sons, Joseph-Louis and Joseph-Jean-Baptiste, died before their first birthdays. Another daughter, Melanie-Therese, died when she was not yet two months old. Less than three years later, Zelie gave birth to her last child, Thérèse. Only God's grace can bring comfort in the presence of such painful losses.

Zelie developed breast cancer and traveled to Lourdes to pray for healing; she died when Thérèse was only four years old. Louis was able to see all five of his daughters grow up. He bravely accepted lifelong separation from four of them when they asked to enter cloistered religious life. He suffered two strokes, became mentally unstable (though still devout), and died three years later. Both parents suffered greatly during prolonged illness, yet they each maintained their deep faith in God throughout it all—yet another gift to their children.

Saint Thérèse has been acclaimed a Doctor of the Church based on her letters and her autobiography. She wrote this autobiography in three parts under obedience to her superiors. In her writings, we learn a great deal about Thérèse's faith, hope, and charity, most obviously through her "little way" of following Jesus. Thérèse's "little way" teaches us that one need not do great things—evangelize on the other side of the world, write detailed theological treatises, or govern large numbers of Catholics—to fulfill one's vocation. Each of us can simply look for seemingly ordinary ways to practice faith, hope, and charity in our daily lives, such as trusting in God when the pain of illness seems overwhelming, looking to Heaven when earthly honors are lost, and reaching out in kindness to those we find difficult. In her autobiography, Thérèse describes doing all these things. Not surprisingly, Thérèse's writings and family letters show that her parents did them too.

The gift of holy families

Although there are many saints who were opposed by their own parents when they pursued God's call to religious life, that is not always the case. Many of the Church's greatest saints had one of the greatest possible advantages from childhood: holy parents.

- Joan de Guzman was the beautiful wife of a Spanish governor in Spain in the twelfth century. Her holy personal life and spirituality caused her to be acclaimed Blessed Joan by the Church. An even greater proof of her holiness lies in the fact that her three sons all became holy priests, and the youngest, Saint Dominic, founded the Dominican order.
- Saint John Bosco's religious order serving boys in nineteenth-century Italy might never have existed if his mother, Venerable Margaret Bosco, had not encouraged his faith from a young age.

Margaret raised her two sons on her own when she was widowed at the age of twenty-nine; she spent the last ten years of her life as a surrogate mother to the boys living in the group home organized by her son.

- Saint Joseph Mary Tommasi faced an interesting dilemma while still a young man living in seventeenth-century Sicily. His wealthy father wanted to give all his wealth and his position to Joseph so that he could leave the world behind and enter religious life. Joseph somehow managed to talk his father into letting *him* enter the priesthood instead. Later, Joseph's mother and four sisters entered religious life too.

- We do not know the names of the parents of Chad, Cedd, Cynibil, and Caelin, but we do know that these four brothers were born in Northumbria in the seventh century and that all four became priests. Chad and Cedd became bishops and are now known as saints. Remember what Saint Gregory of Nazianzus wrote about the likely reason behind multiple siblings becoming holy adults?

- Blessed Bartolo Longo (1841–1926) had strayed so far from the Catholic faith in which his parents had raised him that he became a satanic priest when he was a young man. But his parents did not give up on Bartolo or on God. With the help of a Catholic priest and his parents' prayers, Bartolo returned to the faith and became a devout layman and leader of many spiritual and charitable works in Italy.

Saints Benedict and Scholastica prove that it is possible for siblings to do more than disagree with one another. They were born as twins into a noble Christian family in the year 480 in the Italian town of Nursia. Benedict ran away from his planned education in Rome while still a young man to avoid the immorality he found there. He became a monk and gradually developed the Benedictine Rule of Life that has been followed by thousands of monks since. Scholastica entered a convent as a young woman and eventually became the superior of a community of nuns near Montecassino. In a famous story, at one point Benedict went to see Scholastica for a brief visit. Following his own Rule carefully and minimizing time spent away from his cell, Benedict planned to return to his monastery the same day. Scholastica, apparently aware that she was not going to live much longer, bowed her head and prayed as he was about to leave. A storm arose that made travel dangerous, and Scholastica pluckily explained to Benedict that while he had refused her request for them to spend more time together, God had answered it. Brother and sister spent the rest of the evening drawing closer to God and to each other; she died a short time later.

God calls us all to be saints; it is clear that some Catholics have made it easier for their family members to hear and respond to that call.

Not-so-perfect families

While many canonized saints came from pious and intact families, not all were so blessed. Some learned to trust in God through less-than-perfect family dynamics.

When Saint Francis de Sales (1567–1622) left Geneva to try to bring fallen-away Catholics of the Chablais region of France back into the fold, his father was furious and wrote many angry letters to his son to dissuade him. He thought the assignment was too dangerous, and he was right. Francis was almost killed by assassins and wolves more than once. Eventually, his father calmed down. Saint Joseph of Cupertino (1603–1663) lost his father at a young age and was a failure when he tried to become a shoemaker, a Capuchin Franciscan brother, and a Conventual brother. His mother managed to convince another Franciscan friary to accept him as a servant, but only because she thought he was a nuisance and did not want him to come back home again.

But the patron saint—literally—of dysfunctional families is Saint Eugene de Mazenod (1782–1861). Eugene's mother was from a wealthy family, and his father was from an aristocratic but poor one. On paper, it was a good arrangement for both families. But his parents' stormy relationship eventually ended in divorce, which was very uncommon at that time in France. Eugene later said that he was torn between the life of wealth offered by his deeply unhappy family and the life of sacrifice and peace offered by the example of a holy priest. Eugene chose the latter and became a priest and the founder of a religious congregation.

In the lives of these imperfect families, we can find many encouraging signs. First, one need not be born into a happy family to become a holy person; God supplies what family may have omitted. Second, while we can never wish for any child to experience estrangement from his family, the experience of suffering can lead us closer to Christ. He has already promised to help us carry our crosses, particularly the most painful ones, and these saints were living witnesses to His faithfulness in trials.

This side of Heaven

Saint Rita of Cascia (1381–1457) is often called a patron saint for impossible cases. One might say this is so because she endured so much suffering in her family or because she lived through four vocations in her life: wife, mother, widow, and nun. Just as heroically, Rita earned her title because, by God's grace, she brought her abusive, unfaithful husband to repentance.

Her husband's conversion did not happen overnight, however. She had lived through eighteen years of an unhappy marriage, born him twin sons, and spent many years praying and witnessing through a life of Christian charity before, *finally*, her husband asked for her forgiveness. Shortly afterward, he was murdered, and then Rita prayed and witnessed to her sons, begging them not to seek revenge against their father's murderer. Her sons became ill, and, as Rita cared for them, they repented of their plans to kill their father's murderer. Then they, too, died. Because she was a widow, not a virgin, she was initially refused when she asked to enter a nearby convent, which she had desired since she was a young girl. Eventually, the nuns agreed to allow her to join them, and she lived a model life of humility, obedience, and deep prayer.

If Rita were the only saintly wife who had ever endured abuse from a cruel husband, it would still be a tragedy. But, sadly, Rita is not the only one.

Saint Catherine Fieschi of Genoa (1675–1737) also had a cruel and unfaithful husband whose conversion occurred only after he had spent himself into bankruptcy. Catherine gently led her husband back to the faith, and the couple lived as brother and sister for years. Saint Elizabeth of Portugal (1271–1336) was a princess of Spain when she married Denis, the king of Portugal. Her husband tolerated her deep prayer life and charity for the poor, but he, too, was repeatedly unfaithful to her. He also favored his illegitimate sons, which fed the jealousy of Elizabeth and Denis' legitimate son, almost leading to a civil war. Blessed Victoire Rasoamanarivo (1848–1894) of Madagascar was married for twenty-four years to her violent, unfaithful husband before he repented and asked for Baptism and her forgiveness shortly before his death. Blessed Elizabeth Canori Mora (1774–1825) was married to a Roman lawyer who abandoned her and their two children to live with his mistress. He was with his mistress when Elizabeth died, but, as she predicted, he repented after her death and even became a priest.

Most Catholics think of Saint Monica (322–387) as the mother who prayed her wayward son, Saint Augustine of Hippo, into the Church, and she certainly did that. But she was also the wife of Patroclus, an unfaithful, hot-tempered pagan, and it took many years for Monica to pray and lead her husband into the Church shortly before his death.

Perhaps one of the most tragic female saints in the Church is Saint Godelva of Gistel, who lived in eleventh-century Belgium. Her mother-in-law hated her and turned Godelva's husband, Bertulf, against her even before the wedding reception had ended. Godelva was locked in a tiny room and almost starved to death before she was able to escape. Through the intervention of the local bishop, Bertulf began to treat Godelva better for a time, but then he became abusive and paid two servants to drown his wife in a nearby pond. There was no proof of his involvement in the murder, but everyone knew he was responsible for the crime. Several years later, Bertulf's daughter by his second wife was cured of blindness through prayers for the intercession of Godelva, healing the girl and bringing Bertulf, finally, to repentance.

In Genesis 3:16, God warns Eve that her choice to disobey Him will lead to brokenness in the relationship between husband and wife, and that prediction has been fulfilled innumerable times throughout history. But when Jesus Christ showed us the way to destroy sin—through humble acceptance of our crosses and by following His magnificent example of perfect, self-sacrificing charity—He showed us how to break out of the spiral of hate caused by sinfulness. These seemingly powerless women showed themselves to be better Christians than their seemingly powerful husbands. And if, as Christ said, our Heavenly Father cares for every hair on our heads, He knows and cares about every harsh word, unfaithful act, and cruel gesture that these women endured out of love for Christ.

Just as sadly, it is likely that every person reading these stories personally knows a woman who has endured physical abuse and infidelity from her husband. The Sexual Revolution has multiplied the number of these dysfunctional relationships just as it has multiplied the number of modern STDs. To point out that specific Catholic women have been able, by God's grace, to remain faithful to abusive husbands and bring them to repentance and conversion is not to say that wives should accept mistreatment. The point is that God supplies the grace and wisdom we need to respond to every suffering—including the ones inflicted upon us by those who should be most caring—if we trust in Him.

Surprisingly, there does not seem to be a male corollary to these wounded wives in the list of canonized saints. In the history of the Church, there are a few male saints who left their wives for religious life, but the motives for those decisions are not clear. Perhaps past cultures are more likely to overlook adulterous wives; perhaps those details have been omitted; perhaps men do not share such painful, personal details with others as women generally do.

But there is one example from Scripture that shows such an abandonment is not impossible and shows the Judeo-Christian response. The prophet Hosea, who died around the year 750 B.C., married a woman named Gomer. She was repeatedly unfaithful to him, yet Hosea forgave her and repeatedly took her back as his wife. In the book that bears his name, Hosea explicitly connects the adultery of his wife to the idolatry of the Chosen People. This is not merely the anger of a betrayed husband. Hosea is pointing out a deeper truth; that is, God desires each person to be closely united to Him in the same way that a man and woman united in marriage become one. Therefore, adultery and idolatry are, in a sense, the same horrific sin.

Perhaps the lesson we can learn from all these saints is that their (and our) personal suffering is never overlooked by God and that He will, when we face Him, wipe away every tear from our eyes.[6]

[6]Rev 21:4.

Trust

Our Lord and Savior, Jesus Christ, did not have to be born into a family. Theologians have pointed out for millennia that, being the Son of God and Son of Man, Jesus could have perfectly fulfilled God's righteous anger against the sins of men and atoned for all our sins by something as simple as snapping His fingers. Jesus could have mysteriously materialized, *Star Trek* transporter-style, in the middle of the Temple, rather than being born in a stable. Since He proved that could walk on water and through doors, He could have levitated in the city of Jerusalem to prove His divinity. He could have made legions of angels visibly appear at His side to protect Himself from the Crucifixion.[7] He could have appeared out of nowhere on the first day of His ministry, with no history at all, which is apparently what some of the Jewish people expected Him to do.[8]

But He did none of those things. Instead, He chose to be born into a family. Not only an ordinary human family, but a poor one from an unknown village. The man and woman who were invited to become the father and mother of the Son of God were not mere props; they were and are the most perfect human examples of how to be a holy father and mother precisely because they were chosen to participate in the greatest and most holy human family that has ever existed.

Because we have heard the story of the Nativity so often, we overlook details that would have surprised Jesus' contemporaries. For example, the Old Testament tells us of other angels who were sent to announce the great news of a long-awaited pregnancy. Abraham was visited by three angels, one of whom predicted the pregnancy of his postmenopausal wife.[9] An angel visited Manoah and his wife to predict and explain the vocation of their future son, Samson.[10] In both those cases, the words of the surprised father and mother are completely human. Sarah laughed. Manoah thought he would die because he had seen God in the guise of one of His angels. Neither couple could immediately understand how the angel's prediction could be possible.

---

[7] Mt 26:53.
[8] Jn 7:27.
[9] Gen 18:1–15.
[10] Judg 13:2–25.

The Virgin Mary, however, did two profound things. First, though face-to-face with an angel and hearing a miraculous message, she listened and pondered his words before she responded.[11] Second, she asked for clarification—"How can this be?"[12]—and then accepted the angel's mysterious response without complaint, laughter, or fear.

The most well-known mystical dreamer and interpreter of dreams in the Old Testament is clearly Joseph,[13] one of the twelve sons of Israel. Yet, Joseph famously made an almost fatal mistake by chattering on about his dreams to his brothers. They understood exactly what those dreams meant and later sought to kill him. After all, it is not wise to tell your much older brothers that you had a dream in which they would bow down before you someday.

On the other hand, when Joseph of Nazareth dreamed of an angel telling him that Mary's child was the Savior of the world,[14] he did not need to go consult a holy man to interpret the dream. He not only discerned its meaning on his own but also he obeyed it. He trusted and believed a seemingly dangerous and sudden inspiration, precisely because he trusted and believed in God.

According to Mosaic Law, when a woman gives birth to a son, the son should be circumcised on the eighth day.[15] After forty days,[16] the woman should offer a sacrifice to make atonement for her uncleanness from the birth. One could argue that the Son of God did not need to be circumcised as a sign of His covenant with God and that the Immaculate Virgin Mary did not need to offer a sacrifice to be made clean from anything. But Joseph and Mary showed their humility by being obedient to the Law, and that humility was rewarded with prophetic encouragement about the Child from two strangers—Simeon and Anna[17]—in addition to the host of angels and shepherds who had previously been invited by God Himself to Jesus' birth.

Today's news is full of words and images showing us the dangers of being an immigrant. A father will typically take his family away from

[11] Lk 1:26–29.
[12] Lk 1:34.
[13] Gen 37:5–11.
[14] Mt 1:20–24.
[15] Lev 12:2–8.
[16] Lev 12:1–4.
[17] Lk 2:22–38.

their homeland only because he believes it is no longer a healthy, safe place for them. Traveling from one country to another poses risks from thieves, lack of access to food, and natural dangers. There is also no promise that the new country will be any safer.

Saint Joseph knew well enough that ancient pagan Egypt was not a spiritually welcoming place for Jews, although a Jewish community existed there; that is why the Jews had left during the time of the Exodus in the first place. Crossing a desert with a young child with any ancient form of transportation would have been difficult. But Joseph obeyed directions from an angel in a second,[18] third,[19] and fourth[20] dream unhesitatingly. While not every father is given angelic advice about how to protect his family, every Christian father can trust that, like He did for Saint Joseph, God will provide that advice if he learns to listen for it.

Every parent knows the terrifying fear of a lost child, even if it is only for a few moments. Mary and Joseph lost their child when He was twelve years old,[21] old enough for Him to have explained the reason for His disappearance beforehand. Though homilies often imply that Mary and Joseph were irate when they finally found Him, they had raised the Child Jesus for twelve years at this point and were probably mostly puzzled, once the shock and anxiety of the search ended. Their thoughts probably ran along the lines of "He was always such a *good* boy; what could have happened to make Jesus do such a thing?" But this episode, as with the other stories that we have about Jesus' early life, is not given to us for a superficial reading. Like the Blessed Mother, we should ponder[22] the truths that our Lord—and our children—teach us and keep them in our hearts.[23] For this is how God makes married men and women into saints.

---

[18] Mt 2:13–15.
[19] Mt 2:19–21.
[20] Mt 2:22–23.
[21] Lk 2:41–51.
[22] Lk 2:19.
[23] Lk 2:51.

Praying like the Saints

When the Gospels tell us that Jesus' disciples asked Him to teach them how to pray,[1] our eyes tend to glaze over because two thousand years of Christianity have drilled His answer into our memories. We think instantly of the Lord's Prayer, and maybe we even remember some insights we have learned from priests' homilies over the years. Jesus' answer is rightly important to us, but we overlook the importance of the question.

The apostles' query about how to pray was not a trivial question or a staged event. Jews weren't the only people who prayed—so did the pagans who lived among and around the Chosen People. Prayer is, after all, merely communication between God (or gods, for those who believe in multiple gods) and human beings. Communicating with a friend is called conversation; communicating with God is called prayer.

Just as a conversation between two friends depends a great deal upon the characteristics of each person as well as the relationship between the two, so prayer depends a great deal upon how the person trying to pray sees the God with whom he is trying to communicate.

Before examining the writings of holy men and women who have thought and taught about prayer over the centuries, it is important to point out that this subject is unlike the subject of the other chapters in this book. One can name all the popes in the history of the Church or list major religious orders. But because prayer is communication with our omnipotent, infinite God, the depths of prayer are inexhaustible. *Every* saint prayed, or he is not a saint, although God may choose to communicate with individuals in very different ways and at very different levels. All this chapter can do is introduce briefly some of the many people who can teach us about prayer from their own experiences.

[1] Lk 11:1.

Early Christian understanding of prayer

A Christian understanding of God defines the parameters for Christian prayer. For example, God is sometimes referred to as "Father" in the Old Testament, but the fatherhood of God is not a central teaching of Judaism. For that reason, when Jesus referred to God as "Father" and encouraged His followers to do the same, some of the faithful Jews listening to Him were scandalized. Islam sees Allah as the divine Master and all His creatures as mere servants or slaves. This is the opposite of how Jesus described God's tender care for His people.[2] In the polytheism of the ancient Greeks and Romans, the pagan gods were unpredictable and powerful and cared nothing about having relationships with mere mortals, unless it pleased them for some selfish reason. When you wanted to obtain a favor from a pagan god, you simply followed predetermined rules. For example, pagans believed that if you made an offering to a pagan god and something went wrong, perhaps accidentally, you simply had to sacrifice another animal, again and again if necessary, until you got it right in order to (hopefully) obtain the desired result. Or perhaps not even then, because the gods were known to be capricious and detached from humanity.

When our Lord came as the perfect revelation of God and His love for us, it was not only theology and morality that needed to be adjusted to this new understanding. The manner of prayer changed too.

We can easily see this in the New Testament letters written by Saints Peter, Paul, James, Jude, and John. They knew how faithful Jews prayed because they were faithful Jews, but their understanding of prayer developed through their experience of following Jesus. For example, Saint Peter quotes an Old Testament psalm to explain that God hears the prayers of those who act righteously,[3] as was believed by his Jewish listeners, but his explanation of what it means to be righteous points not to the Old Testament but to Christ's personal example in turning the other cheek.[4] Saint Paul frequently encourages the recipients of his letters by telling them that he is praying for them, emphasizing the importance of unity among the Christian

[2] Mt 5–7; Lk 12.
[3] 1 Pet 3:12.
[4] Mt 5:39; Lk 6:29.

faithful, as well as indicating that intercessory prayer is important to Paul and should be important to us.[5] Saint James explains the value of praying for those who are sick, as well as the real power that Christians wield when they pray.[6] Saint Jude tells us to "pray in the Holy Spirit", an expression that makes sense only in light of Trinitarian theology.[7] Saint John teaches that we should pray for those who are committing venial sin (a Christian concept) but (in a much-debated passage) indicates that praying for those who commit mortal sin is something rather different.[8]

After the death of the apostles, the Fathers of the Church developed our understanding of God, building on what they had learned from their predecessors. But in addition to developing theological terms through discussion, letters, councils, and debates, they taught us how to pray.

Saint Augustine of Hippo (354–430) is generally credited with writing the first autobiography, but his *Confessions* is the opposite of typical modern autobiographies, which tend to be self-congratulatory, self-aggrandizing, and self-centered. Augustine's reason for writing about his own life was not to further his political or financial success; he wrote his *Confessions* as a confession. That is, in this book, Augustine leads his reader through the course of his own life, frankly admitting his mistakes and sins, showing the reader how a Christian should examine his own sinfulness, and teaching the reader how to talk to God about those sins.

Large sections of the *Confessions* are extended prayers to God, in which Augustine debates theological points, asks God questions, and humbly asks for His forgiveness and help. Augustine not only invented a literary form, but he also shows us how to examine our lives and our sins with God. Along the way, since he was a brilliant theologian, he teaches us about God Himself.

One Father of the Church who is not acclaimed a saint—for reasons previously explained in this book—wrote so brilliantly about prayer that his writings are quoted in the Church's Divine Office. That man is Tertullian.

[5] For example, see Eph 3:16; Col 1:3; 1 Thess 1:2.
[6] Jas 5:13–16.
[7] Jude 20.
[8] 1 Jn 5:16.

In Tertullian's work *On Prayer*, he concludes his discussion of Christian prayer—as distinct from the kind of prayer practiced by all those who lived before the time of the New Testament—with a fiery exposition on the power of prayer. He explains that all creatures, from angels to birds to wild animals and even human beings, pray. "Who are you," Tertullian seems to say, "to think that you are too busy, too unimportant, or not suited to pray?" After all, our Lord Jesus Christ Himself prayed.

Tertullian also writes that our prayers are like walls of faith. That is, they are the means by which we protect ourselves from God's righteous anger and "vanquish" (Tertullian's word) God Himself. This is reminiscent of the patriarch Jacob's nighttime wrestling with God in prayer during a dangerous and uncertain moment of his life.[9] Just as it would be worthwhile for us to emulate Augustine's willingness to face his own sinfulness in prayer, so it would be worthwhile for us to emulate Tertullian's call to a persistent, no-holds-barred commitment to prayer.

Monks and nuns

How many Christian religious communities have arisen over the past two millennia! What a profound impact they have had not only on Christian living but also in secular life and even among nonbelievers!

There are many differences among Catholic religious orders. These differences may be very practical, as, for example, monks living in the desert may have different diets and support themselves in different ways than do those monks who live in the mountains. Some differences are due to the primary goal of the religious order's founder, such as encouraging Adoration of the Blessed Sacrament (Saint Peter Julian Eymard's Congregation of Priests of the Blessed Sacrament), providing retreats for the laity (Saint Teresa Couderc's Congregation of Our Lady of the Retreat in the Cenacle), or caring for orphans (Saint Jerome Emiliani's Somaschi). But Saint Benedict of Nursia's famous counsel to his monks to "pray and work"—that is, order one's day so as to both spend time in prayer and spend time

---

[9] Gen 32:24–30.

laboring for one's daily bread—succinctly summarizes an important balance in religious life.

Saint John Cassian (369–c. 435) was a French monk, priest, abbot, and founder of monasteries. But it was his writings about cenobitism (the practice of monks living together in community) that monks and nuns still read today for encouragement in living religious life. His writings deal with practical matters, such as the meaning behind certain items of monastic clothing and the proper times to pray, but also with such timeless topics as dealing with one's principal faults and engaging in the spiritual battles that are faced by every person who seeks to follow Christ. And he describes prayer.

Each man's soul is like a feather, Saint John writes in a memorable passage.[10] When a soul is weighed down by sin, it can rise up to God in prayer only with difficulty. One goal of religious life, therefore, is to drop the weight of sin so that the soul can rise up to God.

Two centuries later, another John, now known as Saint John Climacus (579–649), was a monk and abbot living in a religious community at Mount Sinai in Egypt. His brother monks had noticed his deep devotion and asked him for advice about how to draw closer to God. John essentially told them, "Climb the ladder of wisdom and virtue that God has dropped down to us," and he carefully described the rungs of that ladder in his famous work, *The Ladder of Divine Ascent*. While John obviously wrote his spiritual guide for monks, attempting to be more detached from possessions, trying to be more truly humble, and fighting unchaste thoughts are not struggles fought only in monasteries. Any Christian can become more perfectly united with God, if he takes Saint John's advice.

Several centuries later, a man now known to us as Saint Anselm of Canterbury (1033–1109) had lived a worldly, dissipated life before finding peace in a Benedictine monastery in France. Finding him to be a highly intelligent and well-educated man, Anselm's brother monks asked him to write down his prayers so that they could pray to God with them too. He obliged, and his prayers to God and the saints, as well as his deeply personal meditations about seeking God and virtue,

---

[10]John Cassian, *Conference* 9, 4–5, trans. C. S. Gibson, in *Nicene and Post-Nicene Fathers*, 2nd series, vol. 11, ed. Philip Schaff and Henry Wace (Buffalo, NY: Christian Literature Publishing, 1894). Revised and edited for New Advent by Kevin Knight, NewAdvent.org, 2021, http://www.newadvent.org/fathers/350809.htm.

were eventually circulated within and beyond his monastery. Anselm later became archbishop of Canterbury in England, and he eventually became known as one of the greatest theologians and philosophers of his time. But he was apparently happiest when he was among his brother monks in the monastery, encouraging them to pray fervently and humbly, and trying always to better understand our hidden God.

Anselm had been dead for only a few years when the future Saint Bernard of Clairvaux (1090–1153) showed up on the doorstep of the first monastery of the Cistercian order, asking to become a postulant. Even from the beginning, it was clear that Bernard was a natural leader; he had talked twenty-nine men into joining him in leaving the world behind and entering the monastery. In addition to living a quiet life as a monk, Bernard spent the rest of his life preaching to large crowds, giving advice to kings (even when they did not ask for it), and resolving political disputes. One of his most famous writings is a collection of sermons he gave to his brother monks about the Song of Songs. The Song of Songs is a short biblical book, a love song between a Bridegroom and a Bride. The Christian tradition has always read the book metaphorically, in that the description of a woman longingly seeking for her true love is a symbol of each Christian soul (both male and female) seeking Christ Himself, the true Bridegroom. Bernard's eighty-six sermons about this one biblical book offer interpretations for the Christian soul about grace, salvation, and virtue, but also provide wisdom about the mystical gifts that God bestows on His beloved, such as a mystical kiss given to the soul who loves Him above all else.

Saint Hildegard of Bingen (1098–1179) spent almost her entire life in a Benedictine convent in Germany. Yet she became famous all over Europe during her own lifetime for her brilliance and holiness. How many people in that time or our own can write books about topics as diverse as botany, music, natural history, and religion? Many men and women in the history of the Church have claimed to receive visions; few have described visions that reveal deep truths about God (rather than merely personal messages) and been recognized as a Doctor of the Church. If anything could convince us to be careful about asking for visions from God and to be aware that we might spend the rest of our lives trying to understand them, surely Hildegard's books of visions, such as *Scivias*, should give us a greater respect for the power of visions and prayer.

Although Guigo II, also called Guigo the Carthusian (d. c. 1188), has not been officially canonized by the Catholic Church, his book *Ladder of Monks* has been helpful to Christians for centuries. (Carthusians are notably uninterested in publicity, even for their holiest members.) A Carthusian monk and prior in France, Guigo wrote about four "rungs" on the spiritual ladder that help us climb to God in our study of Sacred Scripture: reading, meditation, prayer, and contemplation.[11] Rather than reading the Bible quickly, he encourages us to ponder slowly a passage through these four steps. By reading the passage slowly and repeatedly, meditating on the passage's meaning, talking to God about what has been considered, and then allowing God to speak through contemplation, we can learn how to hear God's voice. This careful, meditative approach is not a ladder for monks only; it can be used by anyone.

Gregory Palamas (c. 1296–c. 1357) is also not a canonized saint of the Catholic Church, although he is honored by the Orthodox churches for his personal holiness and wisdom. Gregory was a monk, theologian, and archbishop of Thessaloniki, Greece, and he is best known today for a work called *The Triads*, his explanation of what is now called hesychasm. Hesychastic prayer emphasizes interior stillness in the search for union with God in prayer. During his lifetime, this was a hotly debated topic; was hesychastic prayer more like Buddhist meditation, trying to eliminate thoughts of God Himself and using a repetitive prayer like a mantra? Or does silence open the Christian to God's voice? Ultimately, both Orthodox and Catholic theology accepted that the latter was true. It was Gregory's explanation of hesychasm, above and against all other explanations, that explained how silent but Christ-centered prayer is a true path to the true God.

Great thinkers who changed our understanding of prayer

We tend to think of Saint Thomas Aquinas as being only a Catholic philosopher and theologian, but, being a saint, he was also outstanding at another occupation: praying.

That is, Thomas Aquinas' voluminous writings include his thoughts about complicated moral and theological issues but also his reflections

---

[11] The practice is known as *lectio divina* (divine reading).

on prayer and his actual prayers. Those writings include prayers he wrote down for his own use and for the use of others, direct and indirect advice about how to pray to God, and his hymns.

In some ways, Thomas is completely unlike another great Catholic thinker to whom he is often compared: Saint Augustine of Hippo. Thomas never wrote a deeply personal autobiography, as did Augustine, and we know about Thomas' famous spiritual experience—in which he was so moved during prayer that he stopped working on his magnum opus, the *Summa Theologiae*—only because his friend recorded what Thomas told him about it. But Thomas has been able to influence how Catholics pray for centuries through the clear, theologically sound prayers he said before and after receiving Communion, and (of particular use to students) his prayer to be prayed before studying. More profoundly, the hymn he composed for the (new at the time) Feast of Corpus Christi has been sung in Catholic churches during Exposition of the Blessed Sacrament, virtually ever since he wrote it. When Thomas says in the hymn *Pange, Lingua, Gloriosi* that he is unable to find words to explain the mystery of Christ's Presence in the Blessed Sacrament, the rest of us can certainly agree with him and sing along.

As a young man in Spain, Saint Ignatius of Loyola (1491–1556) directed his energies toward winning glory in battles that would increase his wealth and popularity; after his conversion, he was just as single-minded about winning spiritual battles that would draw him closer to God. During his convalescence after a serious injury, he reluctantly began to read about Christ and the saints. In a profound insight, he realized how reading secular literature was enjoyable at the time but left him dissatisfied afterward. The opposite occurred when he prayed and read about the faith; that is, he felt great joy as a result. This realization and many others that he made during his spiritual journey led to the *Spiritual Exercises*, his writing about a vivid method of prayer combined with simple but profound meditations to help a soul "choose Christ", just as Ignatius had done. Ignatian retreats and books based on his exercises have been helping Christians in their spiritual growth ever since.

Saint Teresa of Avila (1515–1582) and Saint John of the Cross (1542–1591) lived at about the same time as Ignatius and were also born in Spain. During their lifetimes, Teresa and John were perhaps better known as founders of the new Discalced Carmelite order and for enduring considerable persecution for their desire to live more penitential lives as vowed religious. But today, they are best known for their profound writings about prayer. Neither of them wrote about prayer to make money or impress others with their holiness; they wrote either because they were ordered to do so by their superiors or because of a desire to help those individuals who were directly under their care follow a safe path and grow in holiness.

Teresa begins her autobiography by explaining that her confessors commanded her to write it and complains that they would not let her describe her past sins in greater detail. But the sin that she bemoans most often is the fact that she gave up spending time in mental prayer with God, even though she was living as a nun. As she explains the circumstances that led her back to the habit of praying daily and deeply, along with other biographical details, she throws out spiritual gems about how to live a spiritual life, discusses amazing mystical experiences in a completely matter-of-fact manner and talks about our Lord so vividly that the reader can tell that she *knows* Jesus Christ as a real Person and intimate friend. She bemoans her previous "chattiness", her tendency to spend hours conversing with friends in the convent's parlor before her deep conversion, but her talkative nature allows her to describe complex personal experiences that we would generally consider inexpressible. This is one of Teresa's greatest charms as a writer.

Like Saint Teresa, Saint John of the Cross is also known as one of the most influential writers on mystical theology in the history of the Church; his works were also written for the express purpose of helping individuals grow in holiness. Unlike Teresa, he rarely discusses the events of his own life. Though his writings include short spiritual maxims and a systematic study of the stages that a soul passes through during its journey toward union with God, three of his most famous works are poems. These poems, which are considered masterpieces in Spanish literature, are indeed beautiful even from a secular perspective, but John's commentaries on each of them reveal great spiritual depth hidden in the seeming simplicity of his poetry. John is perhaps best known for his teaching about "nada", the Spanish word for "nothing". This teaching is easily misunderstood; simply put, John reminds us that Christ Himself

taught us that we must give up everything and anything that sepa-
rates us from Him. When we renounce everything and have nothing that we can call our own, God gives us everything we truly
need or want.

Both John and Teresa used vivid images to explain their mystical
experiences. Teresa wrote about "mansions", that is, the rooms that
we pass through in the great castle of our souls as we travel toward
God Himself at the center of that soul; John wrote about "dark
nights", that is, stages of prayer that we pass through, sometimes not
realizing that we're praying at all because of the darkness in our souls.

Both writers were also countercultural. Teresa would allow any
woman with a proper disposition to enter one of her convents, completely unlike her contemporary culture, which demanded that the
postulant "donate" enough money to feed and clothe her in the future
and which created a stratified culture within each convent based on
the wealth and nobility of one's family before entry. She might have
summed up her criteria for determining whether a woman was suitable for religious life with the modern phrase "Do you have a personal relationship with Christ?"

These four saints were famous even within their own lifetimes.
But their writings on prayer have remained perennially effective to
new generations of Christians, simply because of their personal commitment to prayer.

Devotions to Christ

From the time of the prophet Elijah (roughly eight hundred years
before the birth of Christ) to the time of the prophet Malachi (roughly
four hundred years before Christ), God inspired many holy but ordinary men to speak His words to His people. Generally, the Old Testament prophets were like nagging parents or a tough coach, repeatedly
harping on very simple but truthful themes to their audiences, such
as how much it displeased God when His people acted like He didn't
exist. God's Chosen People often trusted in political solutions and
even dabbled in worshipping false gods rather than turning to Him
first and foremost, and the prophets of the Old Testament confronted
their countrymen about those sins. The prophets also shared their

personal experiences of prayer in their writings. For example, Elijah described how he recognized God's presence through a whispering sound, not an earthquake,[12] and Isaiah described what he saw when God invited him to the very throne room of God in Heaven.[13]

Although God's public revelation of Himself definitively closed with the closing of the canon of the Bible, that does not mean that He does not continue to reveal Himself through private revelations. As Catholics, we are careful to distinguish between *public* revelation versus *private* revelation. According to the *Catechism of the Catholic Church*, "[Private revelations] do not belong ... to the deposit of faith. It is not their role to improve or complete Christ's definitive Revelation, but to help live more fully by it in a certain period of history."[14]

Sometimes God inspires individuals with messages for their own sanctification and uses their words and holiness to draw those around them closer to Himself. Saint Bridget of Sweden (c. 1303–1373), a happily married wife, mother of eight children, and member of the Swedish nobility, received mystical visions starting at the age of seven. Her unabashed faith and spiritual insights—along with her private revelations—allowed her to influence the king and queen and many others while she was serving in the Swedish court. Similarly, Saint Frances of Rome (1384–1440), a wife and mother to a wealthy family, received mystical visions, including a bodily vision of her guardian angel and revelations about current political matters, Purgatory, and Hell. Both women knew hardship during political turmoil, the deaths of their children and (eventually) husbands, and other sufferings, along with spiritual ecstasies.

But sometimes God's messages are not meant only for the sanctification of an individual or even a nation. For example, four Catholic devotions that are universally known and practiced today owe a great deal of credit not to theologians or popes but to simple nuns. Through the open, sensitive hearts of these four women, God found a means of revealing an aspect of Himself that benefited not only them and the members of their communities but also Catholics up to the present day.

[12] 1 Kings 19:9–13.
[13] Is 6:1–13.
[14] *CCC* 67.

The woman we now know as Saint Gertrude the Great (c. 1256–c. 1302) was just a twenty-six-year-old Benedictine nun when she began receiving vivid, complex visions involving theological mysteries. Deeply moved, she stopped her mostly intellectual studies so that she could pursue a better understanding of theology and therefore more clearly understand what God was revealing to her. A true daughter of the Church, she submitted all her visions to the authority of the Church and waited patiently for experts to determine eventually that what she had seen was from God, not His enemy.

The image of Christ that startled her and, once approved, spread rapidly throughout the Christian world through her writings was one that seems commonplace to Catholics today: the Sacred Heart of Jesus. The representation of our Savior with His human heart exposed, bleeding, yearning for His people visibly has been deeply moving to Catholics for centuries. Jesus Christ had a human heart when He walked the streets of Jerusalem, and His heart could be bruised, broken, and hurting, just as our hearts can be bruised, broken, and hurting by the interior and exterior events that fill our days. Through Saint Gertrude's writings, we are reminded that Jesus was truly both God and man, that His loves, cares, emotions, and sufferings are joyful and painful just like our own.

Saint Juliana of Liege (c. 1192–1258) was a Norbertine canoness in what is now Belgium. At one point, she began to receive a series of visions that focused on an image of a full moon with a dark spot. She prayed about and pondered this puzzling image for some time, and she gradually realized that the troubling dark spot indicated a troubling omission in the Church calendar: there was no feast day to commemorate our Lord's Presence in the Blessed Sacrament. She began speaking and writing about the importance of remembering Jesus' Presence in the Eucharist on a given day of the year, and gradually people began to listen and agree with her. Although the Church did not formally add the Solemnity of Corpus Christi until a few years after Juliana had died, it was her persistent promotion of the practice that eventually propelled others into action.

During the seventeenth century, a heresy known as Jansenism became particularly popular in France. Father Cornelius Jansen was a devout French Catholic priest; when he died in 1638, he left behind a speculative writing in which he postulated that many people, even good Catholics, presume too much on God's mercy. Many Catholics, he reasoned, including some who frequent the sacraments and appear to be living devout lives, might actually be destined for Hell without realizing it. Although Jansen also explicitly stated his willingness to accept the final judgment of the Church on his speculative ideas, his suppositions raised uncomfortable questions in the hearts and minds of many ordinary Catholics. People began to believe Jansen's teachings and live accordingly, presuming themselves doomed to Hell whether they practiced their faith or not. As a result, many Catholics only rarely considered themselves worthy of receiving the sacraments.

Into this gloomy atmosphere, Saint Margaret Mary Alacoque (1647–1690) became a nun of the Visitandine order at Paray-le-Monial, France. When she was twenty-six years old, she, too, received visions in which our Lord appeared to her, showing her and speaking of His Sacred Heart. Under obedience to her superiors, Margaret Mary described the revelations she received in writing and explained what our Lord had told her about the value of meditating on Jesus' Heart. In time, Margaret Mary's testimony and personal holiness led to the celebration of the Solemnity of the Sacred Heart of Jesus on the Friday after the octave of the Feast of Corpus Christi.

Saint Faustina Kowalska (1905–1938) was a Polish sister from the Congregation of the Sisters of Our Lady of Mercy; she also experienced mystical visions, as described in the journal that she wrote out of obedience to her superiors. The vision of Christ that she received—and which our Lord told her to have painted and reproduced for others to venerate—showed Him with rays flowing from His heart, rays that symbolized His great love for all mankind. According to Faustina's diary, our Lord also told her to pray a set of prayers that emphasized this message; this has come to be known as the Divine Mercy Chaplet. Saint Pope John Paul II even established a date on the calendar so that all can remember and celebrate this devotion; the second Sunday of the Easter season is now Divine Mercy Sunday.

But these four women are not the only saints in the history of the Church to promote specific devotions for our Lord as a result of their experiences in prayer. As has already been mentioned, Saint Bernardine of Siena was personally devoted to the Most Holy Name of Jesus and popularized it in his preaching in the fifteenth century. Blessed Henry Suso (c. 1295–1366) was a German Dominican friar also noted for his preaching, and he often talked about God under the title of "Eternal Wisdom". The French priest Saint John Eudes (1601–1680) formed a religious order devoted to the Sacred Heart of Jesus; he was so eloquent in his explanations of the spirituality of the Sacred Heart and the Immaculate Heart of Mary that he has been proposed as a future Doctor of the Church.

Inspirational titles are not limited to titles for God. Devotion to the Immaculate Heart of Mary can be explained from the Gospels themselves.[15] Many saints, such as Saints Anselm of Canterbury and Bernard of Clairvaux, also wrote about devotion to the heart of the Mother of God. The Miraculous Medal, which depicts Mary's compassionate heart for sinners and was popularized by Saint Catherine Laboure, helped spread this devotion.

In each of these cases, it is not difficult to see why God would inspire certain holy people to promote these devotions. The people of each age face different trials, so by inspiring holy women and men with particular words and images, God draws His people back to Himself. The fact that these devotions have outlasted the earthly lives of their saintly promoters indicates that the impetus for each of them came from Heaven, not earth.

Lesser-known teachers of prayer

In the biblical book of Judges, there are twelve individuals who are identified as "judges"—that is, eleven men and one woman who "judged" the twelve tribes early in its history.

The Jews had only recently conquered and settled in the Promised Land, and they existed more as a group of tribes than as a united people. Over a period of perhaps a few hundred years, the pagan tribes that surrounded them tried to steal from and conquer the tribes of Israel. Each time that the Chosen People asked for God's help, God inspired an individual to provide the strong leadership that the tribes needed to protect themselves. Scripture describes some of

---

[15] See particularly Lk 2:35.

these judges, such as Samson and Gideon, in considerable detail. But although we believe each of the twelve judges provided essential leadership during pivotal times, all we know about some of these judges is their names. They inspired their people, but God has not seen fit to tell us much more about them than that. Similarly, there have been many Catholic men and women throughout history whose writings on prayer have been highly influential to Christians for centuries but who are not canonized by the Church.

Thomas à Kempis (1380–1471) was a member of the Brothers and Sisters of the Common Life, a simple religious community that no longer exists but that was widespread in Germany during his lifetime. Thomas became a priest, and, in addition to writing instructions for his community's novices and editing a biography of a local saint, he wrote several treatises about living a faithful life. One of them, *The Imitation of Christ*, has been a favorite of Christians all over the world for centuries and has been a favorite book for many saints. For example, Saint Thérèse of Lisieux commented in her autobiography that she had entire chapters of *The Imitation* memorized, apparently long before she entered the Carmelites in her late teenage years. Though this book was clearly written for those living religious life like himself, much of his advice is applicable to any Christian, in any state of life. For example, one of the most beautiful chapters of *The Imitation* describes how suffering unites us to Christ and is fittingly titled "The Royal Road of the Cross".[16]

Fewer people are aware of the writings of the Franciscan friar Francisco de Osuna (c. 1492–c. 1540), although if there had been a "spiritual bestsellers" list in sixteenth-century Spain, de Osuna's works would have been at the top. The focus of his writings, such as *The Third Alphabet*, is the value of entering into your heart, resting in God's presence, and raising your heart up to Him. Saint Teresa of Avila was inspired to deepen her prayer life by de Osuna's writings, as she described in her *Life*.

The Cloud of Unknowing was written anonymously and in English in the fourteenth century. People have been debating for centuries about the identity of its author and a few other works commonly attributed to the same person. But the name of the author is clearly

---

[16] Thomas à Kempis, *The Imitation of Christ*, Book 2, Chapter 12.

less important than the content of the book. *The Cloud* was written as a medieval guide to contemplative prayer and is well summarized by the title: enter into the "cloud of unknowing", surrender your mind to accept what we cannot know about our Almighty God, and in that surrender, you will begin to understand Him.

Brother Lawrence of the Resurrection (1614–1691) was a French Carmelite priest. Another priest collected Brother Lawrence's letters and records of conversations with him, forming what is now called *The Practice of the Presence of God*. A key aspect of Lawrence's spirituality was the disarmingly simple emphasis on being aware of God's presence at all times. Modern prayer books—Catholic and non-Catholic—often recommend *The Practice of the Presence of God* for its simplicity and applicability for every Christian.

Jean Pierre de Caussade (1675–1751) was a French Jesuit priest who served as a spiritual director for nuns of the Visitation order. After his death, the letters of spiritual advice that he wrote, primarily to nuns, were collected, arranged, and given the title *Treatise on Abandonment to Divine Providence*. This book emphasizes the spiritual benefits of abandoning oneself completely to God's Providence in the ups and downs of daily life. Every event in our lives, de Caussade teaches us, has already been planned and arranged by a good and loving God, so why not accept each event with patience and trust? Another popular way of describing this teaching is encapsulated in the phrase "the sacrament of the present moment", pointing out that we are called upon to accept each moment of life as a divine gift from God by which we can receive grace.

All these writings have been read and appreciated by people of very different cultures and are as inspirational to people today as they were to their contemporaries. Unfortunately, popular discussions of these works tend to focus not on their spiritual value but rather on catty, speculative arguments about whether the presumed authors actually wrote them. One might almost say that modern discussions seem calculated to make the reader focus on wild suppositions and hearsay about potential authors based on inconclusive data, just to distract the reader from the genuinely effective teachings offered in the books themselves.

This might be due in part to the lack of detailed biographical information about the authors. While we do have some details about the

lives of Thomas à Kempis, Francisco de Osuna, a few possible authors
of *The Cloud*, Brother Lawrence, and Jean Pierre de Caussade, the
information is relatively sparse. Also, the Church has not declared any
of them canonized saints. That fact raises some important questions.

Have these men not been declared saints because, although they
wrote persuasively about how to grow in holiness, they were not
able to persevere and follow their own good advice all the way to
the end of their lives? Or is there a much more prosaic reason, such
as a humble desire to remain anonymous (like the author of *The
Cloud*) or the lack of an existing religious order to promote the
cause for sainthood (like Thomas à Kempis)? Unverified rumors can
besmirch someone's reputation long after death, such as the gossipy
story that Thomas à Kempis' body, when exhumed, showed signs
that he might have been buried alive and tried to escape from his
coffin. Even if true, the desire to live is a healthy, human desire that
God placed in all our souls, not a sin, and that would not eliminate
Thomas as a candidate for sainthood. He would not be the first holy
man whose reputation was marred by unjust accusations before and
after death. After all, the fallen angels have a vested interest in keeping those of us who are alive from recognizing the holiness of those
who have passed on to Heaven.

However, given the fact that these writers are not canonized saints,
why have Catholics found their works so helpful over many generations? What makes these books so effective?

In each of the works described above, the author was able to establish a balance between two extremes in the spiritual life that are dis-
couraged by the Church. Unlike our contemporary culture, which
sees "spiritual journeys" as an unquestioned good—as long as the
journey doesn't lead to Christianity—the Church cannot forget that
our Lord Himself talked about wide and broad paths that lead to
destruction, and narrow ones that lead to eternal life.[17]

Saint Thomas Aquinas famously explained that virtue is generally
achieved through a balance between two extremes. The same is true
for developing a relationship with God. It's important to abide by
the rules and teachings of the Church, but it's also important that we
not judge our relationship with God solely on external factors, such

[17]Mt 7:13-14.

as the number of Rosaries or Masses we accumulate, lest we become like those Pharisees who were so fixated on rules that they denied the Savior the right to heal people from illness at "inappropriate" times and places. It is important for our prayer with God to be deeply personal, but it is also important for our prayer to reflect our lowly place compared to the King of the Universe. Additionally, if we want our words to be of help to other Christians, we should use theological words and terms correctly so that they are not led astray by a lack of precision.

Two modern examples prove the point. A popular Catholic writer from the late twentieth century often used the same literary device as used by Thomas à Kempis; he made his points through imaginary dialogues between Christ and a disciple. However, unlike Thomas, the author introduced Buddhist teachings and concepts that made it difficult to discern where faithfulness to Christ began and ended in his works. In another modern movement, centering prayer has become a popular method of prayer for many Christians, and some of the language used to describe it can sound like Brother Lawrence's "practice of the presence of God". However, Christian arguments in favor of centering prayer as a technique fall apart when proponents make the fatal mistake of saying that one can draw closer to Christ by being so focused on inner silence that one "kicks out" our Lord if He shows up during prayer to communicate with us.

But these two modern examples are not the first occurrences of an apparent "expert" to try to steer Catholics into dangerous waters by adding concepts from other religions, taking a good idea to an unhealthy extreme, or focusing on the "flashier" gifts of the Holy Spirit. From the followers of Montanus, a second-century leader from a region of modern Turkey who claimed to have ecstatic visions and to literally *be* the incarnation of the Holy Spirit, to seventeenth-century followers of the Spanish priest Miguel de Molinos, who created the false teaching called Quietism when he taught that truly advanced souls reach a point where they should not even *try* to pray, it's clear that just because writers encourage people to pray, that doesn't mean that they are using the word "prayer" the way the Church uses it.

So far as we can tell, Thomas à Kempis, Francisco de Osuna, the author of *The Cloud*, Brother Lawrence, and Jean Pierre de Caussade never claimed to have private revelations from God about the perfect way for all people to pray. They simply communicated the truths about prayer that they had learned and passed them on to others. They all appear to have lived and died as faithful Catholics, receiving the sacraments and submitting their teachings to the final judgment of the Church. They were humble men who took seriously God's call to spend time alone with Him, learned from Him, and shared what they learned with others through their writings.

It is possible that at some point in the future, biographical details about one or all of these men might be miraculously discovered so that any remaining questions about their sanctity could be resolved. That would not be unthinkable; Saint Louis de Montfort's writings were completely lost and then rediscovered about a hundred years later. It is possible that the Holy Spirit Himself might someday move the Church to acknowledge one or all of these men for their holiness and acclaim them as saints. We cannot know the future. However, since they are not currently considered saints, we cannot treat them or their works with the same regard that we treat canonized saints and their works, at least in terms of the orthodoxy of their teachings.

Imagine you were planning to run a marathon, and you had two friends who offered to help you prepare. One friend had completed a couple of marathons and placed respectably; the other friend had won Olympic medals in marathons. All other things being equal, it would not be difficult to decide which friend you should choose to help you achieve your goal.

There are many spiritual writers who have written excellent works on prayer that have benefited Catholics for centuries. We will do our Lord no dishonor by sitting at their feet and learning from them, so long as we are careful to measure what they teach against the teachings of the Church. And we can hope that someday we will receive the true answer about which of these writers are now in Heaven when we, please God, join them there.

Simply praying

According to tradition, the practice of praying the Rosary was given by our Blessed Mother to Saint Dominic de Guzman as a means of countering the heresy called Albigensianism, which was misleading many Christians in twelfth- and thirteenth-century France. That is, the Blessed Virgin Mary told Saint Dominic that not only would he and the members of his religious order grow in holiness if they meditated and prayed about events in the life of Christ while using words from the New Testament that referred to our Lord and our Lady, but that others would benefit from the practice as well.

Another tradition says that the Rosary developed when laypeople emulated the monastic practice of praying all 150 psalms from the Bible on a regular basis. Since working people did not have the time, books, or literacy required to pray all the psalms on a regular basis, they repeated short prayers 150 times instead. (Note that praying fifteen decades of the Rosary was the standard practice before Pope Saint John Paul II added five decades in 2002.)

Whatever combination of divine inspiration and human desire to grow in holiness was involved in the development of the Rosary, the fact remains that it has become a standard method of prayer for Catholics all over the world. Through the Rosary, people of every age and educational background can draw close to God, whether in a busy environment or a quiet place. The practice is tactile (rosary beads), visual (images of the mysteries for each of the twenty decades), and auditory (when said aloud alone or as a group). Although the practice of saying a few prayers many times sounds mind-numbingly repetitive, that repetition is actually perfect for human beings like ourselves with physical bodies that respond to natural rhythms. Meditations on the mysteries can involve short descriptions, passages of Scripture, or images.

The nineteenth-century book called *The Way of the Pilgrim* describes the spiritual journey of a holy Russian man who takes part of the verse of 1 Thessalonians 5:16—"Pray constantly"—very seriously and very literally. The book recounts how he travels all over Russia, talking to and learning from other Christians while he constantly and lovingly recites the Jesus Prayer.

The Jesus Prayer is a very ancient prayer and has various common forms; one of them is, "Lord Jesus Christ, Son of the Living God, have mercy on me, a sinner." The practice of praying this prayer was promoted in Egypt during the days of the early Desert Fathers and Desert Mothers, was encouraged as it spread through the lands of the

Eastern churches over the centuries, and continues to be practiced today, particularly by members of the Orthodox churches and Eastern Catholic rites.

This simple prayer, just like the Rosary, requires minimal memorization, so it can be prayed by any Christian, of any walk of life, at any time. Modern medicine has recently "rediscovered" the benefits of repetitive prayer practices, and while the secular world may encourage such prayers for their calming effects, there is much more to the practice of praying the Rosary and the Jesus Prayer than a modest improvement in blood pressure. Both of these prayers, like all heartfelt prayers we offer up to God, have the admirable ability to help ordinary people reach from earth up to Heaven. For that, we can thank God.

Learning about prayer

The *Catechism of the Catholic Church* is much more than a catechetical explanation of what Catholics believe; it also includes an excellent major section on prayer.[18] The *Catechism* explains the practicalities of prayer—such as the types of prayer and how prayer can be a spiritual battle—as well as analyzes the greatest of all prayers, the one that our Lord taught us Himself. Another excellent resource is the *Catholic Encyclopedia*, originally dated 1917 and now commonly called the *Old Catholic Encyclopedia*; it has excellent entries on prayer and mystical theology.[19]

Before the coming of Christ, the Jewish people did not just read the psalms; they *prayed* them. The psalms, after all, are sacred hymns. Christians, particularly those in monastic life, established a routine for praying the psalms, along with passages from both the New and Old Testaments, over the centuries. That has developed into what is commonly called the Liturgy of the Hours or the Divine Office. Certain prayers are prayed at specific hours of the day, according to the liturgical season and following the calendar of saints of the Church. Even busy members of the laity can participate in the liturgical prayer

[18] Part Four, *CCC* 2558–65.
[19] The entire 1917 *Catholic Encyclopedia* can be found at NewAdvent.org.

of the Church by praying Morning Prayer and Evening Prayer on a weekly or even daily basis, alone or with their families.

Many of the greatest saints in the Church never left behind instructions about how *they* prayed. But those that did write about prayer are worth listening to and learning from. Note that the works of some saintly writers are no longer in print or not available in English. Note also that since prayer is an essential part of the life of every Christian, the following list of their writings about prayer is certainly not exhaustive.

Name	Dates	Location at Time of Death	Select Writings on Prayer
Saint Cyprian of Carthage	d. 258	North Africa	Treatise 4, *On the Lord's Prayer*
Saint Augustine of Hippo	354–430	North Africa	*Letter* 130; *Sermon* 30; treatise *On the Sermon on the Mount*; *Confessions*
Saint John Cassian	c. 360– c. 435	France	*Conferences 9–10*
Saint Bernard of Clairvaux	1090– 1153	France	*Sermons on the Song of Songs*
Saint Hildegard of Bingen	1098– 1179	Germany	*Scivias*
Saint Bonaventure	c. 1221– 1274	France	*The Soul's Journey into God*
Saint Thomas Aquinas	c. 1225– 1274	Italy	Hymns and prayers
Saint Mechtilde (Matilda) of Hackeborn	c. 1240– 1298	Germany	*Book of Special Grace*
Saint Gertrude the Great	c. 1256– c. 1302	Germany	*The Herald of Divine Love; Spiritual Exercises*
Saint Angela of Foligno	1248– 1309	Italy	*The Book of the Blessed Angela of Foligno* (includes *The Memorial* and *The Instructions*)

Name	Dates	Location at Time of Death	Select Writings on Prayer
Blessed Ramon Llull	c. 1232–1315	North Africa	The Book of the Lover and the Beloved
Blessed Henry Suso	1295–1366	Germany	Wisdom's Watch upon the Hours
Saint Catherine of Siena	1347–1380	Italy	The Dialogue; Letters
Blessed John van Ruysbroeck	c. 1293–1381	Netherlands	The Spiritual Espousals; The Sparkling Stones
Saint Catherine of Bologna	1413–1463	Italy	The Seven Spiritual Weapons
Saint Catherine of Genoa	1447–1510	Italy	Purgation and Purgatory: The Spiritual Dialogue
Saint Ignatius of Loyola	1491–1556	Italy	Spiritual Exercises[20]
Saint Peter of Alcantara	1499–1562	Spain	Finding God through Meditation
Saint John of Avila	1499–1569	Spain	Listen, Daughter; Letters
Saint Teresa of Avila	1515–1582	Spain	The Book of Her Life; The Interior Castle; The Way of Perfection
Saint Louis of Granada	1505–1588	Spain	The Sinner's Guide; The Quest for Happiness
Saint John of the Cross	1542–1591	Spain	The Ascent of Mount Carmel; The Dark Night; The Spiritual Canticle; The Living Flame of Love
Saint Mary Magdalene de Pazzi	1566–1607	Italy	The Forty Days; The Dialogues
Saint Francis de Sales	1567–1622	France	Introduction to the Devout Life; Treatise of the Love of God

(continued)

[20]Note that the Spiritual Exercises were not designed to be read; they were written for spiritual directors to lead directees on retreat.

Name	Dates	Location at Time of Death	Select Writings on Prayer
Saint Margaret Mary Alacoque	1647–1690	France	*Autobiography*
Saint Thérèse of Lisieux	1873–1897	France	*The Story of a Soul; Letters*
Saint Faustina Kowalska	1905–1938	Poland	*Diary*

The following writers are not canonized saints of the Church, but many Catholics have found their writings helpful in the spiritual life.

Name	Dates	Location at Time of Death	Select Writings on Prayer	Cautions
Tertullian of Carthage	c. 160–c. 220	North Africa	*On Prayer*	Tertullian's earlier works are highly regarded, but he chose to die outside the Church.
Origen of Alexandria	c. 185–254	Egypt	*Prayer*	Origen's many writings are brilliant, but his theological speculations in some areas have caused many controversies over the centuries.
Pseudo-Dionysius the Areopagite	Unknown[21]	Unknown	*On Prayer*	The writings of this Dionysius have been studied and admired by Christians including Saint Thomas Aquinas, for centuries, but details about the true identity of this author are sparse and uncertain.

[21] If this Dionysius is the saint who was converted by Saint Paul, he probably died in the early first century. If, as is more commonly believed, he was a Christian writer who chose to write under the pseudonym of Dionysius, he may have lived sometime during the fifth century or later.

Name	Dates	Location at Time of Death	Select Writings on Prayer	Cautions
Hugh of Saint Victor	1096–1141	France	*Noah's Ark; The Soul's Three Ways of Seeing*	None; Hugh was a monk, philosopher, theologian, and mystic.
Richard of Saint Victor	d. 1173	France	*The Mystical Ark*	None; Richard was a monk and theologian.
Guigo II, the Carthusian	d. c. 1188	France	*The Ladder of Monks*	None; the Carthusian order avoids the publicity associated with seeking canonization of its members.
Dante Alighieri	1265–1321	Italy	*The Divine Comedy (Inferno, Purgatorio, Paradiso)*	Dante was a poet, not a saint. But he was a thoroughly Catholic man and an excellent poet.
(Meister) Johann Eckhart	c. 1260–1327	Germany	Sermons, commentaries, treatises	Eckhart was a gifted Dominican preacher and mystic, but his imprecise use of terms repeatedly caused him to be suspected and investigated for heresy during his lifetime.
Richard Rolle de Hampole	c. 1300–1349	England	*The Fire of Love*	Richard was a hermit and mystical writer. Suspicions about the orthodoxy of his writings appear to have been due to corrupted versions of his works.

(continued)

Name	Dates	Location at Time of Death	Select Writings on Prayer	Cautions
Gregory Palamas	c. 1296– c. 1357	Greece	*The Triads*	Since Gregory was an Orthodox monk, he is not canonized by the Catholic Church.
John (Johann) Tauler	c. 1300– 1361	Germany	Sermons, conferences	Tauler was a gifted Dominican preacher and mystic; his reputation was damaged by his friendship with the controversial Meister Eckhart, listed above. Some argue that the many writings attributed to Tauler have not been analyzed to determine that all are his genuine works.
Anonymous	Unknown	England	*The Cloud of Unknowing*	The author is unknown.
Juliana of Norwich	c. 1342– c. 1423	England	*Revelations of Divine Love*	The writings of this Benedictine nun concern the visions she received from God.
Jean de Charlier de Gerson	1363–1429	France	*On Mystical Theology*	Gerson was a brilliant orator and a mystical theologian, but his career was upended when he was drawn into the political problems associated with the Avignon papacy.

Name	Dates	Location at Time of Death	Select Writings on Prayer	Cautions
Nicolas of Cusa	c. 1400–1464	Germany	On Seeking God	Nicolas was a philosopher and cardinal who was drawn into political battles and died of ill-treatment as a result.
Thomas à Kempis	c. 1380–1471	Germany	The Imitation of Christ	There is no clear reason why he has not been canonized.
Francisco de Osuna	c. 1492–c. 1540	Spain	The Third Spiritual Alphabet	There is no clear reason why he has not been canonized.
Brother Lawrence of the Resurrection	1614–1691	France	The Practice of the Presence of God	There is no clear reason why he has not been canonized. Note, however, that The Practice of the Presence of God was compiled by others after his death, not by him.
Jacques-Benigne Bossuet	1627–1704	France	Meditations for Advent; Meditations for Lent; Meditations on Mary	He was a brilliant French orator and bishop, but some say he was too authoritative and a bit too cautious about hurting other people's feelings.
Jean Pierre de Caussade	1675–1751	France	Abandonment to Divine Providence	There is no clear reason why he has not been canonized. Note, however, that Abandonment to Divine Providence

(continued)

Name	Dates	Location at Time of Death	Select Writings on Prayer	Cautions
				was compiled by others after his death, not by him. Critics have accused him of the heresy of Quietism, but since he takes pains to point out the errors of that teaching, he is perhaps only guilty of living in France when Quietistic ideas were widespread.

The Hard-to-Understand Saints

Most non-Christians respect, in some manner, the saints described in the other chapters of this book. Medieval warlords understood that popes have power. Pagan peoples had their own priests and priestesses to assist them in their worship. Individuals will sometimes sacrifice their lives for a cause. Even modern culture has developed associations for like-minded people to join and support one another, sometimes for life, such as clubs and fraternities. But there are some Catholic saints whose behavior consistently mystifies non-Catholics, and some Catholics as well.

This category of saints includes those who seemed to welcome pain and suffering through their penitential practices, as well as those whose mystical gifts sometimes looked like magic. Why would anyone wear a metal chain around his waist, as did Venerable Matt Talbot? How could someone be cheerful and encouraging to other people throughout decades of sickness, as was Blessed Alexandrina Maria da Costa? How can Christians pooh-pooh extrasensory perception and still believe in Saint Pio of Pietrelcina, who could read the consciences of those who came to him for confession?

The easy answer to all those questions is Jesus Christ and His profound effect on the lives of those who took Him seriously. But explaining how that is possible is much more complicated.

The penitents

When Jesus Christ began His public ministry, He went from town to town, preaching and healing. That sounds very dramatic, but it was probably also very dusty and exhausting. He apparently traveled entirely on foot; the only time it was noted that he rode an animal for transportation was less than a week before His death.[1] He invited

[1] Mt 21:7; Mk 11:7; Lk 19:35; Jn 12:14.

men to follow Him,[2] but He did not make any promises about living a comfortable lifestyle. Sometimes there was not enough food to eat.[3] One gets the impression that, although He and His followers were sometimes invited for dinner and perhaps given a bed to sleep in,[4] they often slept under the stars. When Jesus died on the Cross, the soldiers split His meager possessions among themselves; there were so few items involved that they had to argue about whether to split one of them in two.[5]

Poverty for the sake of poverty was not Jesus' ultimate goal, and it is not the ultimate goal for us. Instead, His point is beautifully encapsulated when He explicitly tells us not to worry about food, clothing, and all the rest but instead to place all our trust in God's loving care for us.[6]

The Church has clarified many times over the centuries that there is nothing wrong with a person seeking the basic necessities of life, such as food to eat and a place to live. The Church has also never been outdone by any other organization in her dedication in providing those necessities to those who are poor. But the Church encourages us to detach ourselves from our material desires so that we might be more perfectly attached to God Himself. We are all called to imitate Christ's example of self-abnegation, adapting it to the vocation to which God has called us.

For this reason, we find many saints throughout the ages who have voluntarily inverted the typical priorities of human life. Saint Angela Merici (1470–1540) grew up in a wealthy home in Italy, but she decided as a young woman to practice penances such as sleeping on the floor; living on bread, water, and vegetables; and wearing simple clothes. By giving up legitimate comforts, she was able to dedicate herself to serving others, specifically by forming what ultimately became the first teaching order of nuns in the Church, the Ursulines. Saint Arsenius (d. 449) was a wealthy Roman before he decided to leave the world behind and live as a monk in the Egyptian desert. He was particularly known for his prolonged silences, and he explained

[2] Mt 4:18–22; Mk 1:16–20; Lk 5:1–11; Jn 1:35–42.
[3] Mt 14:16–17; Mk 6:37–38; Lk 9:13; Jn 6:7–9.
[4] Lk 10:38.
[5] Jn 19:24.
[6] Mt 6:25–33; Lk 12:22–31.

that while he had often been sorry for the things he had said, he had never been sorry for not saying anything at all. In silence, as the great masters of Christian prayer teach us, it is easier to hear God.

Religious vows such as those of chastity and obedience mystify our contemporaries. But Saint Paul explained why someone could choose to never marry; for example, without a spouse and children, one is more free to serve God completely.[7] Several of the New Testament letters remind us of the importance of obeying rightful authority. Choosing to be obedient, rather than demanding your own freedom, is a powerful means of imitating Jesus Christ, who humbly obeyed mere human beings during His time on earth.

Three of the most famous penitents of the Church—that is, people who chose radically simple lives as a means of doing penance for their past sins—are all women. Saint Mary Magdalene was the first disciple to see the risen Lord, but she was also possessed by seven devils before she met Christ. Tradition says that she spent the rest of her life doing penance for her past sins. Saint Margaret of Cortona, Italy (1247–1297), became a man's mistress; when he died suddenly, she was struck to the heart with shame over her sinful life and lived the rest of her life in poverty, long nights of prayer, and physical mortifications. Saint Mary of Egypt (344–421) was a prostitute when she was overwhelmed by a knowledge of her sins and God's love; she spent the rest of her life living in the desert.

Some penitential practices are easier to understand than others. Non-Christians today will often give up food or sleep or will undergo painful regimens for pleasure, better health, or participation in a sport. Choosing to live in poverty also makes sense to those who willingly choose to serve the poor, whether for religious or secular reasons. But why would someone unnecessary live for decades on a pillar as a penance, as Saint Simeon the Stylite did? Why was a chain found around the waist of Venerable Matt Talbot, a reformed alcoholic, when he unexpectedly dropped dead on a street in Ireland? Why did some saints flog themselves with a knotted cord, popularly called "the discipline"?

Since not every canonized saint has participated in such radical mortifications, such things are obviously not required. Such practices

[7] 1 Cor 7:25–35.

do make sense, however, if you listen to the explanations that these holy men and women gave for doing them. First and foremost, each saint recognized that he had not always been punished for the wrong things he had done or had not made complete restitution for the people he had hurt. Even one cruel word can damage another person in a way we never intended and can never undo.

Penances also can help us grow in holiness as a simple reminder to do or not do something. Venerable Matt Talbot (1856–1925) was a day laborer in Ireland and an alcoholic when he asked the Lord to free him from his addiction. After decades of sobriety and holy living, Matt collapsed on a street and died. That was when people discovered that he had been wearing a chain under his clothes. Although Matt never told anyone why he did so, it is not difficult to see that the chain may have served as a constant reminder to help him daily overcome his addiction to alcohol. Another great saint of the Church, Camillus de Lellis (1550–1614), proves that God can help a humble, penitential soul become free of addiction; Camillus was penniless and addicted to gambling when he turned to God for help. He repented, turned his life around, and spent the rest of his life serving the sick—even founding a religious order to do so—despite his own physical infirmities.

Saint Francis of Assisi also teaches us the power of physical penance to help us grow in holiness. Francis, who suffered from the pain of the stigmata, as well as blindness, called his body "Brother Ass". Like a donkey, our bodies do not always obey us, and our physical desires frequently lead us into trouble. By mortifying our desire for all sorts of physical pleasures—from a favorite food to extra sleep—we make it easier to bridle our desire for other pleasures.

Just as every person who has attempted a physical mortification during Lent can attest, not every such inspiration is easy or perfect. There have been saints who tried a specific physical mortification and later decided to abandon it. Saint John Vianney was not the only saint who later repented of damage to his body caused by excessive fasting when he was a young man. Although Saint Mark of Vertou (527–601) lived a very penitential life in a cave, a holy friend told him that he had gone a bit too far when he tied himself to the cave with a chain.

But perhaps one of the most mystifying penitents in this list gives us a final insight into the benefit of physical penances. Saint Simeon the Stylite (390–459) came from a poor family in modern Turkey before becoming a monk. He imposed such severe penances on himself that the other monks asked him to leave their community. Either his greater tolerance for pain made them ashamed that they could not do the same, or it was disruptive to their community life to have someone behaving so differently from the other monks. Perhaps both. Simeon left to live in a hut, then a cave, and then on top of a short pillar. He ate little and prayed much. In time, crowds of people came to see the seemingly crazy but holy man living in the middle of nowhere, asking for his advice, his prayers, and his instruction. He reluctantly became a preacher to his visitors, teaching them about compassion and about living a moral life. His lifelong battle to "take every thought captive to obey Christ"[8] bore fruit in his own life first as his physical desires obeyed Christ. Then he was able to teach others to do the same.

Saint Simeon was an athlete for Christ, a marathoner of the spiritual life; we can learn from him and the other penitential saints of the Church about detaching from our desires for physical comfort by making our own little acts of physical self-discipline each day.

The victim souls

Every person has felt some sort of physical pain, whether it be due to illness, hunger, an accident, or even emotional trauma. That is probably one of the reasons our Lord Jesus Christ chose not to redeem us through some seemingly detached act of the will. We can recognize the great sacrifice He made for us because we can imagine the pain of being beaten, of not being allowed to sleep, of being scourged, of having nails pounded in our hands and feet, and of dying slowly, publicly, and innocently, while people mock.

Many men and women throughout the centuries have known incredible physical pain and hardship, sometimes for years on end, and have born that burden with deep faith in God. While most of us complain, become angry, and try to escape from such pain because of our fallen human nature, some great saints have showed a different

[8] 2 Cor 10:5.

way to follow Christ in their suffering. Note that since even describing the pains some of these saints have suffered can cause us sympathetic pain, revulsion, or fear, this discussion will focus more on their responses, rather than the details of their maladies.

Saint Julie Billiart (1751–1816) was a young woman living on a farm in France when her life changed forever; the shock of seeing someone fire a shot at her father caused her to become paralyzed. Whatever psychological cause modern psychologists might attribute to her condition, the fact remained that she was still physically unable to walk. Her physical weakness, however, did not slow her down; she was a fearless protector of Catholic priests in France during the French Revolution. Once anti-Catholic fervor had calmed somewhat, she was a leader in her community as she helped reestablish the practice of the faith, supported the poor, and educated children. After having been confined to a chair for decades, a priest-friend asked her to pray a novena for an unspecified intention. After a period of time had elapsed, he apparently told her that she had been praying for her own healing because he asked her to "stand up and walk"[9] in honor of the Sacred Heart of Jesus. Which she did. Her complete healing allowed her to finish the work of establishing a teaching order of sisters, but it was her many years of suffering and powerlessness that taught her to trust in God, even when He seemed to be asking the impossible.

But not all saints are healed miraculously. Saint Pacificus of San Severino (1653–1721) was an Italian Franciscan friar and a professor of philosophy when he lost his sight and hearing at the age of only thirty-five. Later, he lost his ability to walk. Saint Benedict Biscop (628–690), a holy abbot with a great love of learning, spent the last four years of his life paralyzed. Such a disability leads some to bitterness and anger, but these men accepted their suffering with peace and trust in God, inspiring those around them as well.

Though he does not appear to be formally recognized as a blessed by the Church, the man generally called Blessed Herman the Cripple (1013–1054) also shows us that physical limitations do not limit our spiritual growth. Herman of Reichenau, Germany, was born what we would call a special-needs child; descriptions of his condition

[9] See Mt 9:2–6; Mk 2:3–12; Lk 5:17–26.

indicate that he had a cleft palate, spina bifida, and cerebral palsy. He was placed in a monastery to be educated, which was not an unusual choice for noble families of the age, but his parents also seem to have recognized that his disabilities would make it difficult or impossible for him to live in the secular world. It was very difficult for Herman to use his hands to write—but he learned how to anyway. During his lifetime, he became such a famous poet, historian, and writer on many subjects, including mathematics, astronomy, and languages, that students flocked to study in his monastery and learn from him. Even with all his physical disabilities, Herman was known for his loveable personality and virtuous life, showing that he had learned the lesson of the Cross through his profound physical limitations.

Saint Rafqa (Rebecca) Pietra Choboq Ar-Rayes (1832–1914) was born in modern Lebanon; her mother died when she was seven years old, and her father sent her to work as a household servant when she was eleven. When she returned home a few years later to live with her father and stepmother, they pressured her to marry, but she felt drawn to religious life. She entered the convent of Our Lady of Deliverance when she was a young woman; she ran the convent kitchen, taught the catechism and other subjects, and helped establish a new school for girls for her order. During a time of transition in her congregation, a dream involving Saint Anthony the Great inspired her to enter the Lebanese Maronite Order. There, she lived a life of solitude, silence, and austerity for almost thirty years.

In October 1885, Rafqa began to pray, and in her prayer, she asked Jesus to allow her to experience some of the suffering He endured during His Passion. Immediately she began to experience incredible pain in her head and eyes, pain that continued for years; her condition did not respond to treatment or improve with surgery and slowly led to blindness in one eye. Later, she experienced many other painful physical ailments that left her blind and disabled. The only tasks she should perform for her order were humble ones: making clothing and knitting socks. But throughout more than a decade of suffering and constant pain, her sisters noted that she remained uncomplaining and peaceful, even thanking God for the gift of participating in Jesus' suffering.

Shortly before Rafqa died, she asked God for her sight to return for just an hour so that she could see the face of her beloved superior;

He granted that favor. (Another sister made her prove the miracle by asking Rafqa to identify items in the room.) After her peaceful death, Pope John Paul II declared Rafqa a saint due to the miraculous healing of a woman of uterine cancer and due to Rafqa's Christlike acceptance of suffering.

Blessed Alexandrina Maria de Costa (1904–1955) was born on a farm in Portugal. She almost died of an infection when she was twelve years old, and when she was fourteen, she and her sister were attacked by three men. To avoid being sexually assaulted, Alexandrina jumped out of a window and fell more than a dozen feet to the ground. The doctors told her that the injuries she suffered were irreversible. Alexandrina was able to drag herself to church for several years, but by the time she was nineteen, she had become permanently paralyzed.

At first, she prayed for a miraculous healing, but she eventually accepted that it was not to be. Instead, she drew closer to Christ in her suffering and offered her many aches and pains to Him for the salvation of others. Unable to become a missionary in the world, she became a missionary from her bed, as her family, friends, and visitors were touched by the peace and joy that the bedridden woman exuded.

What makes it possible for people like these saints, who bore seemingly unbearable pain, to be peaceful and joyful? The same thing that makes it possible for mere human beings to become lightning rods for the miraculous.

The miraculous saints

The word "miracle" comes from the Latin word for "wonder". A miracle is therefore quite literally something that causes us to be amazed or full of wonder. But while we might experience wonder when seeing a gorgeous scene in nature or watching a magician perform a trick, those are not the most common uses of the word "miracle" today. Rather, we generally think of a miracle as an event that seems to transcend natural limits—something that we cannot explain through our reason, physical senses, or the created world around us; something that, to a believer, can only be explained as the action of God Himself.

While the Old Testament certainly describes God acting through many miracles—the plagues of Egypt, the crossing of the Red Sea, the healings obtained by the prayers of the prophets Elijah and Elisha, for example—Jesus' First Coming was accompanied by an outpouring of miraculous events. Yes, He taught and traveled like other rabbis, but He also cured people of every known malady.[10] He multiplied and transformed food for hungry people.[11] He read the very hearts of the people to whom He spoke.[12] He commanded demons, and they obeyed Him.[13] The good angels accompanied Him too.[14] His physical appearance changed as He was transfigured in prayer on a mountain.[15] The marks of His Crucifixion remained on His body after He rose from the dead,[16] and He repeatedly proved that He was still alive.[17]

Jesus said that His followers would not only do works like His but also would do even greater things than He had done.[18] And so they have, as saints have mystified believers and unbelievers for millennia through the miracles that seem to follow them like daily companions.

Not all saints are known for miracles that occurred during their lifetimes; some quietly lived holy lives without any "flashy" signs to attract crowds. Our Blessed Mother is perhaps the most obvious example of how much God values the hidden holiness of His saints. But sometimes God allows His saints to be lightning rods for miracles even during their lifetimes, and, rather than focusing on the exciting aspect of these signs, perhaps it is better to wonder why. That is, why does God permit signs and wonders to accompany His saints?

In our modern age, which idolizes the word "choice", even believers tend to overemphasize the role of our intellectual faculties over the material world. The Church, on the other hand, teaches us that each of us is composed of both a body and a soul. What we do with our bodies certainly matters from a moral perspective, but

[10] Mt 4:23; Mk 3:10; Lk 7:21.
[11] Mt 15:36; Mk 8:6; Lk 9:16.
[12] Mt 9:4; Mk 2:8; Lk 5:22.
[13] Mt 8:16; Mk 1:34; Lk 4:41.
[14] Mt 4:11; Mk 1:13; Lk 4:10.
[15] Mt 17:2; Mk 9:2; Lk 9:29.
[16] Lk 24:39–40; Jn 20:27.
[17] Acts 1:3.
[18] Jn 14:12.

our physical health, whether good or bad, can also affect our mental, emotional, and spiritual health. If Jesus Christ came to earth only to educate our minds and be a good example, why did He bother to heal people as He traveled all over the Holy Land? Clearly one of the reasons that Christ performed physical miracles was to recognize the value of our material bodies, which were, after all, created by God. But His response to suffering people was not merely a calculated ploy to get people's attention, because Christianity is not a religion of stoic resignation to calamities. To be a follower of Christ means that you open your heart to share in the suffering of others, just as Christ did when He healed suffering people out of compassion.[19]

We know very little about one of the most long-standing and miraculous saints: Januarius of Benevento, Italy (d. c. 305).[20] According to tradition, Saint Januarius was the bishop of the town when the Roman emperor Diocletian began his severe persecution of Christians. While visiting deacons in prison, Januarius was arrested, imprisoned, and executed. Witnesses preserved some of his blood in a vial. Since 1389 his blood has liquified on his feast day and on the Saturday before the first Sunday in May. This miracle seems inexplicable and even perhaps bizarre, but clearly God desires us to remember the faithfulness of this saint and imitate it in our own lives.

Saint John Joseph of the Cross (1654–1734) was a young, devout Franciscan friar living in Italy when he went through a painful period of aridity in prayer. Not only did this trial deepen his prayer life, but people soon noticed that his prayers resulted in physical healings and even the miraculous multiplication of food on at least one occasion. He became so well known as a healer that he had the awkward experience of being acclaimed as a saint when he returned to his home-town to visit his dying mother. Saint Colette Boylet (1381–1447) lived alone in a hermitage as a Franciscan tertiary before God gave her a vision and called her to reform the religious life of nuns in her native France. Colette founded seventeen religious houses and reformed the practice of life in many others during her lifetime, but she was more famous to the people of her time for her miracles, which

---

[19] Mt 14:14.

[20] Sometimes he is also called Saint Januarius of Naples; Naples is approximately thirty miles from Benevento.

included raising someone from the dead. In Saint John Joseph's case, it appears the gift of healing accompanied (perhaps was a side effect of) a deepening of his prayer life. With Saint Colette, the gift may have been given for a more mundane reason: to convince members of the Church, as well as the rich and powerful, that her mission to bring radical poverty to Franciscan nuns all over Europe—the same poverty she personally practiced—was from God Himself.

Another way that our Lord passes on the gift of miracles to His saints is by enabling them to participate in the re-creation of the world. Since the day that the serpent tempted Adam and Eve in the Garden, fallen angels have tempted their children. Jesus Christ showed His power over demons by exorcizing possessed people and by ordering devils around like waiters. There have been exorcists in the Church since before the year 304, when Saint Peter of Rome, a priest and exorcist, died as a Church martyr, up through the time of Saint Vincent Pallotti (1795–1850), a deeply devout priest and exorcist who also served in Rome, up until the present day. God's curse on mankind after the Fall of man in Genesis 3:14–19 teaches us that even the dust of the earth now fights against us and the animals with whom we share creation are no longer completely subject to us.

But the saints show us that Christ has won that victory too. There are stories of early Christians being led into the arena to be killed by wild animals, but the animals refused to harm them. This happened in the case of Saints Abdon and Sennen in third-century Rome. Some saints have possessed a seemingly supernatural ability to communicate with animals, such as Saints Blaise, Caradoc of Wales, Francis of Assisi, and Mamas. Even the damage done to our relationship with animals in the Garden of Eden can be healed by God.

Since the time of the Tower of Babel,[21] the fact that we speak different languages has made it difficult for one group of people to communicate with another. That tragedy was undone at the time of the coming of the Holy Spirit at Pentecost,[22] and the gift of tongues continues in the saints ever since. For example, when Dominican priest Saint Louis Bertrand left his native Spain in 1562 for modern Colombia, he spoke only Spanish and had to use an interpreter

[21] Gen 11:1–9.
[22] Acts 2:1–11.

to communicate with the native peoples. However, the Holy Spirit seems to have supplied whatever Louis lacked on a natural level, as his gift for preaching and the gift of tongues allowed him to bring thousands of people to the Christian faith.

Our modern world is dismissive of accounts of mystical visions, bilocation (someone appearing in two places at the same time), or levitation. To unbelievers, stories about such phenomena are simply that: stories made up by overzealous followers. Or they assume that there was a purely natural explanation that uneducated people from the ancient or medieval world were too ignorant to understand.

But even if you set aside the many reported experiences of miraculous mystical phenomena from before, say, the sixteenth century, there are many examples of saints demonstrating those same phenomena. For example, no one thought much of Saint Joseph of Cupertino (1603–1663) when he was a Conventual Franciscan friar in Italy. But on many occasions, multiple witnesses—primarily his fellow friars, who respected his humility but knew he was also uneducated and not too bright—saw him physically levitating during prayer. In her biography, the great Saint Teresa of Avila (1515–1582) describes the visions and ecstatic experiences of prayer that swept her away and off the ground for days on end, and once again, multiple people witnessed these events. Saint Gerard Majella (1725–1755) was just an uneducated Redemptorist lay brother with poor health when people noticed that the humble man was also a wonder-worker; in addition to miraculous healings through his prayers, there were reports that he appeared in more than one place at the same time. For example, two men both said they spoke with Gerard at the exact same time: one was a brother Redemptorist in his monastery, and the other was a sick man living in a cottage some distance away. Saint Sharbel Makhlouf (1828–1898) was a monk and priest in Lebanon before he left to live as a hermit. Though he lived alone, people began to seek him out for his advice and prayers. Because of those pesky laypeople, we know that he was so devoted to the Blessed Sacrament that he would spend hours preparing himself before he celebrated Mass and that he sometimes levitated while he was praying.

All these saints hid, ignored, or played down their amazing experiences in prayer. Their favorite topic of conversation was God, not God's gifts. Perhaps that is why God gave them those gifts. They were given these experiences not just for their own benefit but also for ours, to remind ordinary Catholics that our devotion to communicating with God in prayer should be so profound that we might just be lifted up off the earth, that He might tell us something important that needs to be shared with others, or that He might trust us to be in two places at once because there is no one else who can say the right words to the right person.

Saint Francis of Assisi was the first person to receive the gift of the stigmata, that is, wounds in his body that mimicked the wounds of our Savior. Francis' wounds in his hands and feet, as attested by multiple witnesses, appeared spontaneously, with no physical explanation, bled constantly, and caused him great physical pain. How can we as Catholics explain that? All we can say is that Francis loved his Lord so much that he asked for the gift of sharing Christ's pain and was granted that gift. Since the time of Francis, more than fifty holy men and women have asked for and been granted that gift, including Saints Catherine of Siena, Catherine de Ricci, Gertrude, Rita of Cascia, and John of God. Sadly, there have been charlatans who faked the signs and even at least one nun who literally made a deal with the devil to receive fake stigmata.[23] But the modern saint Pio of Pietrelcina (1887–1968) proved this was not merely a hysterical condition or fiction from more pious ages. The Capuchin Franciscan from Italy was the first priest to receive the stigmata, and his physical signs were examined by perhaps more medical personnel for a longer period of time than any other stigmatic. Doctors were mystified by the wounds themselves, his ability to survive continual blood loss, and the cause of the wounds. Pio's other famous gift—the ability to read the consciences of his penitents during confession and discern their spiritual state, whether they told him or not—is no less mystifying.

But these amazing gifts, along with all the other miraculous gifts given to the saints described above, are most inexplicable to us because they do not seem to have "normal" causes. In the ordinary manner of things, we would not be surprised by someone pretending to have a gift for monetary or selfish reasons or by a few inexplicable events that we could write off. But when God

---

[23] See Fr. Benedict Groeschel, C.F.R., *A Still Small Voice: A Practical Guide on Reported Revelations* (San Francisco: Ignatius Press, 1993), pp. 45–46.

THE LEAVEN OF THE SAINTS

allows something extraordinary to occur in the life of a holy man or woman, it is not random or selfish. Each of these miraculous happenings—healings, visions, speaking in tongues—occurred precisely because God had established a profound relationship with a man or woman, and mystical phenomena erupted as a natural result. The halos shown around the heads of God and His saints in paintings are not just an artistic effect; the saints show us that the closer a person draws to the fire of God's love, the more that person will shine with His light.

Fourteen helpers from Heaven

During the fourteenth century, the bubonic plague spread throughout Europe, killing millions of people suddenly and without warning, resulting in starvation, lawlessness, and fear. Some people turned to superstition and violence, but Christian Europe, by and large, turned to Heaven for help. Gradually, Catholics created a list of "Fourteen Holy Helpers", saints who were called upon by the survivors for healing from the unknown disease and supernatural help.

Name	Description[24]	Why a "Holy Helper"? (Possible Reasons)
Saint George of Palestine	Christian soldier in the Roman army who was martyred	He displayed soldierly courage in the face of unexpected death.
Saint Margaret of Antioch	Virgin-martyr who may have been tortured by being thrown into boiling oil	The pains of her martyrdom are reminiscent of the pains of the plague.
Saint Eustace of Rome	Second-century convert to the faith from paganism who died a martyr by being burned alive in a bronze bull	The pains of his martyrdom are reminiscent of the pains of the plague.

[24] The cities and time periods of many early Church martyrs are debated.

Name	Description	Why a "Holy Helper"? (Possible Reasons)
Saint Barbara of Nicomedia	Third-century woman who was killed by her own father with a sword for daring to become a Christian	The pains of her martyrdom are reminiscent of the pains of the plague.
Saint Christopher	Third-century martyr who served the poor out of love for Christ	He provided merciful care of the poor.
Saint Denis of Paris	Third-century bishop who converted many pagans and died a martyr	The pains of his martyrdom are reminiscent of the pains of the plague.
Saint Pantaleon	Third-century physician who died a martyr	He provided medical help.
Saint Acacius of Byzantium	Fourth-century soldier in the Roman army who was martyred	He displayed soldierly courage in the face of unexpected death.
Saint Blaise of Sebaste	Fourth-century bishop and martyr who miraculously saved a boy from choking	He was a miracle worker during his lifetime.
Saint Catherine of Alexandria	Fourth-century virgin-martyr who was tortured on a toothed wheel before execution	The pains of her martyrdom are reminiscent of the pains of the plague.
Saint Cyriacus of Rome	Fourth-century nobleman and deacon who performed exorcisms and died a martyr	He provided protection against the devil.
Saint Erasmus of Formia	Fourth-century bishop and martyr who was tortured by having his intestines wound around a windlass	The pains of his martyrdom are reminiscent of the pains of the plague.

(continued)

Name	Description	Why a "Holy Helper"? (Possible Reasons)
Saint Vitus of Lucania	Fourth-century Christian whose prayers resulted in miracles and who was executed by being boiled to death in oil	The pains of his martyrdom are reminiscent of the pains of the plague.
Saint Giles	Eighth-century hermit who, though crippled by an injury, became a wonder-worker through prayer	After his death, his monastery became a famous shrine; many sick and poor people went to pray there.

A final example

One modern blessed offers us a perfect example to summarize the lessons that holy men and women with miraculous gifts teach us.

Blessed Anne Catherine Emmerich was born in 1774 into a large farming family in Germany. She was pious from a young age and wanted to enter religious life as a young woman, but she was too poor to pay the dowry required at most convents. Finally, a convent of Poor Clares agreed to accept her, but only if she could learn to play the organ. She became a servant in the house of an organist so that she could learn, but the organist's family was so poor that she not only did not learn how to play but also gave up some of her earnings to help the family pay their bills.

Fortunately, another convent was willing to overlook her inability to play the organ, and she entered the convent with a friend and became an Augustinian nun. As is often the case for holy people, she soon became a source of division within the community. Anne was careful to be obedient to the order's rule; some were inspired by her pious example, but those who were not so obedient to the rule were annoyed. Anne was also frequently caught up in ecstasies while she prayed; similarly, some believed she was truly caught up in prayer, while others thought she was showing off.

From 1802 to 1814, the German government decided to place Church properties under their direct control. This meant that monasteries all over the country, for no reason besides anti-Catholic animus and a desire for greater government control, were closed down. Anne and her sisters were forced to leave their convent.

She accepted a position as housekeeper for a priest, but she became ill so soon afterward that she became a patient, rather than a servant, in the house. Her younger sister, Gertude, agreed to take over her duties as housekeeper. It was at this point that her invisible stigmata, which she had apparently born in silence for some time, became visible to others.

For the rest of her life, she was often bedridden, endured great pain, and experienced vivid visions, particularly of the Passion of Christ. The anti-Catholic spirit in Germany had unexpectedly given birth to a renewal movement among Catholics, and many faithful and prominent Catholics came to visit the sick and ailing; but the inspirational young woman received all her visitors with great kindness, despite her own pain. One of those visitors was a poet and novelist named Clemens Brentano, who wrote down and posthumously published Anne's visions in a book now known as *The Dolorous Passion of Our Lord Jesus Christ*. There has been debate ever since about how much of the content of that book was from Anne and how much was from Clemens. Anne herself never intended her private revelations to become a public matter, but people of faith have been inspired by these visions for centuries, including at least one modern movie producer.[25]

Another suffering that Anne experienced came, yet again, from the German government. This sick woman's heroic life became so widely known that the authorities sent investigators to try to disprove her stigmata, besmirch her reputation through innuendo, and have her followed like a public enemy. When medical science could not explain her stigmata, they simply said she was lying. (The false government reports, more than any other factor, are also partially responsible for the delay in her beatification.) After Anne's death, rumors that her body had been stolen caused it to be exhumed. Surprising only the authorities, her body was found to be incorrupt.

What lessons does the life of Blessed Anne Catherine Emmerich teach us today? That visions, stigmata, and other miraculous events

---

[25] Some details of Mel Gibson's movie *The Passion of the Christ* were reputedly taken from *The Dolorous Passion*.

are merely signposts that God plants in the lives of His saints so that the rest of us will slow down and notice His power working in mere mortals.

Patron saints of the miraculous

People do not usually call on a saint for help if they want to cross a street or make dinner. They do, however, if they cannot find the right street (Saint Anthony of Padua, patron of seekers of lost articles) or the kitchen is on fire (Saint Florian, patron of firefighters). The following table lists some of the more common patron saints and explains why they have become known as patrons for those in need of big and small miracles.

Do you need help in your spiritual life?

Spiritual Need	Saint	Why This Saint?
Desperate situations and lost causes	Saint Jude (Thaddeus)	It is generally thought that because he shared the same name as the infamous Judas and because little else is known about this apostle, he is a helpful intercessor when all else has failed.
Memory and lost items	Saint Anthony of Padua	He was a brilliant man with an incredible memory, and he (successfully) prayed for years for someone to return a book.
Poverty	Saint Lawrence the Deacon	He famously brought the poor people supported by the Church to the authorities when he was asked to turn in the Church's treasure.
Prayer	Saints John of the Cross, Teresa of Avila, Thérèse of Lisieux	They not only knew how to pray deeply but also wrote about it to help others.

Spiritual Need	Saint	Why This Saint?
Purity and chastity	Saints Agnes of Rome and Maria Goretti	Agnes was put in a brothel to try to make her give up her faith; Maria resisted her attacker rather than be raped.
Repentance	Saint Mary Magdalene	Mary was freed by Christ from seven demons and, unlike others He healed, followed Him as a penitent for the rest of her life.

Do you need help in your family life?

Family Need	Saint	Why This Saint?
Babies	The Holy Innocents	These children were martyred by King Herod, for the sake of Christ.
Children, difficulties with them	Saint Monica	She prayed for years for her son Augustine's conversion.
Grandparents	Saints Joachim and Anne	These are traditional names given for the parents of the Blessed Virgin Mary.
Household chores and homemakers	Saint Martha of Bethany	See Luke 10:38–42.
Husbands and fathers	Saint Joseph	He was the foster father of Jesus Christ and spouse of the Blessed Virgin Mary.
Orphans	Saint Jerome Emiliani	He founded homes for orphans.
Pregnant women	Saint Gerard Majella	He was falsely accused of fathering a child but patiently waited for the woman to admit her lie.
Teenagers	Saint Aloysius Gonzaga	He was a devout young seminarian who died after caring for the sick during a plague.

(*continued*)

Family Need	Saint	Why This Saint?
Wives and mothers	Blessed Virgin Mary	She is the Mother of God.

Do you need help with a physical problem?

Physical Need	Saint	Why This Saint?
Breast conditions	Saint Agatha	She was tortured by having her breasts cut off before dying as a martyr.
Cancer	Saint Peregrine Laziosi	He miraculously recovered from cancer when our Lord healed him.
Deafness and hearing	Saint Francis de Sales	As a priest, he used sign language to communicate with deaf people.
Digestive system problems	Saint Erasmus of Formia	He was tortured by having his intestines removed from his body before being martyred.
Eyes, blindness, and vision	Saint Lucy	She was tortured by being blinded.
Headaches	Saint Teresa of Avila	She suffered from headaches for many years.
Heart problems	Saint John of God	He had many medical problems of his own, despite his vocation of caring for the sick.
Mental problems	Saint Dymphna	When her clearly unbalanced father tried to marry her, she ran away. He killed her.
Stomach ailments	Saint Timothy	He was an associate of Saint Paul, who wrote to Timothy advising him to drink a little wine to help with his ailing stomach.
Teeth problems	Saint Apollonia	An angry mob attacked her because she was a Christian and pulled out her teeth before she died.

Physical Need	Saint	Why This Saint?
Throat ailments	Saint Blaise of Sebaste	He cured a boy with a fish bone stuck in his throat.

Do you need help with your vocation?

Vocational Need	Saint	Why This Saint?
Accountants	Saint Matthew the Apostle	He was a tax collector.
Artists	Saint Luke the Evangelist	He is said to have been an artist.
Athletes and soldiers	Saint Sebastian	He was a soldier who died bravely after being shot by arrows.
Authors and journalists	Saint Francis de Sales	He was a highly influential writer during his lifetime.
Carpenters, engineers, and builders	Saint Joseph of Nazareth	He was a carpenter.
Doctors, nurses, and hospitals	Saints Luke the Evangelist and John of God	Luke was a physician. John was the founder of a religious order serving the sick.
Farmers	Saint Isidore the Farmer	He was a farmer.
Gardeners	Saint Rose of Lima	She helped support her family by growing flowers.
Lawyers	Saint Thomas More	He was a lawyer.
Musicians and singers	Saint Gregory the Great	Gregory reformed sacred music, leading to what is now known as Gregorian chant.
Police officers	Saint Michael the Archangel	He "cleaned up" Heaven by casting the bad angels out when they rebelled.

(continued)

Vocational Need	Saint	Why This Saint?
Priests	Saint John Vianney	Although he almost flunked out of the seminary due to his inability to learn Latin, he was a holy priest and confessor.
Scientists	Saint Albert the Great	He wrote voluminously on many subjects.
Students and teachers	Saint Thomas Aquinas	He was both a brilliant student and a brilliant teacher.

Do you see the trend? In general, saints become patrons of causes and conditions that they faced during their lifetimes. This means that this very brief list of patrons is incomplete; for practically any situation, there are several saints who faced something similar and who know exactly how to help you figure out "What would Jesus do?"

Our Popes

There have been 266 popes in the history of the Church. Many popes have been given the title of saint, blessed, venerable, or servant of God, starting with Saint Peter himself; they are listed at the end of this chapter. Those ninety-three men teach us a great deal about how difficult it is to be both a holy man and the Vicar of Christ on earth.[1]

It is certain that Jesus Christ desired each of the men who have led the Church to be saints—just as He desires all the people in the pews to be saints—but it hasn't worked out that way. Because holding the title of "pope" gives a man the ability to have a profound effect on all the members of the Catholic Church, this chapter examines many saintly popes, as well as the men who were far from holy.

The danger of being pope

Being the pope has not always been seen as a comfortable job. Setting to one side the sudden and accidental deaths of several popes, as well as the deaths of early Church martyrs (described in a previous chapter), simply examining how some of our popes have died provides an overview of the ups and downs of papal power and papal sanctity.

- Saints John I (r. 523–526) and Silverius (r. 536–537) were imprisoned and starved to death by powerful political leaders.
- Saint Martin I (r. 649–655) was arrested, flogged, and then banished by the Byzantine emperor Constans II before dying of poor treatment in exile.

---

[1] For this reason, there will be no mention of the two men who have most recently held the title of pope. As of this writing, Pope Francis is not yet finished "working out his salvation with fear and trembling" (see Phil 2:12), and it will take time for Catholics and the Church to weigh the spiritual legacy of the late Pope Emeritus Benedict XVI, as pope, as theologian, and as a man.

- John VIII (r. 872–882) was a strong leader who was active in political affairs. Perhaps not surprisingly in such violent times, he was assassinated by being poisoned by someone in his court.
- It is still not clear if Saint Adrian III (r. 884–885) died of natural causes or unnatural ones; if he was murdered, it was probably because of his attempts to make peace between feuding leaders.
- Stephen VI (r. 896–897) was imprisoned and strangled when popular opinion turned against him.
- Leo V (r. 903) reigned for only a month before he was imprisoned and almost certainly murdered by the man who succeeded him as pope, Sergius III.
- John X (r. 914–928), Leo VI (r. 928), and Stephen VIII (r. 928–931)—three popes in a row—were imprisoned and killed by different leaders of powerful Italian families.
- Benedict V (r. 964) was deposed and sent away from Rome by Emperor Otto; he died shortly afterward.
- Benedict VI (r. 973–974) was imprisoned and strangled by the powerful Crescenti family; the same thing happened to John XIV (r. 983–984) a decade later.
- Sergius IV (r. 1009–1012) was elected with the support of the Crescenti family, and he died a few days after a Crescenti leader died. Therefore, Sergius was probably killed to make way for his papal successor, who was supported by the Tuscalini family.
- Clement II (r. 1046–1047) was probably poisoned because of his advocacy of Church reform. Damasus II (r. 1048) may have died so quickly after he was elected because of poison too.
- Lucius II (r. 1144–1145) died as a result of the wounds he received while trying to lead an army to retake control of Rome from the Roman Commune.
- Boniface VIII (r. 1294–1303) never recovered fully from injuries he received after being captured and tortured by agents of the French king. His successor, Blessed Benedict XI (r. 1303–1304), may have died by poisoning, perhaps because of his attempts to punish those who had mistreated Boniface.
- Urban VI (r. 1378–1389) appears to have been paranoid about potential enemies; it is likely that one of his many real enemies poisoned him.

- As befitting the worst stereotype of a Renaissance pope, Paul II (r. 1464–1471) died of a stroke after gorging himself.
- Clement XIV (r. 1769–1774) was troubled by a fear of being assassinated; some say he was poisoned since his body decomposed very rapidly after his death.

Popes of the early Church

Although the early Christians were persecuted primarily by Jews, who rightly saw Christian teaching as a challenge to their own theology and practice, the Roman authorities did not immediately condemn Christians. Instead, they initially saw Christians as merely an annoying sect within that annoying religion of Judaism. The ancient Romans had learned the hard way to tolerate Judaism, precisely when they saw, in practice, that Jews were willing to go to any lengths, including death, to avoid offending their God. But when the Roman emperor Nero (r. 54–68) decided to blame Christians for a fire that did great damage to the city of Rome in the year 64, he created a legal precedent that was followed for more than two hundred years.

During those years, the level of hostility toward Christians rose and fell. That is, although the law that made it an act of treason against the state to be a Christian was in effect for all those years, the law was sporadically enforced. Like the waiting for the mythical sword of Damocles to fall, Christians could never be sure when or where they might be called before the local authorities and be ordered to give up their faith by simply offering a little incense to one of their many pagan gods. There were certainly periods of time in which the danger was greatest—during the reigns of emperors Decius (r. 249–251) and Diocletian (r. 284–305), for example—but the threat never went away. Along with the governmental threat of an angry emperor or a fiercely pagan local governor, there was always a more local danger to a Christian's life, such as a vindictive next-door neighbor reporting him to the authorities for personal or financial motives. During the times of greatest persecution, the Roman authorities obviously went to much more trouble to find every Christian priest, bishop, and pope possible, though they were willing to do the same to poor Christian peasants as well. During the reigns of some emperors, less prominent Christians were sentenced to service in the mines of Sardinia. This was virtually a death sentence because of the harsh conditions, which is why Pope Saint Soter (r. 166–175) was noted for his generosity in sending food and comfort to those Christians.

Therefore, until the Roman emperor Constantine famously permitted the practice of Christianity[2] in the empire in 313, for a man to accept the title of pope was truly a courageous act. Or, you might say, a death sentence. Every one of the first thirty-two popes, from Saint Peter to Saint Miltiades, knew that they were unlikely to die of old age once they accepted election to the papacy. Pope Saint Sixtus II (r. 257–258) was simply celebrating Mass in the catacombs when Roman soldiers showed up. Not bothering to waste time with a trial, the soldiers beheaded him while he was still sitting on his papal chair. Pope Saint Fabian (r. 236–250) was elected pope because a dove landed on his head when he entered an assembly that had been called to select a new pope. All those present considered it a sign of God's favor, but one wonders if the other more likely candidates to the papacy heaved a sigh of relief at having avoided that honor. Fabian eventually died a martyr too.

Today, scholars argue about which popes actually died as martyrs because ancient records do not always mention how each pope died. In a few cases, the pope died during a period when persecution appears to have waned, so it is not unreasonable to be skeptical. However, the fact remains that each pope knowingly risked his life to be the leader of the underground Church.

But all that changed when the Roman emperor Constantine took the throne, claiming that his success in battle was led by a Christian vision. Suddenly, the hated but hidden Christians, of whom there were many in the city of Rome, were welcomed and able to practice their faith in public. This was a dramatic improvement, but it came at a price.

---

[2] Note that Constantine did not mandate the practice of Christianity, as is commonly implied today. He became a follower of Christ, although he was not baptized until shortly before his death. It is certainly true that many former pagans became Christians, perhaps to curry favor with him and his government. But Constantine did not require that everyone in the Roman Empire become a Christian.

The popes and heresy

One of the most important duties of the pope is to separate truth from error, to protect Christian teaching from heresy; popes have found this necessary from the very beginning. Saint Peter himself warned the early Christians about false prophets and teachers who will "secretly bring in destructive heresies".[3] The early popes, who often had to celebrate Mass in underground catacombs to avoid detection, also had to deal with debates among Christians over heretical teachings. For example, the early heresy of Gnosticism was a mishmash of Christian teachings and other religions, packaged with the alluring promise of "secret knowledge", not unlike modern New Age teachings. Popes like Saint Hyginus (r. 136–140) had to explain that, no, just because someone talks about Jesus, it does not mean what they are teaching is Christianity.

Much later than Pope Hyginus, the Church solemnly declared the doctrine of papal infallibility. This controversial and complicated teaching was defined precisely to point out the limits of the pope and strengthen the faith of Catholics. The following statement, quoted in the *Catechism* and originally from the documents of Vatican Council I, says:

> "The Roman Pontiff, head of the college of bishops, enjoys this infallibility in virtue of his office, when, as supreme pastor and teacher of all the faithful—who confirms his brethren in the faith—he proclaims by a definitive act a doctrine pertaining to faith or morals.... The infallibility promised to the Church is also present in the body of bishops when, together with Peter's successor, they exercise the supreme Magisterium," above all in an Ecumenical Council.[4]

Practically speaking, what this means is that we, as Catholics, can trust what the pope says when he is making a definitive proclamation on a matter relating to faith or morals; this does not apply to a pope's ordinary words, personal actions, and airplane interviews. Papal infallibility points us to one of the central tasks of any pope: to lead the faithful toward the truth and away from any heresy.

[3] 2 Pet 2:1.
[4] *CCC* 891, quoting *Lumen Gentium*; cf. Vatican Council I: DS 3074.

From Saint Peter to the present day, popes have had to weigh in on the heresies of Gnosticism, Donatism, Arianism, Nestorianism, Pelagianism, Monophysitism, Manichaeism, Monothelitism, iconoclasm, Albigensianism, Jansenism, and Modernism, to name just some of the more important heresies since the time of Christ. Pope Liberius (r. 352–366)—the first pope who was not acclaimed a saint in the history of the Church—appears to have signed a heretical statement about Arianism in the fourth century under pressure from the Roman emperor Constantius II. Since Liberius had already been banished by that emperor once for not supporting Arian doctrine, he was probably threatened with torture and death if he failed to comply. Liberius' later actions and words were more faithful to Church teaching, so he apparently recovered his faith after making a poor decision, like Saint Peter.

But what is a heresy anyway? According to Saint Thomas Aquinas, a heresy is "a species of infidelity in men who, having professed the faith of Christ, corrupt its dogmas".[5] By this definition, Judaism, Islam, Buddhism, and other religions are not technically heresies; they are different religions. There are degrees of seriousness in heretical teachings, ranging from outright heresy of a central tenet of the faith, such as saying that Jesus is not God, to some lesser rejection of Catholic teaching, which we might call dissent—all the way down to confusing statements that can be interpreted multiple ways.

Not every pope after Pope Liberius was acclaimed a saint, but Pope Honorius I (r. 625–638) was perhaps the most disappointing pope to follow him. In an explanation of the true teaching of the Church, as opposed to the then-common heresy of Monophysitism, Honorius used an "unfortunate" term in a letter to the patriarch of Constantinople. Because of the scandal and confusion that his lack of theological precision caused, the Church later anathematized his writings. Honorius' goal was clearly to lead the followers of Monophysitism back to the Church, but the terms he used to do that made things worse, not better.

One has to travel much further forward in time to find another clear failure on the part of a pope to deal with heresy. Well, actually you could name three popes: Leo X, Adrian VI, and Clement VII. All three of these men appear to have led moral lives, loved the

[5] William Joseph, "Heresy", *The Catholic Encyclopedia*, vol. 7 (New York: Robert Appleton, 1910), NewAdvent.org, 2021, https://www.newadvent.org/cathen/07256b.htm.

Church, and did other praiseworthy deeds for the Church. But they reigned during the early sixteenth century and the time of the Protestant Revolt, and their inability or unwillingness to act allowed the spread of Protestantism. All the many wars and deaths that resulted from what was at least as much a political struggle as a religious struggle rest on their heads. As all Catholics know, we can sin by *omission*, as well as by *commission*.

Today, it is not helpful to call Protestants "heretics". They do share many of our beliefs, including, depending on the denomination, those we state every Sunday in the Nicene Creed. However, as Catholics, we can say that many core teachings of Protestantism are heresies. We can also say that those three popes could have done better in responding to the challenges of Protestant leaders because their successor, Paul III (r. 1534–1549), did. That is, he convened the Council of Trent, and he and many of his successors instituted reforms to respond to the genuine abuses and honest criticisms that had been leveled at the Church. Of course, we shouldn't be too critical of Pope Clement VII (r. 1523–1534), the last of the three above-named popes. He almost died at the hands of a mob and was able to escape only because his Swiss Guards sacrificed their lives for his sake, and he even spent two years imprisoned by his enemies.

There are so many heretical distortions in the modern world that it is hard to name them all or determine precisely when they started. Pope Saint Pius X (r. 1903–1914) famously collected all the false teachings prominent in his day and named them Modernism. He even demanded that all clergy and Catholic educators take a formal oath against these heresies in 1910.

> Thus I hold steadfastly, and shall continue to hold to my last breath, the faith of the Fathers in the sure charism of truth that is, has been, and always will be "in the succession of the bishops from the apostles", not so that what seems better and more suited according to the culture of each age should be held, but so that the absolute and immutable truth, which from the beginning was preached by the apostles, "should never be believed, never be understood, in a different way".[6]

---

[6]Heinrich Denzinger, *Enchiridion symbolorum definitionum et declarationum de rebus fidei et morum, Compendium of Creeds, Definitions, and Declarations on Matters of Faith and Morals*, 43rd ed., ed. by Peter Hünermann, Robert Fastiggi, and Anne Englund Nash (San Francisco: Ignatius Press, 2012), no. 3549, p. 712.

The effectiveness of this oath in halting dangerous cultural teachings was and is still debated; the Congregation for the Doctrine of the Faith, with the approval of Pope Paul VI, rescinded Pius X's motu proprio that contained the oath in 1967. What is not debated is that Pius took the threat of heresy seriously and did his best to respond to it for the sake of all Catholics.

It is safe to say that as long as the universe exists, fallen man will sometimes misunderstand, distort, confuse, and fail to follow the truths of the faith. But the Church will remain the "pillar and bulwark of the truth",[7] despite the weaknesses of her members and, occasionally, a pope.

The popes and secular power

Because so many of us are uneducated about the complex history of the papacy and its relationship with secular power, we tend to assume that the popes of the past had the same international role as do popes of modern times. That is, there is a common belief that the pope's job is to make an occasional decision about Catholic teaching, travel around the world and shake people's hands, and meet with international leaders to make statements about the moral value of their public policy. But that's not what Christ told Saint Peter to do.

Jesus Christ's final words to His apostles are beautifully summarized in Mark 16:15: to bring the Good News of Jesus Christ to the ends of the earth. But the entire book of the Acts of the Apostles paints a vivid picture of how quickly that command to preach involved confrontations with local authorities. The hostility that Jesus Himself faced from Jewish leaders only intensified for His followers. Saint James was the first apostle to be martyred, and all because the local ruler (Herod) was willing to let an innocent man be executed in hopes that it would diminish religious tensions in Jerusalem. It didn't. Saint Paul traveled extensively to bring the Gospel to those who had not yet heard it, and he found himself in trouble with local authorities practically everywhere he went. While Jesus never told His disciples to challenge the leadership of secular authorities directly,

[7] 1 Tim 3:15.

it is clear that, even from the beginning, there have been tensions between civil authority and the authority of the Church. The pope, as the leader of the Church, has always been an obvious target or, in better times, the obvious spokesman.

During the first few centuries after the time of Christ, Catholicism was generally practiced in secret, not in public. Why then, if the Church was truly powerless during these centuries, did the third-century Roman emperor Decius make the famous statement that he'd rather lose his throne than find out that another pope had been elected? Precisely because Christians were quietly changing the culture, not through uprisings or legal battles, but simply by living the Gospel.

Before Emperor Constantine's Edict of Milan, the pope had authority only over Christians. Proving that people will fight over practically anything, the right to lead the underground Church as pope—despite constant danger from the imperial authority—was challenged on two different occasions even at that early stage. Two bishops, Hippolytus and Novatian, at two different periods of time, decided that they knew better than the pope in certain matters, so they claimed to be the true pope and gathered followers. Hippolytus was reconciled to the Church while serving in the mines with the true pope for the crime of being a Christian; Novatian was not.

But everything changed when Emperor Constantine declared tolerance toward the practice of the Catholic faith. Suddenly Christians could publicly state that they were Christians, they could own land and build churches, and they could discuss and debate the teachings of the Church more freely. Unfortunately, Constantine made the same mistake that many political leaders have made in every century since: he thought that being in charge of civil matters gave him the right to control the Church as well.

When heretical teachings arose among Christians, many Church leaders, including the pope, debated and issued theological statements for the sake of the faithful. More than once, Constantine and other subsequent Roman emperors were tempted to believe that their political power and financial generosity to the Church gave them the right to decide Church teaching, as if they had a personal veto over the Holy Spirit. These attempts by secular power to influence the teaching of Christ through money, lobbying, threats, public opinion, and similar means are alive and well today.

When the Roman Empire fell apart around the fourth century because of invasions by Germanic tribes, there was no longer
a Roman emperor. In modern-day dystopian visions of life after a
nuclear war, we are asked to imagine all the things of our ordinary
lives that would simply disappear without our government, such as
access to food, safety, medical care, and transportation. The ancient
world after the Roman Empire lived out that nightmare. In this
power vacuum, the leader of the Catholic Church was the only
leader left who could unite and lead large numbers of people when
they dealt with desperate realities such as war, famine, and plagues,
as well as theological heresies.

From the time of Pope Felix III (r. 483–492)[8] all the way to Pope
Pius X in the twentieth century, political leaders have tried to—and
often succeeded in—interfering in the election of the pope. Despite
being elected pope because he had the support of the Ostrogothic king
who had political control over Rome, Felix III was a strong leader and
is acclaimed a saint. Pius X is also considered a saint today, but there
was interference during the conclave that elected him; an emperor
tried to veto a particular candidate. Pius was elected instead of that
candidate, but his first act as pope was to change the laws to prevent
any such interference in the future. Some things never change, and
there will always be those who think of the office of the papacy as a
political chess piece to be controlled, rather than as the Chief Shepherd
of Christ's flock.

In the 1,400 years between Felix III and Pius X, there were other
successes and tragedies in the battle between popes and secular
power. Before the seventh century, the pope and the entire Christian
world were caught up in conflicts between the Ostrogothic leaders
from Germanic tribes, Byzantine emperors in Constantinople, and
Lombard leaders from other Germanic tribes. The strong leadership
of Saint Gregory the Great (who will be described more fully later)

---

[8] Note that several popes, including those named Felix, are sometimes counted in different
ways. Over the history of the Church, it has not always been clear whether a given pope
should be counted as the second one by that name or the third, for example. This is due to
the presence of anti-popes during a pope's reign (it has not always been easy to tell which man
is the real pope and which is the anti-pope until the dust has settled) or other complications,
such as popes who died very quickly after election. To avoid making this book even more
confusing, the second, optional numbering is omitted for those popes in this book. Felix III
is sometimes named as Felix III (IV), for example.

set a new precedent of respect for the papacy and its dealings with political leaders. Later, when Saint Leo III (r. 795–816) crowned Charlemagne, the king of the Franks and Italy, as Holy Roman Emperor, he created another precedent, one in which a king (usually German) was given imperial status. This relationship between pope and emperor was healthy in some time periods, as in the early ninth century when Pope Leo III and Charlemagne each truly lived their Christian vocations. Leo was a good pope who settled theological disputes, as well as disputes between kings and bishops. Charlemagne was a good ruler who created a cultural revival of literature, the arts, and intellectual pursuits.

At the other end of the spectrum, the Italian house of Theophylact controlled the government of civil and Church matters so completely in the early tenth century that the pope himself had very little power. Well, that is if the pope enjoyed breathing. For example, Pope Stephen VIII (r. 928–931) was arrested, imprisoned, and killed (probably by strangulation or starvation) because he did something to offend Alberic II, a leader of the Theophylact family.

In the following centuries, other Italian families, then French kings, and ultimately most European nations placed their influence behind various papal candidates in attempts to control the papacy and therefore the Church. Balancing the desire for being a Christlike leader of the Church with the need for diplomatic wisdom with secular leaders was not an easy one for many popes. It must be said that not every man who held the office of pope worked strenuously at the former.

But a large number of popes have valiantly demanded the right for a pope to act as the head of Christ's Body on earth. Alexander III (r. 1159–1181) punished King Henry II of England for his role in the murder of the archbishop of Canterbury, Saint Thomas á Becket. Innocent III (r. 1198–1216) tried to stay out of political disputes but would, when needed, write to kings about problematic situations and encourage them in a virtuous direction, as a pastor speaking to a member of his flock. Multiple popes tried to prevent and have tried to heal the eleventh-century schism that still exists between the Orthodox churches and the Catholic Church, up to and including Pope Saint John Paul II.[9]

[9] See, for example, John Paul II, Encyclical on Commitment to Ecumenism *Ut Unum Sint* (May 25, 1995), https://www.vatican.va/content/john-paul-ii/en/encyclicals/documents/hf _jp-ii_enc_25051995_ut-unum-sint.html.

A key point to be remembered in this centuries-long battle for balance in the roles of the pope and secular power is that, then as now, real-world situations often—perhaps constantly—push the barque of Peter into stormy seas. Popes only of extremely short reigns have the pleasure of spending their papacies in peace and quiet inside Vatican walls.

Today, the Church is challenged by the family trauma resulting from the immorality proposed by the Sexual Revolution, cultural and financial changes due to technological advancements, the fear and violence experienced by those experiencing persecution under Communism and terrorism, and the personal and material damages resulting from war, poverty, famine, and illness. Is that so different from the following challenges in other times in history?

- Early Christians living in the Roman Empire, including the pope, had to explain the immorality of infanticide, abortion, polygamy, and other practices that destroy the family to their pagan neighbors.

- When European nations enslaved native peoples to mine the gold that made journeys to the New World profitable in the sixteenth century, Pope Paul III condemned the practice, explaining that these people were also created by God.

- The violent conquest of the Holy Land by Muslim forces—which resulted in the death of many Christians and the destruction of Christian holy sites—caused Pope Urban II to call for the First Crusade in the eleventh century, with the goal of reclaiming those lands so that Christians could safely travel on pilgrimage to the land where Christ had lived.

- Popes Leo the Great (r. 440–461), Gregory IV (r. 827–844), Benedict XV (r. 1914–1922), and Pius XII (r. 1939–1958) tried vigorously to prevent the destruction of Rome by, respectively, the Huns and Vandals, Italian civil war, World War I, and World War II. Some popes, like Clement X (r. 1670–1676), were successful in avoiding wars between nations simply by maintaining good relationships with secular rulers. Pope Saint Boniface IV (r. 608–615) was a pillar of strength as Italy recovered from famine, plagues, and earthquakes during his short reign. Pope Stephen V (r. 885–891) used his own money to feed those who were starving during a famine.

The popes and reform

But Jesus Christ often spoke of two polar opposites: the kingdom of God and "the world". He did not call Saint Peter to be the foundation of His Church to serve worldly powers but to serve the kingdom of God. An important focus of every pope should be to help the members of the Church on earth become as holy as possible. Just as each individual Christian needs to constantly reevaluate his behavior and make changes, so the Body of Christ is in constant need of reform.

When Gregory I, commonly called Gregory the Great, became pope in 590, the effects of political instability were being felt by Christians and non-Christians alike. The Roman Empire no longer existed; instead, the former regions of the Roman Empire were caught up in battles between Germanic tribes and the Byzantine emperors. Since there was no real local government, the pope administered civil matters in Rome and nearby areas. More importantly, he initiated several reforms that affected all Catholics. Since he had personally given up his responsibilities as a Roman prefect to live as a monk before becoming pope, he encouraged monastic life and promoted monks to positions of authority in the Church. He regularized sacred music used in the liturgy and elevated liturgical standards everywhere. He also educated others through his prolific writings about the faith. In the reigns of subsequent popes, there was a seesaw effect regarding the effect of monasticism in Church leadership, as one pope would promote monks within the hierarchy, while the next would prefer priests and deacons instead. But Gregory's reform in many areas had lasting ramifications for the Church.

Unfortunately, by the tenth century, monastic life had spread so widely that it, too, needed to be reformed. And another problem had become a significant threat to the medieval Church: simony.

Monasteries had become so much an important part of European society (what a wonderful problem to have!) that they were also wealthy and powerful. Similarly, the position of bishop or archbishop was a position that wielded wealth and power over an area because medieval European society had largely embraced the Gospel. So, of course, it was tempting for those who were rich or powerful to want to control—or be—the man with so much control over a region. What better way to control it than to give a large "donation" to the Church and request that a sympathetic friend or family member be named as bishop? Then that bishop would settle disputes over property, commerce, personal matters, and practically everything else in favor of the wealthy donor.

When Simon Magus wanted to buy the gift of the Holy Spirit from Saint Peter,[10] he probably hoped to perform miraculous healings and speak in tongues to fleece the public of their money, thereby giving himself a comfortable life. In just the same way, medieval leaders always seemed to have an extra son for whom they wanted to purchase a lifelong source of income as a priest, bishop, or abbot. While some of these bribes for religious offices resulted in good and even holy leaders, more often than not simoniacal leaders showed themselves to be greedy shepherds who cared only for their own profit, not Christlike leaders of their flocks. As may be imagined, men who became priests and bishops for the sake of financial stability were not anxious to embrace clerical celibacy, and their concubines were a constant scandal to the faithful.

Therefore, popes like John XIII (r. 965–972), Benedict VII (r. 974–983), Benedict VIII (r. 1012–1024), Clement II (r. 1046–1047), Saint Leo IX (r. 1049–1054), Victor II (r. 1055–1057), Stephen IX (r. 1057–1058), Nicholas II (r. 1059–1061), and Alexander II (r. 1061–1073) were particularly known—and elected pope—because of their stated intentions to stop simony and ensure that monks and clergy lived in a manner appropriate to their state in life. But the efforts of these popes were a mixed bag (note that only one of the men listed above is now acclaimed a saint) until a man named Hildebrand was elected pope in 1073 and took the name Gregory VII. Gregory was a great pope who made the reform of simony and clerical abuses the center of his papacy, and the reform that had been tentatively undertaken under previous popes spread widely under Gregory's leadership. Blessed Victor III (r. 1086–1087) and Blessed Urban II (r. 1088–1099), for example, followed Gregory's lead.

How did they bring about such a change? Pope Gregory refused to back down, even to an emperor and an anti-pope, rather than capitulate to demands that anyone with enough money could be named a bishop of the Church. Pope Urban II, solely on his authority as pope, forced feuding leaders to respect the Truce of God, cease-fires that

[10] Acts 8:9–24.

allowed ordinary citizens to live their ordinary lives of feeding themselves and their families, rather than constantly being caught in the cross fire of largely pointless feudal battles.

More than a century later, Saints Francis of Assisi (1181–1226) and Dominic de Guzman (1170–1221) introduced their own reform: the mendicant orders. The "begging" orders that the two men founded, while very different from one another in some ways, were united in their focus on abandoning the money, property, and comforts that had crept into the lives of too many priests and monks. After meeting Francis in an audience, Pope Innocent III (r. 1198–1216) told his nephew that he had had a dream in which he saw the poor, saintly Francis single-handedly holding up a church building to keep it from falling. Pope Innocent and his successors recognized the truth in the symbols of that dream and encouraged the Franciscan and Dominican mendicant orders precisely because they saw that these orders brought the freshness of the Gospel to the entire Church. (However, it must be said that popes did quibble with these orders on the practicality of some details of their desired rules of life, such as not owning any property at all.)

The word "crusade" has such negative connotations today that it is difficult for us to imagine how the people of the Middle Ages saw things differently. But they did, and so did the popes who encouraged the crusades that occurred in the medieval world.

Islam spread into the Holy Land in the seventh century, but it was not until the eleventh century that the Seljuk Turks threatened the Byzantine Empire enough for the emperor to ask the pope to send troops to help him defend Christian territories. Previously, Christians had been able to safely travel on pilgrimages to the Holy Land where Jesus Christ had lived and walked. When that changed, Christians and Christian Europe became concerned. But safe travel was not the only issue. Christians were brutally killed and enslaved by Muslims during these attacks. Muslim forces gave no sign that they would be content to live only in those lands and not continue to invade other territories. There was also the not insignificant problem that the feudal system seemed to foster endless fighting between one Christian territory and another. Wouldn't it be a good idea to get Christians fighting someone other than one another, for a worthy reason? Fighting for a just cause might help some of these Christians improve themselves spiritually, it was thought, as well as protect Christians near and far from violence.

Therefore, Blessed Urban II called on Christian leaders to embark on what became known as the First Crusade, and other popes followed, from time to time. Since the success of these crusades is debatable, controversial, and covered more extensively in other books, this topic will be concluded with the observation that the crusades were, in a way, a source of reform within the Church.

No one would call Clement V (r. 1305–1314) a reformer pope; in fact, he started a practice that damaged the Church for decades. A Frenchman by birth, he refused to even go to Rome to be consecrated and spent his entire papacy in France, largely listening to the counsel (some would say the direction) of the French king. This shift in power damaged the city of Rome and the Church. Clement's successors were alternately known for the luxurious lifestyles they enjoyed in the French court of Avignon or for living like monks and attempting to bring about some reforms in the Church. Even with the help of one of the greatest saints in the history of the Church, Catherine of Siena, it took the attempts of three reform-minded popes—Saint Urban V (r. 1362–1370), Gregory XI (r. 1370–1378), and Urban VI (r. 1378–1389)—before the seat of the Church was moved back to the city of Rome.

Similarly, it was the lavish lifestyles of the Renaissance popes of the late fifteenth century that fed both the just and unjust complaints that Martin Luther and other Protestant reformers made against the Church in the sixteenth century. Some Renaissance popes engaged in great building projects (Nicholas V and Sixtus IV); wrote poems, plays, and novels (Pius II); were famous for their banquets, gambling, and greed (Paul II); and spent money on expensive wars as well as expensive clothes (Innocent VIII). But, sadly, the popes of the early sixteenth century made the fifteenth-century popes look like amateurs. Granted, today we appreciate the Sistine Chapel and innumerable works of art that were made possible by papal patronage. But these popes largely "fiddled while Rome burned"; that is, they enjoyed themselves while ignoring the damage being done to the Church by the violence and wars between Protestant and Catholic nations. Adrian VI (r. 1522–1523) was a German theologian before he became pope, and he tried to respond to the valid criticisms of the

Church, but the cardinals who surrounded him ignored and opposed him. The practice of nepotism—giving a nephew, friend, or family member a comfortable and important job whether he was qualified or not—reached its zenith (or nadir, depending on how you define it) with most of these popes.

Interestingly, the first pope who bucked the tide and convened the Council of Trent to stop this wound in the Church was a man we might call a "revert". Paul III (r. 1534–1549) fathered four children while he was a young priest, and his sister was one of the many mistresses of the epitome of bad popes, Alexander VI. But long before his election to the papacy, Paul underwent a personal conversion and cleaned up his life. In addition to opening a council to address the Protestant Revolt, he promoted those who, like him, wanted to reform the Church, as well as supporting the Jesuit order. Unfortunately, he was not converted enough to see the dangers of promoting family members to positions of authority, which wounded him personally and as a pope.

Subsequent popes followed the better aspects of Pope Paul III's reign, such as the great Saint Pius V (r. 1566–1572). Though his reign was short, Pius made many changes. He demanded that his leaders *implement* the decrees of the Council of Trent, not just read them. When he found cardinals continuing to live immoral lives, he sent them to live in monasteries to be cared for by trusted Jesuit priests, a brilliant response that probably felt like house arrest to erring prelates. He ordered the publishing of a catechism for the universal Church. An invasion of Turks was stopped at Lepanto only because Pius put all his skills to work to organize Christian leaders to fight and protect Christian Europe. His leadership set the standard for subsequent popes.

Another Pius started another reform a few centuries later. As already described, Saint Pius X (r. 1903–1914) condemned several heretical ideas he called Modernism. By articulating these errors and condemning them, Pius strengthened the Church against their attacks. He also reorganized his Curia of cardinals, reformed Church music, and encouraged the reception of daily Communion.

While one could argue about whether Vatican Council II was focused more on "renewing" or "reforming" the Church, the aftermath of the many changes proposed by the documents of Vatican II is still ongoing. Whether all the changes associated with this council have brought stability or confusion to the Church, Popes Saint John XXIII (r. 1958–1963), Saint Paul VI (r. 1963–1978), and Saint John Paul II (r. 1978–2005) were all Church leaders who recognized the need for this council to help bring the truth of Christ to a modern world that had lost its connection to the Gospel.

Surprising popes

It is hardly surprising that Pope Leo XIII (r. 1878–1903) wrote brilliant encyclicals; he was a scholar and poet before becoming pope. However, it was a great surprise to many people that he reigned for twenty-five years. After all, the cardinals who elected him thought he was in bad health and chose him as a compromise candidate who might not last long. He is not the only pope whose reign didn't turn out as expected.

Pope Silverius inconvenienced the Byzantine empress Theodora when he was elected pope instead of her own preferred candidate. That was a simple problem for a scheming courtesan-turned-empress like Theodora; she forged letters to implicate Silverius as a criminal and then had him imprisoned and starved to death. That left the way open for her puppet, Vigilius (r. 537–555), to be elected. Naturally, the people of Rome hated Vigilius because they knew how he had gotten elected. But not for long, because Vigilius surprised everyone by showing himself to be a faithful proponent of Catholic theology and opposing the heresies of the age, as one would expect of a pope. His faithfulness led him to be captured and imprisoned in Constantinople for several years. He died shortly after being released.

Blessed Victor III (r. 1086–1087) was known as the greatest of all the abbots of Monte Cassino before being elected pope. It might have been better for the Church if he had not been elected, since becoming pope was an honor that he frankly never sought. He was a great religious leader and peacemaker between feuding leaders while an abbot, and he was active in the Hildebrandine reform of the Church under the previous pope, Saint Gregory VII. But either Victor knew he was a better negotiator than a leader or he knew his health was too poor to be able to handle the stress of the papacy. Or both. Either way, he did not survive long as pope and left Rome twice out of frustration with his cardinals, living at the monastery of Monte Cassino instead.

Callistus II (r. 1119–1124) was elected primarily because he was a member of the French nobility and was related to practically every royal house of Europe. It was hoped that he could use his family connections to negotiate an end to a bitter controversy with Holy Roman Emperor Henry V, who demanded the right to select bishops himself. It was a long shot, but it worked. Proving that sometimes family connections can be used for good purposes, Callistus and Henry eventually signed the Concordat of Worms and settled a bitter power struggle between church and state.

Saint Celestine V (r. 1294) was a Benedictine abbot who sent a scolding letter to the cardinals who were sitting in a conclave, demanding that they elect a new pope soon to end the political chaos that was affecting far too many lives. So they did. They chose him. Celestine was a truly holy man and presumably an excellent abbot, but he was a disaster as a pope. Some say his problem was that he was too gullible and believed the people who came to him for favors, agreeing to their requests. When Celestine realized that he had said yes to too many people and for conflicting things, which was causing a political nightmare, he humbly abdicated and planned to return to his monastery. However, the subsequent pope, Boniface VIII (r. 1294–1303), deemed it safer to put a former pope in (a comfortable) prison. Celestine died a few years later. Although Boniface was otherwise a good pope in many ways, his uncharitable treatment of Celestine will forever blemish his pontificate.

Clement IV (r. 1265–1268) was a widower who had entered the Carthusian order when he was elected pope. Showing in yet another way that it is best for the Church for the pope to be celibate, men showed up immediately after Clement's election, begging to marry his daughters. Thankfully, his daughters were happy to enter religious life and help the Christian world avoid facing the difficult problem of what to do with the grandson of a pope.

The fact that Saint Urban V (r. 1362–1370) and Gregory XI (r. 1370–1378) ever even tried to move the papal court from Avignon, France, back to Rome would be a shocking surprise—if they had not had Saint Catherine of Siena gently and persistently encouraging them to do so. Another seemingly impossible situation was resolved several decades later—perhaps Saint Catherine was interceding for it from Heaven—when three men claimed to be pope at the same time. Called the Great Western Schism, it ended only when a council of bishops met, convinced two claimants to resign, excommunicated the third claimant, and elected a new pope, Martin V (r. 1417–1431).

Finally, the reign of Blessed Innocent XI (r. 1676–1689) is surprising for an unusual reason. Innocent was a pious and charitable man who restored the drained papal finances through modest taxation and cutbacks. He also passed laws against gaudy clothing and gambling dens in Rome. Because of his personality and good leadership—and despite his measures against the ever-popular pastime of gambling—he was greatly loved by Romans at the time of his death.

How weak popes have betrayed Christ and His Church

Records of the specific actions of the popes during the time of Roman persecution are spotty. Therefore, it is possible, but not certain, that Pope Saint Marcellinus (r. 296–304) handed over copies of the Sacred Scriptures to Roman authorities. Considering what we know now of those times, it is not unlikely that Roman soldiers, enforcing an imperial edict to take property from an outlawed religion, would have demanded all Church property, including sacred writings. Roman soldiers would not have been afraid to use force to ensure compliance. However complicit Pope Marcellinus was in handing over the writings of the Church, only God knows, and we can hope he paid for any lack of courage on his part through his subsequent martyrdom.

The disappointing popes Liberius and Honorius have already been discussed because of their weak behavior with regard to speaking against heresy. The next major scandal in the Church involved Popes Formosus and Stephen VI and required the actions of two subsequent popes to clean it up.

Formosus (r. 891–896) had the bad luck to be pope while a man named Guy III of Spoleto was the Holy Roman Emperor. Guy was violent, unpredictable, and powerful, and Formosus did not trust him. So Formosus asked for the help of Arnulf, king of the Franks, against Guy. Formosus even crowned Arnulf as Holy Roman Emperor, but he died soon afterward. The next pope lived only fifteen days as pope, but his successor, Stephen VI (r. 896–897), was talked into one of the most bizarre events in the history of the Church by Guy's son, Lambert: the Cadaver Synod. The corpse of Formosus was exhumed and placed in a chair in the assembly and "tried" for various "crimes". This was apparently designed to punish Formosus for taking sides against the powerful house of Spoleto and frighten anyone else from doing the same. But a subsequent earthquake in Rome was widely interpreted as a sign of God's displeasure with the whole gruesome business, and the wicked Spoletan party promptly strangled the complicit Pope Stephen to get him out of the way. Two subsequent popes, Theodore II (r. 897) and John IX (r. 898–900), annulled the synod and its decisions and condemned Stephen for participating in it at all.

Four popes demonstrate the tried-and-true wisdom that it is always a good idea to surround yourself with virtuous friends and always a bad idea to have wicked ones. Sergius II (r. 844–847) was apparently a decent leader, but he made his greedy, simoniacal brother, Benedict, a papal administrator. (It is a bad sign when historians are still calling your brother "odious" twelve centuries later.) Benedict VIII (r. 1012–1024) did encourage clerical reforms and organize resistance to Saracen raids, but he gave considerable power to his younger brother. This brother later became Pope John XIX (r. 1024–1032), who gained election primarily through bribes and kickbacks. Much closer to our own time, Servant of God Benedict XIII (r. 1724–1730) was a genuinely devout man who prayed the Rosary, visited the poor, and passed laws to encourage modesty and temperance. But he gave power to an unscrupulous cardinal who not only controlled the administration of the Church but also stole from the papal treasury. In all these cases, the reputation of the man's papacy is tarnished forever by the actions of those he chose to put in positions of authority.

Neither good nor bad

Just as in politics today, the pendulum often swings from one extreme to the other in subsequent papacies. Paul IV (r. 1555–1559) was a severe pope who arrested monks who chose to live outside monasteries and would even rebuke cardinals to bring them in line. His successor Pius IV (r. 1559–1565) was an easygoing man who walked the streets of Rome to lose weight and freed many prisoners of the previous pope. (However, it must be noted that Pius punished and even executed some of the more notorious recipients of papal favors from the previous pope as well.)

Benedict XIII (mentioned above) banned the Roman lottery and let a cardinal control the papal treasury. His successor, Clement XII (r. 1730–1740), permitted the lottery and tightly controlled papal finances.

Leo XII (r. 1823–1829) was a devout man but made many unpopular changes, such as restricting the sale of wine in taverns, covering some nude statues, and making ineffective changes to financial administration. His successor, Pius VIII (r. 1829–1830), reigned only a short time, but long enough to reverse many of the "police state" measures of the previous pope.

The office of pope is not a light burden, and it is easy to see why some men would be considered disappointing popes in the light of history. It would be difficult to become *more* virtuous when you have so much power. Therefore, we have popes for whom we could use the words "vacillating" (Adrian II, ninth century), "harsh" (Urban VI, fourteenth century, and Martin V, fifteenth century), "bad-tempered" (Boniface VIII, late thirteenth century), and "greedy" (Nicholas III, Clement V, and a long string of popes from the fifteenth and sixteenth centuries).

Clement XIV (r. 1769–1774) buckled to intense pressure from many European noble houses when he gave in and suppressed the Jesuit order. Clement's predecessor had been harassed by the same powerful figures for years; these powerful men resented the fact that Jesuit priests answered directly to the pope and served as advisors and confessors to men of power and wealth. It is not surprising that Clement gave in to their demands, but it is more than disappointing that a pope would agree to the destruction of a religious order precisely because it was successful and effective. Similarly, when Pope Stephen V (r. 885–891) decided the Slavic language was barbaric and forbade its use in the liturgy, it was worse than a mistake. It ultimately led to the loss of many Slavic Christians—including all of Russia—to the Orthodox churches.

Saint Paul the Apostle wrote, "Now we have received not the spirit of the world, but the Spirit which is from God, that we might understand the gifts bestowed on us by God."[11] Although giving in to the spirit of our culture—what Jesus called "the world"—instead of listening to the Holy Spirit is a battle we all fight, it's particularly damaging to the reputation and effectiveness of the Church when a pope succumbs. Therefore, when we read about the reigns of several popes in the tenth century—Anastasius III, Lando, Leo VI, Stephen VII, Leo VII, Stephen VIII, Marinus II, and Agapetus II—we find that each man basically "kept his head down" throughout his reign. The Italian house of Theophylact completely controlled the territory and the papacy itself during this time period. When Pope John X (r. 914–928) came along, he bucked that trend and tried to be a strong leader of the Church, for which he was rewarded by being imprisoned and killed. Similarly, most of the men we call "Renaissance popes" in the fifteenth and sixteenth centuries were so absorbed about producing lasting contributions through the arts and architecture that they failed to reform the behaviors that started and fed the exodus of many Catholics out of the Church and into Protestantism.

Surely one of the worst contributions of the papacy in the history of the world is the very word "nepotism". The tradition of giving high positions in the Church to the pope's nephew—the origin of the word—or his brother, brother-in-law, cousins, and every other greedy relative he possessed did not start in the Renaissance era, but it was certainly very common by then. Modern analyses of past papal actions generally conclude that Innocent IV (r. 1243–1254) was nepotistic and devious, Nicholas III (r. 1277–1280) was nepotistic but otherwise honest, Clement V (r. 1305–1314) was nepotistic and avaricious, John XXII (r. 1316–1334) was nepotistic though personally lived a simple life, and Boniface IX (r. 1389–1404) was nepotistic and shameless about it. And all those men reigned long before the Renaissance, when nepotism was raised almost to an art form!

In the history of the Church, almost one hundred popes are now considered to be saintly men, if not outright saints. Some of the few dozen men described above in this chapter could reasonably be called

[11] I Cor 2:12.

weak popes. That is, their human weaknesses limited or at least seem to overshadow any good that they performed during their reigns. But in terms of truly bad popes, there are only five men for whom we can simply hope in the mercy of God for their souls.

Sergius III (r. 904–911) was a member of the Roman nobility when he was elected. He had also been one of the gutless cardinals who had participated in the Cadaver Synod and consented to the "trial" of the late Pope Formosus. It is possible (some say likely) that he ordered the deaths of his predecessor, Leo V, who was murdered, and an anti-pope who would have been in his way during the time he was lobbying for election as pope. Probably to protect his reputation as a participant in the Cadaver Synod, he declared the reigns of the three previous popes to be null, though later popes overruled his decision. Although his theological understanding of the Catholic faith was apparently sound, his moral behavior as a Catholic was clearly deficient. He fathered a child by a fifteen-year-old named Marozia, who happened to be the daughter of the important and powerful Theophylact family. The illegitimate child of a pope is a scandal, but this child was worse than a scandal because his intelligent, powerful, and unscrupulous mother, Marozia, wanted her son to become pope too.

The five popes who followed Sergius were under the control of the Theophylact family and were basically placeholders until Marozia's son was old enough to reign. So, of course, he did, as John XI (r. 931–935). As pope, John even presided over his own mother's marriage to another powerful leader—which was uncanonical for many reasons, including the fact that the groom was married to someone else at the time. However, Marozia's scheming was her undoing. By marrying a rival leader, she antagonized another son, who recognized the marriage as a threat to his power and led an uprising. Marozia died in prison, and John was controlled by his half brother during the rest of his short reign as pope.

Another of Marozia's sons, Alberic II, also had a son who became pope. John XII (r. 955–963) was Alberic's illegitimate son, but that did not stop the Theophylact family from having him elected as pope when he was only eighteen years old. Though he was very young, he turned out to have some leadership abilities. What makes him a truly wicked pope, however, was the scandalous, immoral life that he lived. Even if we accept that some of the reports about John were exaggerated, it is fairly certain that his chief crime was to live like a worldly, secular leader while also being the pope. That is, he had mistresses—lots of them—gambled, had parties, drank heavily, and basically acted like the teenager that he was. John XII could not escape scandal even in death; it's still not clear whether he was killed by the angry husband of one of the women with whom he'd had an affair, whether he died of a stroke in a woman's arms, or some combination of the two.

A bit further down Marozia's family tree, her great-great-grandson became Benedict IX (r. 1032–1044, 1045, 1047–1048) because his father bribed enough cardinal electors to vote for the twenty-something-year-old man. Because of the heated politics of the times, it is once again difficult to be certain if all the horrible things that were written about Benedict are true. According to milder statements, he raped women (and maybe men) and ordered the deaths of inconvenient people, which was not unusual for an eleventh-century political leader. But if his actions were scandalous in a way that was considered "ordinary", why did the Roman populace rise up and kick him out of the city? Three other men reigned as pope at intervals between the three times that Benedict lived in Rome and claimed the office of pope. One of them, Gregory VI (r. 1045–1046), was Benedict's godfather. When Benedict briefly gave up his desire to be pope and wanted to marry, he bribed his godfather to become pope. Gregory probably accepted the bribe out of the healthy desire to rid the Church of a horrible pope. But married life did not turn out as Benedict had hoped, so he came back to Rome with an army, reigning again a third time until he was finally kicked out by Holy Roman Emperor Henry III. It is not clear what happened to Benedict after that, but the whole Church heaved a sigh of relief that such a wicked man at least no longer wanted to be pope.

Enemies of the Church like to promote ridiculous fiction about a female pope hidden somewhere in the past. The scheming Marozia is the closest thing the Church has ever had to a female pope, and her influence was indirect, as the mother of a pope. But Marozia is, sadly, not fictional, and her worst contributions to the history of the papacy have nothing to do with the fact that she was a woman, but the fact that she was wicked.

Believe it or not, the next candidate for the title of "worst pope" did not arise until four hundred years later. Alexander VI (r. 1492–1503) was a member of the Borgia family, a powerful house of Spanish nobility. Born into wealth, he accumulated considerably more wealth over his lifetime; he was a political schemer as well as a handsome smooth talker who had many affairs and who fathered numerous illegitimate children. Naturally, he heavily bribed the cardinals to elect him as pope, though his first actions as pope were good ones: he restored order to Rome and proposed a crusade. He also worked to create good diplomatic relations between the Church and European leaders. However, it appears that everything Alexander accomplished was done for two selfish reasons: to enrich the treasuries of the house of Borgia and to provide for his own personal comfort and luxury. He gave his illegitimate sons power and wealth, and they used it as scandalously as might be expected. One of the sons apparently killed his brother and threw his dead body into the river, where it was dredged from the Tiber by the pope's servants. The Romans acidly joked that the pope was now truly a fisher of men. Alexander repented—briefly. But his desire for money and pleasure won out over all other concerns, and any good that the man did as pope was spoiled by his innumerable acts of avarice and immorality.

How strong popes have saved Christ's Church

The weak and bad popes in the history of the Church often scandalize us. That is, they can cause us to stumble (the literal meaning of the Greek word at the root of our word "scandal") and lose faith in God. But they should not scandalize us, and for two good reasons.

First, we should all be aware of our broken human nature. We are all sinners. We want to do the right thing, as Saint Paul explains in Romans 7:15–25, but instead we find ourselves saying and doing the wrong things. What is the answer to this perennial human problem? Saint Paul tells us that the answer is Jesus Christ Himself! "The law of the Spirit of life in Christ Jesus has set me free from the law of sin and death."[12] By drawing close to our Savior, we can avoid sin and avoid being scandalized by the sins of others.

[12] Rom 8:2.

Second, we can be encouraged by the positive examples of the great popes that the Holy Spirit has drawn forth for the good of the Church. The headstrong, uncertain Simon who was called by Christ became the bold, courageous Saint Peter who literally laid down his life for his sheep, just like the Lord he chose to follow. According to an ancient tradition, Peter left the city of Rome near the end of his life because of the heated persecution. As Peter walked out of the city, he encountered the risen Jesus, who was walking in the opposite direction. "Where are you going, Lord?" Peter asked Him. "I'm going to Rome to be crucified again," our Lord responded. Humbled, Peter turned around and walked back into the city to accept martyrdom for Christ and for His Church.

Peter and the other early popes were vividly aware of the imminent danger they were in as leaders of the hated Catholic Church. They must be counted as some of the greatest popes because of their willingness to die for Christ. Similarly, we should be encouraged by the bravery of John I, Silverius, Martin I, and other popes whose deaths were mysterious and a bit too conveniently timed to be ruled out as murders because they, too, probably died for the sake of Christ and His Church.

Some holy popes are generally overlooked and should not be. Saint Damasus I (r. 366–384) was validly elected, but the violence of his followers and an anti-pope's followers caused a great scandal. He patiently endured accusations of adultery—they were proven to be false—and faithfully opposed two widespread heresies of the time. But one of his decisions was destined to change the Church for over a thousand years.

At the time of Christ, Greek was widely spoken throughout the Roman Empire, and the Gospels were written and transmitted in that language. Three hundred years later, Greek was no longer the common language; Latin was. There were several partial Latin translations of the New and Old Testaments available at the time, but they were all incomplete and had their faults. Damasus asked his secretary, the brilliant Saint Jerome of Stridon, to make the best possible Latin translation of the entire Bible. It took decades, cost Jerome his eyesight, and had to be completed with the help of his female assistants (Saints Paula and Eustochium, whom he said were better at the job than men), but Jerome finished his translation before his death. Jerome's Vulgate Bible was such an excellent translation that it was used by the universal Church for over a thousand years.

Saints Leo the Great (r. 440–461) and Gregory the Great (r. 590–604) were natural leaders who faced down heresies and invading armies with strength, but also charity. Saint Gelasius I (r. 492–496) was the first to use the title "Vicar of Christ", showing the humility of the position of pope, and he was both prayerful and generous to the poor. Saint Leo II (r. 682–683) did not whitewash his predecessor Pope Honorius' poor word choices in dealing with the heresy of Monophysitism; he accepted a public censure of Honorius' faulty statement and offered explanations for the condemnation of another heresy, Monothelitism, as well.

Saints Gregory II (r. 715–731) and Gregory III (r. 731–741) did not hide their heads in the sand when the ruler of the Byzantine Empire governed through violence and persecution. Gregory II stood up to the emperor about the taxes he had imposed, which were particularly oppressive to the poor. Both Gregory II and Gregory III openly opposed the emperor for his brutal imposition of iconoclasm, in which religious images were destroyed and the faithful—particularly monks—were killed, all in the name of keeping people from falsely worshipping images. Gregory III quietly showed which side of the controversy he was on by rebuilding churches that had been attacked, installing images of our Lord and the saints, and having candles lit in front of them. Both popes also showed their ability to find diplomatic solutions to tough problems by convincing an army not to invade Rome (Gregory II) and by appealing for help from the mayor of the palace of the Franks, rather than the Franks' virtually powerless king (Gregory III).

Saint Leo III (r. 795–816) survived an attack by a mob and formed an alliance with the great king of the Franks and Italy, Charlemagne, which served the good of the Church for centuries. Saint Nicholas I (r. 858–867) faced down an emperor and a siege, and he asserted the rights of the papacy to keep from being made a pawn of other leaders.

Clement VIII (r. 1592–1605) has never been named a saint, but, as the final pope of the Catholic Counter-Reformation period, he deserves our thanks. He personally took the time to visit every church and every charitable institution in Rome, probably at the encouragement of his friend Saint Philip Neri. Yet Clement was also an excellent administrator who knew how to balance the papal finances and ensure that one nation (Spain) did not dominate the decisions of his Curia. He even possessed the wisdom and tact to allow a genuine debate within the Church over the balance between grace and free will, a hot topic of argument between the Jesuit and Dominican orders.

Saint Pius V (r. 1566–1572) and Servant of God Pius VII (r. 1800–1823) showed their strong leadership skills, respectively, in promoting Tridentine reforms and in dealing with the tyrant Napoleon Bonaparte. What many people fail to recognize today is that the current situation of the independent Vatican City State began during the pontificate of another great pope: Blessed Pius IX (r. 1846–1878). His predecessor had ruled with an authoritarian style, unlike Pius IX. When he expressed sympathy for Italian rebels, Pius' charity was misunderstood as support, and riots broke out. He had to disguise himself as a simple priest to escape from Rome and live in exile until a French army restored order in the city. After that event, he opposed the unification of Italy into a single state, refused to acknowledge the Italian government, and lived as the "prisoner of the Vatican" inside the walls of Saint Peter's Basilica. Despite the tumult of Italian politics, he found time to proclaim the doctrine of the Immaculate Conception of Mary, convene Vatican Council I, and issue a list of contemporary heresies. During his reign, the pope changed from being seen as a secular ruler in Italy to being recognized as the pastor of the Church and the world.

The fact that Pius X (r. 1903–1914) was a saint and a strong leader who pointed out the heresies of his time has already been described, but he was far more than a holy leader. He reorganized his Curia, reformed liturgical music for the entire Church, promoted Catholic Action (an organization of lay Catholics who supported one another in living out their faith), and encouraged the daily reception of Holy Communion.

The popes of the twentieth century were endlessly reviled by modern media even before it became known as modern media, but our modern popes have been great witnesses to faithfulness. Pius XI (r. 1922–1939) tried to negotiate with Adolf Hitler for the sake of peace but spoke and wrote scathingly about him and Nazism when Germany broke their side of a treaty. In addition to ordering renovations of Saint Peter's Basilica and writing encyclicals, he showed what he thought of nepotism by making his own family members request permission if they even wanted to come see him. Pius XII (r. 1939–1958) has been criticized for not speaking more boldly against Hitler—but only by people who have never had to deal with a madman who controls one of the world's most powerful armies. When Pius did speak out publicly—and he did—the Nazis responded instantly by killing and imprisoning more Jews, Catholics, and priests. Therefore, Pius quietly changed his strategy and had priests and religious clandestinely hide Jews from Nazis in monasteries and convents all over Europe, including Vatican property, also spending millions of dollars to rescue those being persecuted by the Nazis whenever possible. The Chief Rabbi of Rome during World War II, Israel Zolli, converted to Catholicism after the war precisely because he was moved by the example of Christian charity in action toward Jews. According to many sources, Pope Pius' leadership saved at least seven hundred thousand Jews from imprisonment and extermination.

Saint John XXIII (r. 1958–1963) was a good-humored, honest, practical man but also the author of encyclicals that were controversial and widely misunderstood at the time. For example, the title of his encyclical *Mater et Magistra* was supposed to remind Catholics of the truth that the Church is both Mother and Teacher to the members of the Body of Christ; dissenting Catholics famously said they accepted the Church as *mother* but refused to accept the Church as *teacher.* John's encyclical *Pacem in Terris* explained how to bring peace to the many conflicts in the world at the time, but critics dissected only the section about nuclear war. Of course, his most famous act was the convening of Vatican Council II. Controversial then and now, the council was not convened merely to change inconvenient practices but to ensure that Catholic doctrine was defended and presented more effectively.

Saint Paul VI (r. 1963–1978) continued the same council, saw it to completion, and even managed to prevent a schism while Church leaders and laity differed strongly on the degree of reform to institute. He was almost assassinated, traveled frequently, and, most famously, supported the Church's prohibition of artificial birth control, through a prescient encyclical that accurately predicted the social devastation that would result if contraception was widely accepted (*Humanae Vitae*). He also defended the Church's tradition of priestly celibacy in *Sacerdotalis Caelibatus.*

Some final thoughts about the popes

When examining the long list of popes throughout history, it is easy to see some trends in papal sanctity. So many of the early popes died as martyrs that it is not surprising that many are acclaimed as saints. The bad example of Pope Liberius shocked Catholics into realizing that not every pope was as saintly and wise as he should be, but most popes in the first several centuries were indeed holy men. As the office of pope became more respected and powerful in society, it became a greater temptation to use the papal throne for political gain, and the number of saintly popes decreased in frequency. Almost fifty popes reigned in the tenth century alone, and none of them are likely to be called "holy men". The number of popes seeking holiness for themselves and for the Church became more and more intermittent over the centuries; in the sixteenth to nineteenth centuries there were only one or two saintly popes per century. But the historical change from pope as secular ruler to pope as "pastor of the world" in the late nineteenth century has produced many genuinely devout and holy popes.

For this, we can thank God for the grace He has bestowed on the office of the papacy and every pope.

Holy popes

The following table lists popes who have been recognized as saints, blesseds, venerables, or servants of God by the Church. However, there has been debate in modern times about whether some of these men, specifically the early popes, should be acknowledged as saints.

It is generally easy for us to determine why more recent popes have been acclaimed as saints by the Church; we have a great deal of information about these men and their reigns from secular and Church records. It is much more difficult to examine the lives of some of our earliest popes because less information has survived through the centuries. The information that did survive about these early popes was sometimes written many centuries later, causing skeptical historians to question whether *every* pope from Saint Peter to Saint Julius I was really martyred, for example, or whether every pope was simply acclaimed a saint and martyr at his death until Pope Liberius proved that not every pope has a backbone when dealing with secular power.

Some ancient sources indicate that persecution of the Church was sporadic and that some popes lived through imperial reigns with relative peace. We cannot even be certain of the reigning dates of some of the early popes, much less how they died.

However, it is certain that accepting the call to become pope was potentially dangerous during the early centuries, and if not every pope died a martyr, every pope knew the possibility of dying a martyr was real. In the end, we must simply accept the verdict of the Christians who lived with and personally knew many of the earliest popes and call them *saints*.

	Name	Years of Reign[13]	Description[14]
I	Saint Peter	32–64	As is well known, he was a fisherman when he was called by Jesus Christ. Peter was the first leader of the Church and the first pope; he was martyred upside down on a cross.
2	Saint Linus	67–76	Linus was probably the first Italian pope and was probably martyred.
3	Saint Anacletus	76–88	Anacletus was perhaps a Greek by birth. He divided Rome into twenty-five parishes and died a martyr.
4	Saint Clement I	88–97	Clement was formerly a slave. Several extant writings are attributed to him, including his *First Letter of Clement*. He was probably martyred.

[13] Practically every written source listing the early popes includes different reigning dates for each pope. There is simply not enough certainty about exact dates during this time period. The dates included here are from Matthew Bunson's *The Pope Encyclopedia* and provide a rough idea of the length of each pope's reign.

[14] Many early popes were assumed to be martyrs as well; later research has brought that into question. The table above distinguishes between popes that were definitely martyred (meaning there is strong early evidence that said pope died a martyr) or probably martyred (meaning that although some ancient records declare said pope to be a martyr, early evidence of martyrdom may be lacking).

	Name	Years of Reign	Description
5	Saint Evaristus	97–105	Some say Evaristus was a Jew from Bethlehem; others say he was a Greek by birth. He was probably martyred.
6	Saint Alexander I	105–115	Alexander was perhaps a Roman and was probably martyred.
7	Saint Sixtus I	115–125	According to some traditions, Sixtus created liturgical regulations and set a moveable date for Easter. He was probably martyred.
8	Saint Telesphorus	125–136	Telesphorus was probably a Greek by birth. According to some traditions, he celebrated the first Midnight Mass. He was probably martyred.
9	Saint Hyginus	136–140	Hyginus opposed the heresy of Gnosticism, which reached Rome during his reign. He was probably martyred.
10	Saint Pius I	140–155	Pius was formerly a slave, and his brother, Hermas, was the author of a famous ancient Christian writing, *The Shepherd of Hermas*. He responded to Christian heresies involving Greek philosophy, as well as Gnosticism. He was probably martyred.
11	Saint Anicetus	155–166	Anicetus was a Syrian. He opposed the common heresies of the time and dealt with the ongoing controversy over the proper date to celebrate Easter. He was probably martyred.
12	Saint Soter	166–175	Soter was generous in sending support for Christians who had been sentenced to slavery in the Sardinian mines. He introduced Easter as an annual festival in Rome and was probably martyred.

(continued)

	Name	Years of Reign	Description
13	Saint Eleutherius	175–189	A Greek by birth and probably a deacon when elected, Eleutherius reigned during a generally peaceful time in the empire. He opposed the heresy of Montanism.
14	Saint Victor I	189–199	Reports say that Victor was either a Roman or an African by birth. He enforced orthodox teachings, including the date of the celebration of Easter. Starting with his reign, Latin became the dominant language of the Church.
15	Saint Zephyrinus	199–217	Zephyrinus was criticized by (anti-pope) Hippolytus[15] for being lenient with lapsed Christians. He was probably martyred.
16	Saint Callistus I	217–222	Callistus was formerly a slave and was opposed by anti-pope Hippolytus. Some sources say he died a martyr; some say he died by violence during a riot.
17	Saint Urban I	222–230	Urban was probably of Roman birth. He was opposed by anti-pope Hippolytus.
18	Saint Pontian	230–235	Pontian was opposed by anti-pope Hippolytus. When banished by the emperor, he abdicated to allow a successor to take over. Since he died in exile for the faith, he is generally counted as a "white" martyr.
19	Saint Anterus	235–236	Anterus was opposed by anti-pope Hippolytus. He was probably martyred, which some say happened because he collected written acts of the martyrs.

[15] Hippolytus claimed that the pope was being too lenient in allowing lapsed Christians to return to the Church after persecution had ended. With the support of others, he declared himself the true pope. Hippolytus was the first anti-pope in the history of the Church, but not the last. He is the only anti-pope who later reconciled with the Church and is now considered a saint. His "reign" covered many years and put him in conflict with several true popes.

	Name	Years of Reign	Description
20	Saint Fabian	236–250	A legend says that Fabian was elected when a dove landed on his head as he entered the assembly for electing the pope; this may reflect the later sense of his contemporaries that the Holy Spirit sent him to become the strong leader and able administrator that the Church needed at the time. He was martyred when persecution was renewed.
21	Saint Cornelius	251–253	Cornelius was a Roman priest when elected. He was opposed by anti-pope Novatian for being too moderate with lapsed Christians who wanted to return to the Church and was probably martyred.
22	Saint Lucius I	253–254	Lucius was a Roman by birth. He was exiled soon after his election but allowed to return soon afterward. He was opposed by anti-pope Novatian for allowing lapsed Christians to do penance and return to the Church. He was probably martyred.
23	Saint Stephen I	254–257	Stephen was a Roman archdeacon when elected. He clashed with Saint Cyprian (bishop of Carthage and future martyr) over whether Baptism was valid when performed by heretics. (Cyprian said no.) Stephen was probably martyred.
24	Saint Sixtus II	257–258	Sixtus was an effective peacemaker between the Roman church and the churches of Asia and Africa. He was martyred during a renewal of anti-Catholic persecution.
25	Saint Dionysius	260–268	Dionysius was probably of Greek descent. He dealt with Christian heresies and improved the organization of the Church.

(*continued*)

	Name	Years of Reign	Description
26	Saint Felix I	269–274	Felix was a Roman by birth. He wrote about the Blessed Trinity during his reign and was probably martyred.
27	Saint Eutychian	275–283	Eutychian lived during a time of general peace for the Church. He was probably martyred.
28	Saint Caius (Gaius)	283–296	We have no other information about Caius than some reports that he was probably martyred.
29	Saint Marcellinus	296–304	There is controversy about and incomplete knowledge of Marcellinus' actions as pope. It is possible that he handed over copies of Scripture to Roman authorities when they were demanded.
30	Saint Marcellus I	308–309	Marcellus rigorously restored Church discipline after a time of persecution ended, which made him very unpopular. He was banished by the emperor.
31	Saint Eusebius	309 or 310	Eusebius allowed lapsed Christians to do penance and return to the Church. He was sent into exile for a time.
32	Saint Miltiades (Melchiades)	311–314	Miltiades reigned during a time of fierce persecution under Emperor Diocletian, but he also reigned during a great springtime in the Church as the emperor Constantine issued the Edict of Milan. Miltiades opposed the Donatist heresy and is generally considered a martyr due to his faithfulness during the persecution that occurred early in his reign.
33	Saint Sylvester I (Silvester)	314–335	Sylvester was a Roman priest when elected. He benefited from the emperor Constantine's financial generosity to the

	Name	Years of Reign	Description
			Church, but he also had to deal with Constantine's meddling in Church affairs.
34	Saint Marcus (Mark)	336	Marcus was a Roman. His short reign was overshadowed by the power of the emperor. He founded two new churches.
35	Saint Julius I	337–352	Julius was a Roman. He was a forceful leader who strongly opposed the heresy of Arianism and supported Saint Athanasius against his persecutors.
37	Saint Damasus I	366–384	Damasus was a Roman. He was opposed by anti-pope Ursicinus immediately after he was elected, and the resulting violence on both sides damaged Damasus' reputation. He was falsely accused of adultery at one point; he also opposed the heresies of Arianism and Donatism. He built churches, organized the papal archives, and requested his secretary, the future Saint Jerome of Stridon, to translate the Bible into Latin.
38	Saint Siricius	384–399	Siricius was a Roman deacon when elected, and his election was challenged by anti-pope Ursicinus. Though Siricius was overshadowed by his saintly and brilliant contemporaries (Jerome of Stridon and Ambrose of Milan), he was a strong leader who asserted the primacy of the pope over the Church. He settled the Meletian Schism.
39	Saint Anastasius I	399–401	Anastasius was a Roman. He condemned certain writings of Origen because of heretical interpretations that had arisen after Origen's death.

(continued)

	Name	Years of Reign	Description
40	Saint Innocent I	401–417	Innocent was perhaps the son of Pope Saint Anastasius I and was a deacon at election. He became pope as the Roman Empire was being destroyed by Germanic tribes, leading to political instability. Innocent was a strong leader who tried to negotiate peace, promoted the primacy of the pope over the Church, and worked to relieve the suffering of Romans during famine.
41	Saint Zosimus	417–418	Zosimus was a Greek. He was a strong leader, but he was accused of being tactless and dictatorial, and some of his actions made him unpopular at the time.
42	Saint Boniface I	418–422	Boniface was a Roman priest at election and was challenged by Eulalius, who also claimed to be pope. The emperor decided in Boniface's favor and against anti-pope Eulalius after the political chaos that resulted from having two popes. Boniface was a good administrator, and he was supported by Saint Augustine in his opposition to the heresy of Pelagianism.
43	Saint Celestine I	422–432	Celestine was a Roman archdeacon at election. We still have the letters he wrote to Saints Augustine and Ambrose. Celestine strongly opposed the heresies of the time and sent Saint Palladius to Ireland as a missionary (long before the famous Saint Patrick).
44	Saint Sixtus III	432–440	Sixtus was a Roman. He spent his reign strongly opposing the heresies of Nestorianism and Pelagianism and defending papal authority.

	Name	Years of Reign	Description
45	Saint Leo I, the Great	440–461	Leo was a deacon at election. He strengthened the role of the Holy See, served as a peacemaker during two sieges of Rome, and wrote his famous *Tome of Leo*, which elucidated Church teaching against heresy. His strong leadership as pope earned him the title "the Great".
46	Saint Hilarius	461–468	Hilarius was an archdeacon at election. He protected the rights of the pope over the Church.
47	Saint Simplicius	468–483	Simplicius' reign was overshadowed by the political upheaval that occurred during the fall of the Roman Empire. He opposed the heresy of Monophysitism.
48	Saint Felix III (II)	483–492	Felix was a Roman who was promoted for election as pope by the Germanic king who was ruling Italy at the time. Felix opposed the unorthodox actions of the patriarch of Constantinople, which led to the Acacian Schism. He was a strong leader but was criticized for stubbornness and harshness in some of his actions.
49	Saint Gelasius I	492–496	Gelasius was a Roman. He asserted the authority of the pope over the Church, was the first pope to use the title of Vicar of Christ, and was known for his prayerfulness, humility, and generosity with the poor. He was a strong but often overlooked pope.
51	Saint Symmachus	498–514	Symmachus was a deacon at the time of his election and was opposed by anti-pope Laurentius. Laurentius and

(continued)

	Name	Years of Reign	Description
			his supporters opposed Symmachus' previous strong actions regarding the Acacian Schism, which led to a public confrontation. The civil leader King Theodoric eventually ruled in Symmachus' favor. In response, Laurentius' supporters attacked the pope and killed several priests. Symmachus also opposed the heresy of Manichaeism and burned their books.
52	Saint Hormisdas	514–523	Hormisdas was married before ordination and a member of the Roman aristocracy. He developed good relations with the Ostrogothic king, making possible an end to the Acacian Schism.
53	Saint John I	523–526	John was an Italian deacon at election. He was the first pope to visit Constantinople, which led the Ostrogothic king Theodoric, fearing an alliance between the pope and the Byzantines, to imprison John. He was probably starved to death.
54	Saint Felix IV (III)	526–530	Felix was recommended for election as pope by the Ostrogothic king and therefore had good relations with him. Felix supported Augustine's teachings on grace and original sin, and he indicated his desired successor before his death.
57	Saint Agapetus I (Agapitus)	535–536	Agepetus was a Roman archdeacon at election. He deposed the patriarch of Constantinople for adhering to the heresy of Monophysitism. He was also sent to Constantinople by the Ostrogothic king to deter the Byzantine emperor from invasion; the Byzantine emperor treated him respectfully but invaded anyway.

	Name	Years of Reign	Description
58	Saint Silverius	536–537	Silverius was the son of Pope Hormisdas and was a subdeacon at election. He was elected at request of the Ostrogothic king as a foil against the Byzantines. Empress Theodora wanted her own candidate (Vigilius) to be pope, so she forged letters to implicate Silverius in a crime. Silverius was forced to step down and then starved to death while in captivity because the Byzantines wanted him out of the way quickly.
64	Saint Gregory I, the Great	590–604	Gregory was a member of the Roman nobility who had been a monk and an ambassador before election. Despite his initial efforts to avoid the papacy, his strong leadership as pope initiated what is now called the Medieval Papacy. In the power vacuum that existed from the lack of a local government, he administered civil matters in Rome. He acknowledged Byzantine rulers' authority, but he negotiated peace with the Lombard tribes on his own authority. He encouraged monastic life, was a prolific writer, regulated liturgical music, and encouraged missionaries to go spread the Gospel.
67	Saint Boniface IV	608–615	Boniface was a deacon and monk before election. He responded to the famines, plagues, and earthquakes that occurred during his reign with spiritual strength.
68	Saint Deusdedit (Adeodatus I)	615–618	Deusdedit was a Roman. He promoted clergy rather than monks in the Church, assisted victims of earthquake, and supported the Byzantines against the Lombards, who were threatening Rome at the time.

(continued)

	Name	Years of Reign	Description
74	Saint Martin I	649–655	Martin was an Italian who had served the Church as an ambassador before election. He was a determined and independent-minded pope who declined to seek imperial approval of his election. When he convened a synod to condemn Monothelitism, the Byzantine emperor Constans II ordered his men to drag Martin from his sickbed and bring him to Constantinople. The sick pope was flogged; he was first sentenced to death and then sentenced to banishment. Martin died of the cruel treatment and cold that he received while in exile in Crimea. He was ignored by Romans, who did not even send him blankets or food in his imprisonment. He is considered a martyr.
75	Saint Eugene I	655–657	Eugene was a Roman and had been recognized by Pope Martin as his successor. Eugene opposed Monothelitism, as his predecessor had done; the emperor threatened to flog and banish him too, but he was too busy fighting wars to do it.
76	Saint Vitalian	657–672	Vitalian was an Italian. He opposed Monothelitism but worked hard to repair relations with the emperor, who supported that heresy.
79	Saint Agatho	678–681	Agatho was an Italian Benedictine monk and was one hundred years old when he was elected. Agatho sent legates to a council to condemn Monothelitism, and he was personally generous and good-natured.

	Name	Years of Reign	Description
80	Saint Leo II	682–683	Leo was a Sicilian. He promoted sacred music and condemned Monothelitism. A previous pope, Honorius, had made poor word choices in responding to the Monophysite heresy, and Leo accepted a written censure of Honorius' words.
81	Saint Benedict II	684–685	Benedict was a Roman. His consecration as pope was delayed for a time while waiting for it to be approved by the Byzantines. He restored churches and was personally humble and kind.
84	Saint Sergius I	687–701	Sergius was an Italian. Two anti-popes, Theodore and Paschal, had also been elected at the previous pope's passing, but Sergius had the support of the military, the clergy, and the emperor's representative in Ravenna, making him the true pope. When he refused to accept Emperor Justinian's demands to permit clerical marriage and give the patriarch of Constantinople equal status to the pope, Justinian sent soldiers to arrest Sergius. But Byzantine troops in Rome sided with the pope against the emperor's representative, Zacharias. Zacharias even had to hide under the pope's bed while Sergius negotiated to protect him from the mob. The emperor was overthrown before Zacharias returned from his assignment.
89	Saint Gregory II	715–731	Gregory was a Roman, subdeacon, and the first papal librarian prior to his election. He opposed iconoclasm, and when he also opposed the emperor's oppressive taxes, the emperor tried

(continued)

	Name	Years of Reign	Description
			(unsuccessfully) to have him assassinated or deposed. Showing his diplomatic skills, Gregory personally convinced the Lombard king not to invade Rome. He sent Saint Boniface to bring the Gospel to the Germanic peoples.
90	Saint Gregory III	731–741	Gregory was a Syrian. He was the last pope who had to ask for Byzantine approval before accepting election. He opposed iconoclasm, which was violently promoted by the emperor, but later he helped the emperor recover Italian lands (by not supporting the Lombards), somewhat recovering his relationship with the emperor. When Gregory asked for help from the mayor of the palace of the Franks (rather than the king, who actually had no power), he established a fruitful relationship between the Church and France that lasted for centuries.
91	Saint Zachary	741–752	Zachary was a deacon at election. He negotiated with the Lombards to protect Ravenna, endearing himself to the Byzantine emperor, and he recognized Pepin III as French king over the deposed Merovingian king. He also restored damaged churches.
93	Saint Paul I	757–767	Paul was the brother of a previous pope, Stephen II, and was a Roman deacon at election. He was a good administrator with a strong personality who organized papal territories and used his influence with the Franks to protect Italy from the Lombards. However, his opposition to iconoclasm caused him to have poor relations with the Byzantines. Paul visited prisoners at night to pray with and comfort them.

	Name	Years of Reign	Description
96	Saint Leo III	795–816	Leo was a Roman cardinal priest when he was elected unanimously, but some disliked his style of government, or perhaps preferred the previous pope, which led him to be attacked by a mob. His attackers almost cut out his tongue and gouged out his eyes, but he managed to escape. When he reached safety, he thanked Charlemagne, king of the Franks and Italy, for protecting him and crowned him as Holy Roman Emperor, a tradition that continued for centuries. He also proved to be a capable administrator.
98	Saint Paschal I	817–824	Paschal was a Roman priest and abbot before election, and he requested the approval of the Holy Roman Emperor before accepting election. The emperor Louis granted him significant privileges. Later, Louis crowned his son Lothair as his co-emperor, but anti-Frankish feeling (due to Lothair's blameworthy actions) led to the murders of two Frankish leaders who were in Rome. Paschal was forced, under imperial pressure, to swear an oath that he was not involved in the murders and execute the ringleaders. Some say Paschal was greatly disliked while he was pope, but others say he was a strong voice against iconoclasm and rebuilt many churches.
103	Saint Leo IV	847–855	Leo was a Roman, a Benedictine monk, and a cardinal priest before election. He was elected as pope rather quickly and without imperial approval because of the urgent need for leadership caused by a recent Saracen invasion. Leo built walls

(continued)

	Name	Years of Reign	Description
			and ships to protect Rome from future invasion and advanced papal rights. He was a stern ruler, as when he had imperial officials executed for murdering a papal legate, which got him in trouble with the emperor.
105	Saint Nicholas I, the Great	858–867	Nicholas was a Roman who was elected after another candidate (the future pope Adrian II) declined. He was a strong leader and promoter of papal rights. At one point, the emperor besieged Rome to try to force the pope to capitulate on an issue, but Nicholas (and Rome) rode out the siege. His forceful leadership strained relations with the Byzantines, which led to the Photian Schism.
109	Saint Adrian III	884–885	Adrian was a Roman who reconciled the Church with the Eastern Church. He supported Romans during a famine and may have gotten himself involved in political feuds going on in Rome. His death was possibly not the result of natural causes.
152	Saint Leo IX	1049– 1054	Leo was a German bishop at the time of his election. Though King Henry supported him as a candidate, Leo insisted that the people and clergy of Rome accept his election as pope too. He humbly entered Rome barefoot, as a pilgrim. He was helped in his reform of the Church by the future Pope Gregory VII and by Saint Peter Damian. Leo was captured by Normans while on a military campaign and had to pay a large ransom to be released nine months later. The incursion he ordered into Byzantine

	Name	Years of Reign	Description
			territory strained relations before the final break between the Catholic Church and Eastern Church in 1054.
157	Saint Gregory VII	1073–1085	Gregory was an Italian who had resisted being elected pope in previous elections, but he finally accepted. The reform of simony and clerical abuses within the Church were at the center of his papacy, which became known as the Hildebrandine (Gregory's name before election) reform. Several subsequent popes followed his lead. Gregory's reforms strained relations with German king and emperor Henry IV, which forced the pope to excommunicate him at one point until Henry performed public penance. Henry supported an anti-pope at one point, leading to another excommunication, and Gregory was abandoned by both his cardinals and the Roman people when he refused to back down. Gregory was then rescued by the Norman army, but their acts of violence lost the support of the Romans, and Gregory died in exile from Rome.
158	Blessed Victor III	1086–1087	Victor was a great religious leader, negotiator, and abbot of Monte Cassino before his election, but he never wanted to be pope. Perhaps this was because he knew he was in poor health, or perhaps it was because he knew he was better as a negotiator than a leader. He left Rome for Monte Cassino twice out of frustration.

(continued)

	Name	Years of Reign	Description
159	Blessed Urban II	1088– 1099	Urban was born into the French nobility and was a cardinal bishop at election. He was a pious, intelligent, and eloquent man. His reign was opposed by anti-pope Clement III, who had been supported by Emperor Henry IV to become pope. Though initially lacking in money and support, Urban was gradually able to enter Rome and reign as pope. He promoted reforms against simony and investiture, promoted the Truce of God (a policy of cease-fires to protect civilians), and called for the First Crusade to reclaim the Holy Land. He established good relations with the Normans and improved papal finances.
167	Blessed Eugene III	1145– 1153	Eugene was born into a humble Italian family and was a Cistercian monk before election. During his reign, he was briefly at peace with the Roman government but was then forced to flee the city. He organized the Second Crusade with the help of Saint Bernard of Clairvaux, although it was a military disappointment. He tried to negotiate peace with various warlike leaders and was an able pope, despite his inexperience as a political leader.
184	Blessed Gregory X	1271– 1276	Gregory was an Italian archdeacon at election and a surprise choice after the papal office was vacant for three years. He worked to reform papacy, tried (though failed) to mount a crusade to protect the Christians in the Holy Land, and established a fleeting reunion with the Eastern Church.

	Name	Years of Reign	Description
185	Blessed Innocent V	1276	Innocent was a French Dominican who personally knew Saints Thomas Aquinas and Albert the Great. He tried to organize another crusade to protect Christians in the Holy Land and attempted to reestablish good relations with the Eastern Church.
192	Saint Celestine V	1294	Celestine was an Italian Benedictine abbot. He was also a holy man, but he was a disaster as a pope because of his lack of political skill and education. For the good of the Church, he abdicated. He was essentially imprisoned by the next pope and died a few years later.
194	Blessed Benedict XI	1303–1304	Benedict was an Italian Dominican and cardinal, and he was probably elected because of his courage in standing by a previous pope during torture. Benedict forgave the king for insults to the previous pope, and he forgave erring cardinals, but he also pursued action against those individuals who were specifically responsible for the poor treatment of the previous pope.
200	Saint Urban V	1362–1370	Urban was French, and he was a devout Benedictine who made time for prayers and retained his black habit even when becoming pope. He curtailed court expenses and reformed his clergy. He wanted to return to Rome to live and managed to do so. He tried to reunite the Church with the Eastern Church but was unsuccessful. Because of unrest in Rome and the fact that his cardinals had stayed in Avignon, France, he returned to Avignon after only three years and died soon afterward.

(continued)

	Name	Years of Reign	Description
225	Saint Pius V	1566–1572	Pius was from a poor Italian family and was a devout Dominican, scholar, and prior before his election. Romans worried initially that he (a former inquisitor) would be a severe pope, but he was evenhanded as a ruler. He became a reforming pope who curbed the excesses of his own Curia, and he even sent immoral cardinals to a monastery to be cared for by Jesuits. He implemented the Council of Trent, published the Catechism, and organized European nations to fight and defeat an Islamic invasion at the Battle of Lepanto. Pius acted forcefully on several issues to protect the Church and Christians in danger, though some of his decisions are still controversial.
240	Blessed Innocent XI	1676–1689	Innocent was an Italian Jesuit and cardinal who accepted the papacy only on the condition that cardinals accept his plan for Church reform. As a man, he was pious and charitable. He supported Poles and Austrians against Turkish invasion. Innocent instituted austere measures and modest taxation to restore ruined papal finances, prohibited gaudy clothing and gambling dens in Rome, and resisted King Louis XIV's attempts to control the Church in France. He organized a Holy League force against Turkish attacks and was beloved by Romans at his death, despite his measures against gambling.
245	Servant of God Benedict XIII	1724–1730	Benedict was an Italian Dominican and cardinal who initially refused to accept the papacy. He was a deeply spiritual man who prayed the Rosary,

	Name	Years of Reign	Description
			heard confessions, and visited the poor. He curbed flamboyant dress among the clergy and banned the Roman lottery. However, he gave power to an unscrupulous cardinal who stole from the treasury and controlled administration, which has marred his reputation as pope.
251	Servant of God Pius VII	1800–1823	Pius was from a noble Italian family and was a Benedictine professor and cardinal. He was elected by his fellow cardinals because they thought he was the only one who could face down the emperor Napoleon Bonaparte. Pius was devout, faithful, and gentle by nature. Bonaparte's rule led to anti-Catholicism in the countries he controlled; when the pope refused to bend to Bonaparte's demands, the emperor invaded Rome, annexed the papal states, and arrested and imprisoned the pope. Pius signed an agreement with Bonaparte under pressure but retracted it two months later. When Bonaparte lost power, Pius was freed, was restored as ruler of the papal states, reinstituted the Jesuits, and instituted Church reforms. He requested leniency for Bonaparte during imprisonment and allowed his family to live in Rome because they were not welcome anywhere else.
255	Blessed Pius IX	1846–1878	Pius was an Italian, had suffered from epilepsy in childhood, and was a diplomat and cardinal when elected. He granted amnesty to political prisoners and reversed the authoritarian rule of the previous pope. When he expressed

(continued)

	Name	Years of Reign	Description
			sympathy for Italian rebels, it was misinterpreted and resulted in riots and the assassination of a cardinal. Pius was forced to flee Rome disguised as a priest, and he lived in exile until the French restored peace in Rome. As a result, he was opposed to Italian unification, seeing (accurately) that it would take power away from the pope. He refused to acknowledge the Italian government, called himself a prisoner of the Vatican, and controlled only Rome. He issued a list of heresies, proclaimed the doctrine of the Immaculate Conception, provided strong direction to the Church, and convened Vatican Council I. He was personally kind and charming; he was a transitional figure for the role of the pope, who was now seen as the pastor of the Church and the world, rather than a secular ruler.
257	Saint Pius X	1903–1914	Pius was born into a modest Italian family and became a priest, bishop, and cardinal before becoming pope. Because an emperor had interfered with the conclave and discouraged a different candidate during his election, Pius decreed that there should be no more interference in the future. He condemned Modernism, reorganized the Curia, reformed Church music, and promoted Catholic Action (an organization of lay Catholics who supported one another in living out their faith). Pius was a strong proponent of daily Communion. He died soon after the start of World War I, which he had warned European nations to avoid.

	Name	Years of Reign	Description
261	Saint John XXIII	1958–1963	John was born into a humble Italian family; he was a historian, papal nuncio, and cardinal before becoming pope. He established the number of cardinals and wrote notable encyclicals. His desire for renewal of the Church led him to try to open relations with Russia and reach out to other Christian denominations. He also convened Vatican Council II. John was known to be personally good-humored, practical, and honest.
262	Saint Paul VI	1963–1978	Paul was an Italian priest and Church diplomat before his election. He promised (and kept his promise) to continue Vatican Council II. Paul managed to prevent a schism when some Church leaders differed strongly on the level of reform to be followed from the council. He reduced the trappings of papacy, created cardinals from nations all over the world, and issued a detailed decree on electing a pope. He traveled to many countries, was almost assassinated, promoted ecumenism, and wrote important encyclicals.
263	Venerable John Paul I	1978	John Paul was born into a humble Italian family and was a priest, patriarch, and cardinal before his election. Personally unassuming, he reduced the trappings of the papal office, but he died after only thirty-three days.
264	Saint John Paul II	1978–2005	John Paul was born in Poland, having lived under Nazism and Communism, and was a natural leader. He traveled all over the world as pope and was known for his unbending orthodoxy. He

(continued)

Name	Years of Reign	Description
		initiated extensive reforms in the Church, issued a new catechism for the universal Church, and revised canon law. John Paul was very personable and at home in front of large crowds of people. He survived an attempted assassination by a gunman, instigated by Communists, who rightly saw him as a threat to Communism. He was also a poet and playwright. He issued many profound writings and speeches, including his development of the "Theology of the Body". He encouraged many canonizations and beatifications to promote a better understanding of the universal call to holiness.

And the Virgin's Name Was Mary

In the workplace, most companies require an annual performance appraisal for each employee. An annual assessment is theoretically a great idea so the employer can help the employee remain focused and effective on the job. But in reality, a typical performance appraisal describes the employee in such glowing terms that it is almost laughable. And most people know that if your appraisal is not filled with praise, you need to be looking for a new job.

To a non-Catholic, Catholic descriptions of Jesus' mother, Mary, sometimes sound similarly exaggerated. She appears only in a limited number of passages in the Gospels, so what do we really know about her?

Actually, we know a lot.

The phrase "Holy Trinity" does not appear in the Bible, and yet all Christians profess to believe in it. The Church approved the Nicene Creed in the year 325; we state in that creed that we believe in the Holy Trinity, not because we thought it sounded like a good idea or because we understand exactly what that means, but because this is what God has revealed to us through Sacred Scripture and Tradition. Similarly, we can know many things about the Blessed Virgin Mary even if Jesus Himself did not leave a detailed autobiography of His life growing up in Nazareth.

From a theological point of view, the Church has made some very specific statements about Mary's identity. Examining each of the descriptions of Mary given in the *Catechism of the Catholic Church* would fill a book of its own. The *Catechism* carefully explains[1] her role as Christ's mother by the power of the Holy Spirit; her relationship to the Church; her position in the "economy of salvation"; her lived example of holiness, obedience, and faith; and even how she is

[1] See the index of the *Catechism of the Catholic Church* under "Mary".

to be venerated, rather than worshipped. She has been given numerous titles by the Church; let us examine just one.

Mary, Mother of God

In the early fifth century, an eloquent priest and monk named Nestorius became patriarch of the great city of Constantinople. He was a strong defender of the Catholic faith against the Arian heresy, so he surprised Catholics when he began preaching in his homilies that Mary should not be called "Mother of God". Since Christians, both leaders and laypeople, had been calling Mary "Mother of God" for centuries, his teaching almost immediately caused an uproar. Eventually, the Church, particularly through Saint Cyril of Alexandria, identified his teachings as a heresy, which is now called Nestorianism. But the debate raised some interesting questions.

Nestorius' argument was, in part, that this title could lead non-Christians to believe that we think Mary is a goddess. After all, the mother of the pagan gods and goddesses was thought to be a goddess. How could a human being give birth to God Himself? Nestorius' explanation was that Jesus Christ was a human Person and that he was joined (somehow) to what we could call the Second Person of the Blessed Trinity.

The Church responded that Mary was truly the Mother of God. While she did not give birth to Jesus' divine nature, she did give birth to His human nature, and that nature was united, in what we now call the hypostatic union, with His divine nature. This is explained more thoroughly in the *Catechism*,[2] but why is this term so important to ordinary Catholics that we use that title and even celebrate it once a year on the first day of January?

Though the title may cause us trouble with our Protestant brothers and sisters (as it caused problems with Gnostics in Nestorius' day), it teaches us important things about Mary. Most importantly, the title does what Mary herself did throughout her earthly life: directs our attention to Jesus Christ. Any honor we show her is due first and foremost to Him. In that sense, a common analogy is helpful; if Jesus

[2] See *CCC* 466.

is like the sun, from which we all receive the light that makes it possible for us to live, Mary is like the moon, receiving that light and shining it back to Him more perfectly than any other human being. Mary is not Mother of God because she climbed the highest mountain, was voted more beautiful than any other woman, or otherwise achieved some great personal accomplishment on her own. She is the Mother of God because God *chose* her, and then she said *yes*.

God chooses each one of us for a specific purpose; all we have to do is say yes.

Mary's gifts

But rather than dwell on the theological truths about Mary that have been debated and affirmed over the centuries—about which many, many books have been written—there is another way to see her role in salvation that is more practical.

Imagine that God, in His kindness, speaks to you today. He tells you that you will die tomorrow, and He offers to place your children in the care of another man or woman who will raise your children for you. Since He's God, He gives you the option of choosing any person, living, dead, or yet to be born, to fulfill this role in your place. Is there a mother or father who would *not* examine every candidate carefully, trying to find the best person possible, the person who would be the most loving, patient, faithful, understanding, demanding, and thoughtful replacement? Someone who would have all your best qualities and none of the worst? Would you choose a physically abusive man? A verbally abusive woman? Someone with a towering ego or a terrible temper or an unrepented addiction?

Of course not. Because the gift of motherhood and fatherhood is a blessing from God that allows us to share in His joy as our Creator, we experience it (at least in our better moments, when our children are well behaved and happy) as a great joy. We love them because they are ours as a gratuitous gift from God, not something we earned or deserved. And even when we cannot be around them, we want *them* to know that same joy.

But this thought experiment is not a hypothetical case for God. He really does see into the hearts of every single person that has ever lived or will ever live, so He knew which soul would be the most perfect one to be the mother of the Messiah. Mary was not, as is sometimes shown in bad Christian depictions of Jesus' birth, just an ordinary woman like anyone else who did not really know what was going on. She still had to ponder what the angel told her, and she probably began a serious study of the writings we call the Old Testament to understand what God had already revealed about the coming Messiah. But she received God's invitation with a great openness and obedience.

We tend to think of Mary's Immaculate Conception as a pious title, not a reality. She was born without the concupiscence that all of us share, but she chose, each day, to remain immaculate.

Can you think back to one of your earliest sins, an occasion when you realized you did something wrong and you would be in trouble? You can probably also remember going back over the event and thinking, "If I hadn't done or thought *that*, I wouldn't have made that mistake." God allows us to feel shame when we sin, not as a punishment, but so that we will stop and think about the circumstances that led us to that point. Mary never let herself step over that chasm that led to sin. She was surely tempted innumerable times, just as all of us are. If the devil tempted Jesus Himself—and we know he did—he did not skip Mary. Perhaps the briefest way to put it is that, in every moment, she trusted God.

Perhaps what we can learn from Mary is that, like her, each one of us is the most perfect soul to face our particular family, vocation, situation, and culture, and that all we have to do is trust Him, each day, whether we feel like it or not, whether we understand what's going on or not, and follow in her Son's footsteps.

The following table lists major feasts associated specifically with the Blessed Virgin Mary.

Name of Feast	Date	Reason for Feast
Mary, Mother of God	January 1	Commemorates our belief that Mary is indeed the Mother of God.
Our Lady of Lourdes	February 11	Celebrates anniversary of apparitions of our Lady to Saint Bernadette Soubirous in Lourdes, France, in which Mary told her to pray the

Name of Feast	Date	Reason for Feast
		Rosary, do penance, and pray for sinners; Mary asked for a chapel to be built and declared, "I am the Immaculate Conception."
The Annunciation to the Blessed Virgin Mary	March 25	Commemorates God's invitation, through an angel, to the Blessed Mother to become the mother of His Son.
Our Lady of Good Counsel	April 26	Honors our Blessed Mother under a title and through an image that has inspired Catholics since the fifteenth century.
Mary, Mother of the Church	Monday after Pentecost	Commemorates an ancient title for the Blessed Mother that has been used for centuries but has been reiterated by recent popes: Paul VI, John Paul II, Benedict XVI, and Francis.
Our Lady of Fatima	May 13	Celebrates anniversary of first apparition of our Lady to three shepherd children at Fatima, Portugal; key themes were penance and conversion.
The Visitation of the Blessed Virgin Mary	May 31	Commemorates Mary's journey to see her cousin Elizabeth during her unexpected pregnancy, as described in Luke 1:39–56.
Our Lady of Perpetual Help	June 27	Honors our Blessed Mother under a title and icon that has been inspiring Catholics since at least the fifteenth century.
Our Lady of Mount Carmel	July 16	Commemorates the Blessed Mother as patroness of the Carmelite order.

(continued)

Name of Feast	Date	Reason for Feast
The Assumption of the Blessed Virgin Mary	August 15	Commemorates the Assumption of Mary, body and soul, into Heaven at the end of her life.
Our Lady of Knock	August 21	Celebrates anniversary of the apparition of the Blessed Mother, Saint Joseph, and Saint John the Evangelist, along with angels and Jesus Christ (depicted as the Lamb of God), outside a church in Knock, Ireland.
The Queenship (Coronation) of the Blessed Virgin Mary	August 22	Commemorates the crowning of Mary as Queen of Heaven after her Assumption into Heaven.
Our Lady of Sorrows	September 15	Honors the sufferings of Mary, as the mother of the Crucified Christ, on the day after the Feast of the Exaltation of the Cross.
Our Lady of La Salette	September 19	Celebrates anniversary of the apparitions of the Blessed Mother to two children of La Salette, France, in which she wept and encouraged people to show greater respect for the Sabbath rest and for the name of God.
Our Lady of Mercy or Our Lady of Ransom	September 24	Commemorates the founding of the order of Mercedarians, who ransomed Christians from slavery.
Our Lady of the Rosary	October 7	Commemorates devotion to our Lady through the praying of the Rosary, but also the defeat of Muslim forces by Christians at the Battle of Lepanto in 1571.

Name of Feast	Date	Reason for Feast
Our Lady of the Pillar	October 12	Commemorates the first apparition of Mary, in which she appeared to Saint James the Greater in Saragossa, Spain, along with a wooden image of Mary holding Jesus, while standing atop a pillar.
The Presentation of the Blessed Virgin Mary	November 21	Commemorates the extrabiblical but ancient tradition that Mary was given to God at the Jerusalem Temple when she was only a child.
The Miraculous Medal of the Blessed Virgin Mary	November 27	Celebrates anniversary of the appearance of the Blessed Mother to Saint Catherine Laboure, asking her to have medals with her image imprinted and given out to encourage trust in Mary's prayers.
The Immaculate Conception of the Blessed Virgin Mary	December 8	Commemorates the belief that Mary was immaculate and free of original sin from the time of her conception.
Our Lady of Loreto	December 10	Commemorates the building, currently located in Loreto, Italy, in which the Blessed Mother is said to have lived.
Our Lady of Guadalupe	December 12	Celebrates anniversary of the apparitions and miraculous image of the Blessed Mother to Saint Juan Diego on Tepeyac Hill in Guadalupe, Mexico.

SELECT BIBLIOGRAPHY

To learn more about the saints described in this book, see the following resources.

Books

Akin, Jimmy. *The Bible Is a Catholic Book*. El Cajon, CA: Catholic Answers Press, 2019.

—————. *The Fathers Know Best: Your Essential Guide to the Teachings of the Early Church*. El Cajon, CA: Catholic Answers Press, 2010.

Aquilina, Mike. *The Fathers of the Church: An Introduction to the First Christian Teachers*. 3rd ed. Huntington, IN: Our Sunday Visitor, 2013.

Athanasius. *The Life of Anthony and the Letter to Marcellinus*. Translated by Robert C. Gregg. New York: Paulist Press, 1980.

Benedict XVI. *Doctors of the Church*. Huntington, IN: Our Sunday Visitor Publishing Division, 2011.

Beutner, Dawn. *Saints: Becoming an Image of Christ Every Day of the Year*. San Francisco: Ignatius Press, 2020.

Bunson, Matthew. *The Catholic Almanac's Guide to the Church*. Huntington, IN: Our Sunday Visitor Publishing Division, 2001.

—————. *The Pope Encyclopedia: An A to Z of the Holy See*. New York: Crown Trade Paperbacks, 1995.

Carroll, Warren. *A History of Christendom*. 6 vols. Front Royal, VA: Christendom Press, 1985–2013.

Catechism of the Catholic Church. United States Catholic Conference—Libreria Editrice Vaticana, Second Edition, 2019. English translation of the *Catechism of the Catholic Church*: Modifications from the Editio Typica. United States Conference of Catholic Bishops—Libreria Editrice Vaticana, 1997.

The Catholic Source Book. 4th ed. Huntington, IN: Our Sunday Visitor Curriculum Division, 2008.

Cruz, Joan Carroll. *Saintly Women of Modern Times*. Huntington, IN: Our Sunday Visitor Publishing Division, 2004.

Graham, Albert E. *Compendium of the Miraculous*. Charlotte, NC: TAN Books, 2013.

Kelly, J. N. D., and M. J. Walsh. *Oxford Dictionary of Popes*. New York: Oxford University Press, 2010.

Martyrologium Romanum, Editio Altera. Libreria Editrice Vaticana, 2004.

Ott, Ludwig. *Fundamentals of Catholic Dogma*. Charlotte, NC: TAN Books, 1974.

Rengers, Christopher, O.F.M. Cap., and Matthew E. Bunson, K.H.S. *The 35 Doctors of the Church*. Rev. ed. Charlotte, NC: TAN Books, 2014.

Walsh, Michael, ed. *Butler's Lives of the Saints, Concise Edition Revised and Updated*. San Francisco: HarperCollins Publishers, 1991.

Websites

NewAdvent.org. [Contains many entries from the *Catholic Encyclopedia*, sometimes called the *Old Catholic Encyclopedia* (originally published in 1917). Many entries from this encyclopedia are also available at Catholic.com.]

Vatican.va. [Contains many papal documents, including biographies of saints given as papal addresses.]

NAMES INDEX

Abdon, Saint, 241

Abednego, 19

Abraham (patriarch), 125–26, 200

Acacius of Byzantium, Saint, 245

Achilleus, Saint, 16

Adalbert, Saint, 101

Adam (first man), 241

Adeodatus I (pope), 293

Adrian II (pope), 274, 298

Adrian III (pope), 254, 298

Adrian VI (pope), 258–59, 268–69

Agapetus I (pope), 292

Agapetus II (pope), 275

Agatha, Saint, 13, 250

Agatha of Sicily, Saint, 43

Agatho (pope), 294

Agathopedes, Saint, 139–40

Agnes of Austria, 111

Agnes of Rome, Saint, 43, 249

Alacoque, Saint Margaret Mary, 215, 226

Alban, Saint, 110

Alberic II (house of Theophylact), 263, 276

Alberic of Citeaux, Saint, 149, 158

Albert of Jerusalem, Saint, 149, 150, 158

Albert the Great, Saint, 71, 77, 85, 89, 151, 252, 301

Alexander I (pope), 285

Alexander II (pope), 266

Alexander III (pope), 263

Alexander VI (pope), 269, 278

Alexander of Alexandria, Saint, 35, 50–51, 65, 66

Alexander Severus (Roman emperor), 21

Ambrose of Milan, Saint, 52, 64, 66–68, 82, 88, 173–74, 289, 290

Amidei, Saint Bartholomew degli, 154–55

Anacletus (pope), 27, 27n2, 92, 284

Anastasia of Sirmium, Saint, 43

Anastasius I (pope), 289, 290

Anastasius III (pope), 275

Anchieta, Saint Jose de, 101, 114

Andrew, Saint, 95, 97, 100, 111

Andrew of Crete, Saint, 37, 57

Angela of Foligno, Saint, 178, 224

Anicetus (pope), 285

Anna (prophet), 201

Anne, Saint, 43, 249

Anno II of Germany, Saint, 112

Anselm of Canterbury, Saint, 84, 89, 207–8, 216

Ansgar, Saint, 101

Antela, Saint Benedict dell', 154–55

Anterus (pope), 286

Anthelm of Belley, Saint, 141–43

Anthony of Padua, Saint, 63, 64, 85, 89, 133, 151, 248

Anthony the Great, Saint, 17, 66, 145, 162–66, 237

Antoninus of Florence, Saint, 179–80

Antony of Kiev, Saint, 155–56

Apollinaris of Ravenna, Saint, 21

Apollonia, Saint, 13, 250

Arius, 35–36, 50, 65–67

Arnobius, 41, 60

Arnulf (Holy Roman Emperor), 272–73

Arsenius, Saint, 232–33

Athanasius of Alexandria, Saint, 35, 37, 51, 64, 66–67, 67n2, 81, 87, 140, 162–64, 289

Attila the Hun, 28, 111, 133

Augustine of Canterbury, Saint, 101, 109